KINSALE
HARBOUR
A History

JOHN THUILLIER

The Collins Press

FIRST PUBLISHED IN 2014 BY
The Collins Press
West Link Park
Doughcloyne
Wilton
Cork

A CIP record for this book is available from the British Library.

Hardback ISBN: 978-1-84889-206-4
PDF eBook ISBN: 978-1-84889-847-9
EPUB eBook ISBN: 978-1-84889-848-6
Kindle ISBN: 978-1-84889-849-3

Design and typesetting by Carrigboy Typesetting Services
Typeset in Sabon
Printed in Malta by Gutenberg Press Limited

Contents

Acknowledgements

Kinsale in the 1950s and 1960s, when I was growing up, was at a low ebb economically. Many young men took the option of going to sea for a livelihood. On their return after long voyages one was treated to stories of sailing the oceans and listening to accounts of escapades ashore in foreign ports. Jack O'Driscoll, Charlie Hurley, John Alcock, Gerald Gimblett, Ted Coakley, Tommy Newman, Billy Farren, members of the Kent, Price and Lombard families and others were generous, not just in recounting their own experiences at sea, but drawing on the memories of generations of seafarers who went before them. In any case, the delight of receiving an orange 'all the way from Australia' helped to spark the imagination of the young listener.

My mother, whose family were involved in the fishing industry, provided detailed information on the buyers and auctioneers and records of transporting the catch to Dublin and Liverpool, and to Billingsgate market in London. On my father's side, the family were boatbuilders, owners and through membership of various boards and public bodies were fully engaged in the affairs of the harbour. Detailed records, memoirs, financial statements and work diaries, which provide first-hand accounts of over 200 years marine activity, were invaluable to me in understanding the reality of seafaring life in Kinsale.

Dan O'Shea, the late Harbour Master, Bill Deasy and Neddy Ward of the World's End, were willing to share their appreciation of the harbour while Francie Dempsey, Jimmy Lawton, Eugene Dennis and Jerome Lordan provided invaluable information on the Old Head of Kinsale. Thanks are also due to Captain Phil Devitt for making the harbour records available to me.

I wish to acknowledge the assistance of the Admiralty Office in London and the National Library of Ireland for permission to reproduce charts and photographs. I am grateful to Mary Hegarty, Kevin Goggin and Buddy Irwin for the use of photographs and Liam Fitzgibbon, Kevin O'Sullivan, Dermot Collins and the late John H. Thuillier (my grandfather) for providing illustrations and drawings. Particular thanks are due to Tony Bocking for his interest and knowledge of local history and his archive of photographs, which he very generously made available. Appreciation also to Mary Lombard of the Boole Library, University College Cork, for her kindness and assistance.

The professional photographic skills and technical knowledge of John Collins are in evidence in the high quality of the images reproduced in the book. The role and encouragement, from the beginning, of The Collins Press is much appreciated.

My brothers, Maurice who has spent a lifetime in boats and Joe who is a master mariner, have provided advice and critical comment. Son Bill and daughters Maeve and Jane took a keen interest in the project and were constantly available to undertake proofreading and offer assistance in the technical area. I would like to thank the copyright holders for permission to reproduce the photographs, charts and drawings in the book. Every reasonable attempt has been made to trace ownership. The publisher will be happy to hear from any copyright holders not acknowledged and undertakes to rectify any errors or omissions in future editions. Finally as ever, Margaret, my wife, has provided enormous support and encouragement and was always available with advice, love and support.

John R. Thuillier
2014

1

On Entering Kinsale Harbour

The story of Kinsale is the history of its connection with the sea. Heartbeat-like, the rhythmic ebb and flow of the tide sustains the town. For centuries the impact of the maritime environment has influenced structure and settlement patterns, as it responded to the seaborne traffic that entered the harbour. The Irish name for Kinsale says it all, *Ceann tSáile*, the head of the sea. The town's fortunes over the centuries waxed and waned in response to the possibilities and potential present in its marine setting. The harbour became a focus for drifters, trawlers and hookers attracted to fish the large shoals off the coast. For centuries Kinsale was also an important hub for shipping. No method of transport could compete with the efficiency of ships capable of bearing thousands of tons of cargo over great distances. While dependent on wind and constrained by weather and tide, the sea provided the means by which communication and commercial links were established. Tall ships, square sailed to fore-and-aft rig, filled the harbour, heralding the desire for discovery and colonisation in lands beyond the horizon.

The deep water of the harbour situated on the estuary at the mouth of the Bandon River gave access to shipping at all stages of the tide and provided rest and shelter for many tired and storm-buffeted sailors. Schooners, smacks, brigs and barquentines, pitching and rolling as they came through the robust tidal race off the Old Head of Kinsale, prepared for the final approach to the harbour mouth. Giving Bream Rock a wide berth in the prevailing breeze, the incoming vessels yielded to fluky squalls from the cliffs of the tall promontory and, steering on a course a few degrees east of north, headed for the entrance. Ships arriving from the south-east, the Isles of Scilly or Cornwall picked up the light on the Old Head 30 miles out. Vessels from Bristol on a bearing due west of the Smalls Rocks off the Welsh coast approached Kinsale leaving the Sovereign Islands to starboard. The 1703 ship's log of the vessel on which Alexander Selkirk was sailing master, and on whom Daniel Defoe based his novel *Robinson Crusoe*, describes them as 'very foul'.[1] Closing in on the entrance, sheets are checked as the vessel, yawing in the breaking crests, surges forward. Slowing in the trough, with helm down to counter the broach, the ship awaits the next wave coming up under the stern.

Even for the modern yachtsman approaching the entrance, there is little to compare with the sight of a gleaming smooth wake in a sparkling breeze, as the Sovereign Islands close on Frower Point and vessels enter the embracing shelter of the harbour. Passing Preghane and Eastern Points to starboard and Money Point on the western side, relieved crews with bronzed faces, whitened with drying salt from the spray, relax under the bracken-covered cliff.

> Where no storm comes,
> Where the green swell is in the havens dumb
> And out of the swing of the sea.
> Gerald Manley Hopkins ('Heaven-Haven').

Shelter was just one of the factors which attracted maritime activity to Kinsale. In 1666 it was described by the Earl of Orrery as 'one of the noblest harbours in Europe'. There are numerous references to the harbour 'teeming with ships' and at least to the middle of the eighteenth century its importance was such that it was described as being 'in the roads of the commerce of the world'. Kinsale had the depth of water to take ships of up to 1,000 tons, which were the ocean-going vessels of the day. In the fairway, extending from the mouth of the harbour to Murphy's (Ringfinnan) Point, on the Bandon River, anchorage is available to a depth of two fathoms.

The port is located on a series of bends in the lower reaches of the river which, through erosion and river capture, form three linked harbours making Kinsale one of the most secure anchorages on the coast. The Old Head of Kinsale promontory, stretching 5 miles into the open sea, is a natural breakwater giving the harbour mouth protection from the prevailing south-westerly winds. The prominent headland with its lighthouse is also the ideal landfall for incoming ships.

At the time when vessels were dependent on wind as the only source of power, proximity to the open sea was important, which from the anchorage at Kinsale is approximately one nautical mile. In calm conditions it is possible to drift on an ebb tide to pick up a breeze outside the harbour. The prevailing winds generally give beam-reaching conditions for quick passages to Britain, France and Spain. Regularly voyages to Ushant, off the Brittany coast, were made in two days and in suitable conditions a trip to Bristol, Kinsale's contact port in Britain, could be sailed in under thirty hours.

Another factor in Kinsale's success as a port was the Bandon River and the contact it provided with the extensive agricultural hinterland, north and west of the town. The river was navigable to Colliers Quay above Shippool Castle and from there to Innishannon in flat-bottomed barges and even further to Dundaniel in lighters.

It was inevitable, with this matrix of natural attributes, that sea travellers would discover Kinsale and realise the potential of the harbour. Each wave of settler sought in various ways to improve infrastructure and put in place administrative systems for the orderly operation of the harbour. Development, over many centuries, was gradual and evolved in an ad hoc manner. The main thrust was on extending the sea frontage further into deeper water. Evidence of some early habitation exists in the surrounding area, such as the remains of a dolmen, known as 'the Prince's Bed', on the high cliff at Ballymacus overlooking the Sovereign Islands. Standing stones in the fields above Charles Fort and the undulating patterns in the ground at Dún Cearma on the Old Head indicate settlement in pre-Christian Kinsale.

Later, ring forts at Ballycatten near Ballinspittle, Duneen Upper on the Old Head, and Dunderrow close to the river were the sites for new arrivals from France and northern Spain in the fourth century.[2]

Kinsale town itself emerged as a settlement in the sixth century, gradually evolving in identifiable but overlapping stages. Each was stimulated by a succession of newcomers and an increase in port usage. After the initial discovery as a weather bolthole, the harbour attracted mercantile and naval shipping. Fishing has been a constant activity in the harbour and it too required shore-based facilities. In modern times the harbour has developed facilities for yachting and angling. Traders, fishermen, military personnel, colonisers, adventurers, entrepreneurs and asylum seekers, such as French Protestants escaping from persecution in the seventeenth century, settled in Kinsale and each has contributed to the amalgam that makes Kinsale distinctive and quite unique among Irish towns.

Originally it was to the hills, configured like a horseshoe around the town, that the earliest settlers scrambled ashore and established habitation sites. What is now the flat urban centre consisted of mud and isolated rocky outcrops laced with meandering streams that channelled fresh water from the slopes to the harbour. Twice daily the incoming tide flooded the area lapping the higher ground at Main Street, the Back Glen, Sleveen and the rise close to St Multose at Church Square, the location of the first marketplace. Here the terraced slopes with their thatched mud huts converged. Covered at high tide were the areas which today are the town's shops, public parks, Acton's Hotel gardens, the site now occupied by the Shearwater apartment complex and the Trident Hotel. The physical waterfront was the link to the harbour and consisted of a series of quays and slipways separated by muddy strands. This was the interface of the town with the sea, where wealth-generating cargos were handled, victuals supplied and maritime services provided. The modern street pattern was laid down at this time in stepped linear development on the slopes around the harbour, still evident at Main Street, Fisher Street (renamed O'Connell Street in the 1960s) and the Rampart, converging at Church Square. Cork and Barrack Streets extended the settlement on the eastern side.

In October 1703, Francis Rogers, a London merchant sailing from the West Indies, put into Kinsale following a heavy-weather voyage. As his ship rode at anchor between other vessels, men-of-war and merchant-men, he expressed his relief at being safely in the harbour in terms that were typical of the many voyagers at the time: 'This is a very good harbour secured at the entrance by a strong fort, riding [anchored] quite up to the town being near a mile. It is quite narrow in some places steep home to the rocks on the main side'. His diary goes on to describe the taverns and the pleasant hospitality he enjoyed ashore.[3]

Before reaching this happy position the crew of an incoming vessel would identify the natural features and man-made structures that facilitated navigation and a safe entrance. The ship's master referred to his charts and would call for the assistance of a pilot seeking information on leading lines, the fairway, anchoring, obstructions and to be made aware of the facilities and services available while in port (see plate 2).

For the approaching vessel the first encounter with Kinsale was the cliff and seascape of the Old Head jutting south into the sea, an extension and intrinsic part of the town's multilayered story. The landmark, ranking with the great headlands of these islands, was formed aeons ago of Devonian sand and Carboniferous limestone. The strata twisted and warped deep within the crust of the Earth and when brought to the surface was shaped by weathering and erosion. Tucked away at the western end of Bullen's Bay is the main landing place for the headland itself. Funnel-like in shape, the bay is a deadly lee shore made treacherous by a series of jagged outcrops which are covered at high water. A safe passage is possible through the maze of rocks and inside the natural barrier, small boats are moored or drawn above the high-water mark at Duneen and An Doras Breac (The Speckled Door). Ashore, the splendour of the peninsula may also be appreciated. Looking from the high ground at Kilcolman, above the landing place, the rugged coastline of Bullen's Bay to Black Head and west the beach at Garrylucus appear in a wide vista. There is a tradition that a light was located here, not for the purpose of warning shipping off the dangerous coast but to indicate the landfall for the followers of the earliest settlers. There are references to a light by the Spaniards when they landed at Kinsale in 1601: 'Known to the Dane,

Kinsale's Inner, Middle and Outer Harbours, looking south. *Courtesy Irish Examiner*

the Saxon and Turk. Called by the Spaniard Cabo de Vela'.[4]

The light, however, was not a permanent feature until Charles II came to the throne in 1660, when a patent was issued to Robert Reading to build lighthouses on the Irish coast including one for the Old Head. A cottage light was constructed on gently rising ground some distance from the point itself. Still evident is the dilapidated building with a hole in the roof designed to take the brazier or iron basket in which a fire was lit, using coal or other material. While a great advance, these beacon furnaces had limitations as they were often shrouded in their own smoke and were said to 'hurt mariners and expose them to more danger than if they did not trust them'. They also consumed copious quantities of fuel due to the ferocious draught created by the high winds and inclement weather.[5] Complaints led to the suspension of the light for twenty years in 1783. Then in 1804 Thomas Forge replaced the fire with twelve lamps, fuelled by fish oil and surrounded by copper dishes, which reflected added light in the circular structure.

Advancing technology and the demands of shipping for safer navigational aids encouraged the Dublin

Port Authority in 1814 to appoint George Halpin as supervisor of coast lights. He was responsible for a new lighthouse on the Old Head, which was built close to the cottage structure. It consisted of a whitewashed tower 300 feet above sea level, whose light could be seen for a distance of 25 miles and north towards the harbour mouth. The particular problem it presented, however, was that low cloud and fog frequently obscured it.[6]

In 1853 the lighthouse was replaced by the current structure, built so that the beam is visible from all points seaward and out of Kinsale (see plate 1). The distinctive sequence of flashes that identifies the light, two every ten seconds, is produced by a revolving optic. Originally this involved winding up a weight every forty-five minutes which, as it fell under gravity, turned the lantern at a constant speed. Electrical power replaced the manual operation in 1972. The beam, which is 236 feet above sea level, can be seen from 25 miles and in daylight the tower's alternating black-and-white bands are its distinguishing feature. In poor visibility the warning was a sound signal generated by small explosions at five-minute intervals. For security reasons, the powder was kept in a hut near Duneen and delivered to the lighthouse as required. In 1972 an electric horn replaced the explosive, operating on a light-sensitive system which, when triggered by reduced visibility, produced three sharp ear-piercing blasts in each 45-second period. Of great assistance to navigation was the introduction of a radio direction finding signal. The transmitted OH, the Morse code for Old Head, could be received by vessels up to 25 miles off, giving an invaluable compass bearing, particularly useful when visibility was poor. Modern technology made all of this redundant and in 1987 an automated system was introduced, ending 1,500 years of manned activity on the headland. The iconic slender tower with its characteristic black-and-white bands and flashing light beam remain an essential navigational feature, a safety aid and a beacon for seafarers.

The lighthouse keepers and later the coastguard, also stationed at the Old Head, received supplies landed by tender at steps cut into the cliff on both sides of the promontory at Gunhole, inside Bream Rock on the eastern side and, depending on wind direction, at Cuas Gorm on the western side. The keepers were quite well looked after by eighteenth-century standards. It was reported that they had a constant supply of fuel and food and were provided with accommodation in stone-built whitewashed cottages, which were maintained up to naval standards of tidiness. In addition to an annual income of £12, the keeper kept a cow and grew vegetables in the surrounding land and, of course, had access to a plentiful supply of fish, caught by hand from the rocks.

Because of its prominent position on the coast, the Old Head of Kinsale was used to monitor incoming traffic and convey messages by signalling. It was an aid to navigation, and arriving vessels bound for Kinsale, Cork, Waterford and British ports could be spotted by pilots watching from the high cliffs. They had an advantage over the men in the famous Bristol pilot cutters who, to get the pilotage of ships, were required to stay at sea west of the Isles of Scilly 'seeking' business.[7] When a strange sail was sighted, the crews scrambled down the rocks, boarded the boats and raced to the incoming vessel. Crewed by the pilot and a boy, high levels of seamanship skills were required as the small cutters, identified by the red-and-white signal flag flying from the masthead, approached under the towering lee of the vessel. In rough seas, contact with the bigger ship could be dangerous and was controlled by 'scandalising' the mainsail, using the peak halyard to adjust the height of the gaff to spill wind quickly. Pilots sometimes transferred to the larger ship in a well-found, sea-kindly rowing yawl. In the open sea, even when hove to, there was a constant risk of being run down or catching on the chain plates or the rubbing streaks of the larger vessel in the rise and fall of the sea. The pilot, choosing the correct moment, grabbed the rope ladder on the side of the larger vessel and scrambled over the lee rail in a precarious operation in which he risked slipping and falling between the two boats. With the pilot safely aboard, the cutter was cast off from the larger ship and accompanied her to port.

The pilot provided an essential service in assisting ships arriving and departing the harbour, often the most hazardous part of a voyage. The task was to navigate vessels through restricted shoaling harbour mouths and rock-strewn entrances, drawing on the skills and knowledge gleaned from experience passed down through generations.

For pilots it was rewarding financially. Men with good reputations were well remunerated by the ships' owners and masters. While not regulated, piloting involved crews vying competitively to seek out and be first aboard the arriving vessel. Rivalry existed between the Kinsale and Cork harbour pilots and could be contentious as it was a 'closed-shop' occupation, where usurpers were warned off. As late as 1872, the Kinsale Harbour Board expressed its astonishment at the decision of the Cork Board not to allow 'Kinsale fishermen pilots' to take ships into Cork Harbour.[8] The introduction of the telegraph in 1862 made it possible to have information on arrivals passed directly from the Old Head to Queenstown in Cork, where a pilot vessel was dispatched immediately. Efficiency and speed were increased by the arrival of the steam-powered cutter. In harbour the pilot or members of his family were often engaged in servicing the ship and a visiting captain would be directed to particular suppliers.

The competitive element remained and the garrulous reputation of the pilots was even referred to by James Joyce in his novel *Ulysses*. Emphasising the explosive impact of a fracas in Dublin, Joyce uses the image an umbrella flying through the air and ending up in the sand of Hole Open Bay. Here he is drawing on his father's experience when, as a student in Cork, he had the opportunity of accompanying the Cork pilots to sea and experienced at first hand the uncompromising nature of the pilot's character. The grandness of the Old Head may have been in Joyce's mind when he wrote 'a silk umbrella—embedded to the extent of one foot three inches in the sandy beach of Hole Open Bay near the Old Head of Kinsale'. It is one of very few references to places outside Dublin in the novel.[9]

The Kinsale pilots lived close to the harbour mouth at Lower Cove and used the Old Head, Preghane and Hangman Points as observation positions overlooking the sea to the horizon. Their importance was recognised in 1839 by Samuel Lewis who wrote that they 'have been noted for the goodness of their boats and their excellent seamanship, their services in supplying the markets of Cork and other neighbouring towns and their skills as pilots have procured for themselves exemption from impressment during the last war'.[10] The reference here was to the Napoleonic Wars when many Irish, particularly experienced seamen, were forced to sail and fight aboard English ships.

The importance of piloting remains to the present day. One of the first motions adopted by Kinsale Harbour Board, when established in 1870, was to regularise the practice in its own port. It appointed two pilots for the harbour and a separate pair for the river, which presents specific and quite different navigational challenges.

To assist the pilot, a ship approaching the harbour in poor visibility had a crewman forward with a lead line which was cast ahead of the ship and sank quickly to the bottom. As the ship moved forward, the line rising perpendicularly from the bottom gave the leadsman the opportunity to determine the depth under the vessel by reading the various leather and cloth bunting marks, which he called out or 'sounded'. In this way, the skipper would determine the bottom contour and be aware of shoaling water and distance off land, by interpreting information already on the chart. Retrieving the lead, its tallow-filled cavity brought up an imprint of a hard bottom or a sample of mud, sand or shingle indicating the type of 'ground' and thus the quality of its holding for anchoring purposes could be evaluated.

One of the earliest charts, showing soundings for Kinsale, was drawn by Paul Ivye in November 1601. It was ordered by Lord Deputy Mountjoy so that he could bring in reinforcements from England to 'invest' and recapture the harbour after the Spaniards had landed in September. A navigable channel is indicated on the eastern side of the harbour to Scilly Point and shoal water on the western side is shown by shading. Above Rincurran Point safe anchorage is recommended 'where great ships use to ride',[11] and marked at the entrance off Eastern Point is an unnamed dangerous rock which later came to be known as Bulman.

Another early chart was produced at the end of the English Civil War when Prince Rupert, nephew of the executed King Charles I, arrived in Kinsale in 1649. To keep the Prince confined within the harbour, the Parliamentary navy established a blockade for which a chart was prepared with sailing directions for entry to the harbour:

> Steer NNE from the Old Head to the Harbour mouth
> you must keep to the eastern shore and keep Barry Óg's
> [now Charles Fort] Castle open on the last point in your
> sight to go clear of the rock [now Bulman] that lies off
> the east point. The Castle going up in the Harbour on
> your starboard side and so you go clear of the rock, and
> then run up into the Harbour. When you are almost as
> far as Barry's Castle you may anchor if you please or run
> up further. It is good riding all along the shore on your
> starboard side.

These instructions are excellent and serve well even today.[12]

Later in the seventeenth and eighteenth centuries more accurate charts of ports in England and Ireland were prepared by the hydrographer Captain Greenville Collins aboard his survey vessel *Merlin*. The chart of Kinsale drawn in 1693 and dedicated to Robert Southwell (a member of the prominent 17th-century Kinsale family) names Bulman Rock, and highlights the Harbour Bar and the newly complete Charles Fort (see plate 4).

From 1750, a ship's master could avail of a map inscribed by Charles Smith, 'A New and Correct Map of the County Cork', which included tidal information showing the set, drift and time lag between ebb and flood at different points on the coast. Approaching Kinsale Harbour soundings (normally given in fathoms) of 60 and 70 feet on the map provided important data for the incoming vessel.

A large scale chart was drawn by Bellin in 1764 for the French admiralty which, when discovered by the English, heightened anxiety about plans for a possible invasion. He shows Bulman Rock, the Harbour Bar, the location of the shipyard at Castlepark and Sandy Cove Island, which was then connected to the land. The natural barrier to the sea made Sandy Cove and the Pill a sheltered inlet.

With improving survey methods, charts became more accurate but still required utmost caution from navigators. Eighteenth-century map-makers, for instance Beaufort and Arrowsmith, give two latitude positions for Kinsale, which differ by more than two nautical miles and refer to positions well south of the Old Head.[13] Names of features, taken from the original Irish, were spelt phonetically and were sometimes marked inaccurately. In an otherwise useful chart drawn in 1763 by Captain Murdock MacKenzie, Hangman Point is misplaced at Preghane. All provide information about anchoring positions, including the Bandon River. In the 1830s a major hydrographic survey of the coast was undertaken by the British Admiralty. The data is corrected regularly and remains a valuable source of information for seafarers.

A research report in 1900 undertaken for the Harbour Board included a survey indicating the fairway in the harbour, giving specific transits using identifiable marks ashore. The Railway Station (now the site of Kinsale Holiday Homes) in line with the Blockhouse identified the channel until opposite Sally Port. An alternative course could be held by keeping the old Summer Cove School (halfway down the hill) in line with the Fort battery. Further into the harbour, deep-water anchoring is available off the 'Hotel' (now a private residence on the High Road) at 37 feet, off the Pier at 51 feet and the Ferry Slip at 23 feet.[14]

A number of features, because of their importance to navigation in the harbour, receive particular attention, such as 'the dangerous rock' marked off Eastern Point. The Captain Collins chart shows only 5 feet clearance at low water over Bulman. The name most probably comes from *bolmán*, an old Irish name for horse mackerel,[15] many of which are caught close to the rock.[16] In recent centuries, the danger has been marked by a buoy which lies to the south. Provision for a bell-and-whistle attachment was made in 1908 to assist the mariner at night and in poor visibility. The motion of the water caused the bell to ring intermittently. When the whistle was fitted, air compressed by the rise and fall of the buoy in the sea created an eerie, mournful sound, particularly with the wind from the southeast. The sound could be heard in the town itself. Originally the buoy was a black floating cone shape and later the colour changed to green indicating a starboard-hand mark. The present buoy is a south cardinal IALA mark, a standard internationally recognised system for avoiding isolated dangers.

Before the rock was buoyed, it was described simply as 'a blind rock close to east point'.[17] Early directions say that the rock must be kept to starboard and that the clearing line is Charles Fort open on Eastern Point when entering the harbour from the south and the

Small Sovereign Island open on Frower Point when approaching from the east. In calm weather small vessels may pass through Bulman Sound, a channel between the rock and Preghane Point. The rock itself is a deceptively innocent hazard in anything up to moderate conditions when it breaks. It draws less than a fathom on which leisure craft ignorant of the danger come to grief occasionally and in gales a violent sea over the rock shows the potential for calamity (see plate 3).

Another feature particularly noted in the Collins and Bellin charts is the Harbour Bar indicated by shoal water across the harbour from Money Point to Middle Cove. It became an issue at the end of the seventeenth century as the larger ships then being built required greater depths of water. The debate gave rise to long-term doubts about Kinsale's viability as a port and threats to its status as a naval centre. Edward Southwell in 1703, anxious to keep the channel clear, sought: 'permission from the High Court of Parliament sitting in this Kingdom for the cleansing of the Harbour ... which would make it much spacier and advantageous'. He insisted on maintaining the practice of taking mud and sand from inside the harbour to distribute as a valuable fertiliser for the land.[18] The 'Swallow', the name attributed to the western section of the outer harbour between the Blockhouse and Money Point, was specifically identified. Ironically this sandbank, described in 1652 'as a great shelf that shooted a great way off the land', saved a vessel called the *Peru*. She was damaged below the waterline but managed to reach Kinsale and was gently beached, where repairs were undertaken at low tide. According to Alexander Selkirk in 1703, there was so much sand in the area that it dried out at low water.[19] Despite the constant removal of sand, a valuable resource for agriculture, the build-up of silt was a problem in the harbour. Samuel Lewis in 1839 pointed to the limited depth because 'nearly abreast of Charles Fort is a bar having only 12 feet of water at low spring tides'. Dredging operations were required intermittently when, for example, the Harbour Board in 1905 engaged the services of the steam-powered, appropriately named *Sisyphus,* to continue the unremitting task of removing the endless quantities of silt.

Nevertheless, Kinsale's natural qualities as a port were promoted even though ships were increasing in size. A report of 1652 stated that 'in Kinsale ships may ride at anchor in 8 or 9 fathom of water being defended off all winds'. In 1709 'mercantile vessels and privateers ... put into this harbour knowing from authentic charts the good anchorage facility at all times and speedy exit to the ocean'.[20]

Local knowledge and experience, sailing directions and pilot guides were essential for a safe harbour entry that required clear visual sight lines of physical features to provide the transits, leading and clearing lines. Caution was required as more informal features could change, such as the colour on the gable end of a house, a tree on a headland or the removal of a telegraph pole. For example, Sprayfield House above Cuirtaphorteen, south of Sandy Cove, was a noted mark when arriving from the east. Confusion would arise if the colour changed from its traditional white.

One of the earliest aids to navigation in the harbour was a light placed at Rincurran Point close to Barry Óg's Castle, now the site of Charles Fort. As suggested in the name Rincurran, it is derived from the Irish, meaning the point (*rinn*) of the reaping hook (*corrán*). The name comes from the configuration of the land in the surrounding area, which when viewed from above takes the shape of a sickle, with its point appropriately ending at the rock under the lighthouse, jutting into the harbour. The original light may have been housed in a cottage-type structure similar to that at the Old Head of Kinsale. When Charles Fort was completed in 1680, the light was incorporated into a diamond niche high on an internal building within the walls. In modern times the light is in a small structure on the sea-facing bastion above the White Lady turret. Described as 'the pride and joy of the Irish Lights' the sectored light, with its leading white beam flashing every 5 seconds, visible from the Old Head, gives a clear passage into the harbour.[21]

North of Charles Fort, an incoming vessel at night sailed blind until the Pier Head light was visible when clear of the Blockhouse after the 1880s. During the height of the fishing industry there were calls for a leading light on the Lower Road at Scilly. This demand, however, was eventually superseded by the introduction of flashing red top marks on the three port-hand lateral buoys, known locally as Bostoon, Spit and Scilly, which mark the approach to the upper reaches of the harbour.

When the marina was built in the 1970s other lights were put in place, which have improved pilotage in the harbour. A painting of the landing of King James II in 1689, reputed to be at the Glen, shows a building referred to as the Cuckold light. This image is of the Inner Harbour before the area was filled in to create what is now the town's centre, and may be viewed in Kinsale Museum.

Other dangers in the harbour include Farmer Rock at Bog Hole, south of Money Point and the 'Platters and Dishes' southwest of the Blockhouse. For each, directions on clearing and leading lines were passed down through generations. A boat making the short passage from Sandy Cove to Kinsale must keep the tower of Ardbrack Church open (visible) on Money Point. The clearing line takes the vessel east of Farmer Rock, a deceptive hazard which shows at low-water spring tides. Anxiety about the rock forced the Harbour Board in January 1902 to request the Commissioners of Irish Lights to have it marked with a perch. The appeals were turned down. The Board felt so strongly that warnings were painted on the rocks ashore. These have long since disappeared but the danger remains.

Close to the Blockhouse are the 'Platters and Dishes', named for the flat plate-like shape of the rocky shoreline. These were a favourite picnic and swimming spot but under water they stretch dangerously into the harbour. To avoid them O'Brien's farmhouse, kept in line of sight, south of the Blockhouse will take a boat clear. In other parts of the harbour, threatening seaweed-covered obstructions are no longer dangerous as they have been covered by the Pier Head, in the case of the Town Rock, and Carraig na Roan has been incorporated into the Boatyard Pier at Middle Cove.

Apart from instructions for safely navigating the harbour, numerous features and practices were identified to assist the seafarer. In the past when timekeepers or watches were rare, the 'Half Tide' Rock at Castlepark and other points in the harbour provided direct information on the state of the tide. By looking at the water level in relation to the rock, a fisherman or sailor could determine the time when enough water would be available for a boat to come alongside a quay wall or clear the bar on arriving or departing the harbour. This data, taken with the lunar phases, provided a predictable calendar of tidal ranges. Knowledge of the equinoxes and how they impacted on the heights of the tides that occurred at the 'Patrick's springs', around 17 March, provided a timetable for particular tasks, such as the repair of quay walls, that could only be undertaken at extreme low-water levels.

A major man-made feature, built at the World's End in the seventeenth century, was the Royal Dockyard (now the Trident Hotel). It had the capacity to repair and build ships of over 100 feet in length. After the navy left, it provided docking facilities for coastal shipping. Further upriver the remains of a gun wharf used for stepping masts, handling guns and general provisioning is still visible. The nearby double slipway was the departure point from which the cross-river ferry operated. Both these facilities were accessed by way of the 'drang', a steep narrow incline above the water which existed before the World's End road was constructed. Similarly a pathway through the Folly provided the connection to the stone-faced Lobster Quay with its wide slipway and stone spiral steps curving around its sheltered corner.

The use of the term 'drang', which in Cornish means a lane, illustrates how the World's End section of the town became associated with people from the southwest of England. They also brought a distinctive speech pattern that can still be heard among some of the older inhabitants. It is characterised by the practice of disregarding the letter 'h' at the beginning of words and ironically putting it in when a vowel is the initial letter. A humorous example of the peculiarity is remembered in a response to the whereabouts of a local man, when the enquirer was told that ''e's on the Lobster Quay leathering a pair of hoars', which was the task of attaching leather to oars to protect them from wear.

Apart from the Cornwall link with the World's End the connection with the southwest of England is further indicated by the name Scilly, another settlement in the harbour, which had fishing and boatbuilding links to the Isles of Scilly.

On the same side of the river and a little further west are the Folly steps and Carraig Oisín, or Oisín's Rock, which links Kinsale to the Oisianic saga of Tír na nÓg – the land of everlasting youth. In a fit of temper at the 'people over the water' at Castlepark, the Folly's own giant managed to throw five large stones across the river, landing on the opposite bank. In attempting to lift the sixth stone the giant failed, and the missile remains fixed in the ground close to the steps. The story continues with Oisín arriving on his white horse and, in response to calls from the giant for assistance, dismounted, forgetting that when he stepped on the land he would lose the gift of eternal youth. Suddenly assuming the physical condition of being thousands of years of age he immediately crumbled to dust. The stone was never moved and ever since has been dedicated to Oisín. Across the river on the opposite bank draught net fishermen still refer to that stretch of bank as the Five Stones.

Fresh water was a requirement for all vessels calling to Kinsale and an abundance of spring wells provided a ready supply. Scilly Well with easy access was used most frequently. At a particular stage of a rising tide a punt loaded with empty casks was dispatched from the ship. The containers were placed upright on the aft taut and filled directly from the flowing spring. Timing was critical as the rising tide ensured that the punt, now laden with heavy water-filled barrels, would float but not so far into the duration of the flood that the fresh water from the well would mix with the incoming salt water. Other methods of loading water were also used: 'I went down to the Cove [at the top of the Dam] and here at the upper end Alderman Hoare [Southwell's agent] and his Men of War get their water. They have made a dam head and a spout to run into the hogs' heads and they put the casks into the water and float them to the ships.'[22]

Crews of visiting ships met the people of the small communities living on the shore around the harbour and witnessed the bare subsistence levels on which they survived. At settlements, south of Charles Fort, people scavenged for a living from the sea and land. Similarly, the community on the Old Head, like the nesting shearwaters on the cliff ledges below, clung for survival, in mud and stone huts attached to the ruined walls of older structures.

Both these areas were Irish speaking where names in Irish were used for the smallest inlets and rock features. In modern times the helms of engine-powered boats rarely need to consider the tide in the harbour. Formerly, small boats, dependent on sail and oars, hugged the shore to reduce the effect of a strong countercurrent. Shelter from a sudden squall, the need for rest and landing places for nets and fish were found in little inlets known as 'cushanna' or, in the lee of rocky outcrops, 'carraigheanna'. People had an intimate knowledge of the shoreline. They, together with the lobstermen, operating close inshore, became familiar with features and inevitably gave names to places they encountered frequently. Droichead na Fine off Garrettstown as its name, 'the bridge of wine', suggests was the wreck site of a ship spilling its cargo of wine casks into the sea, no doubt to the satisfaction and pleasure of some in the area. Viewed from the north, The Old Head peninsula takes the shape of a corpulent man facing west, supporting a belly-like feature called Cnoc a' Bolg and on the eastern side the other physiognomical extremity, the Tóin (or Bottom) Point. Faill an Aifrinn (Mass Rock) is the location where Mass was said in penal times, hidden amid the rocks and close enough to the water for people to escape by boat if discovered by the authorities who had banned the practice of Catholicism. A number of other Mass rocks were located on the eastern side of the harbour itself, at Claidhe an Aifrinn (Mass fence) and at Preghane, both locations close to the sea. The practice was noted by Cosimo de' Medici, a member of the Florentine banking family, influential in European affairs, when he arrived in Kinsale in 1669 after his ship was blown off course in heavy weather. He was highly critical of the prohibition on religious freedom.[23] The roar of the sea crashing on the rocks is conveyed in the name Faill na nGlór. On a calm day the blueness of the deep water is well described by Cuas Gorm, just west of the tip of the Head. On the eastern side, boats sheltering crept into the corner of Hole Open to boil a kettle, which is appropriately called An Cistin (The Kitchen). Across Bullen's Bay, Cuas Buí with its yellow-coloured sand was popular for bathing. In contrast, reflecting the tragedies that attach to seaboard life is Cuas an Duinne Bháite where, in circumstances now forgotten, the remains of a drowned sailor were washed ashore. Further towards Duneen is Oileánn Glas – the Green Island – but due to erosion of the soil the grass no longer grows. It was here for security that the explosive powder for the lighthouse fog signal was stored.[24]

Inside the mouth of the harbour itself on the eastern shore, Irish names were prevalent. On the stretch of shoreline from Charles Fort to Ballymacus Point, women, perhaps washing and drying clothes, gathered at Carraig na Ban (Women's Rock) close to Cuas Lár

(Middle Cove). Across the Cove there was Carraig na Rón (Rock of the Seal). Cuas Fáinleoga is further south where swallows gather in the autumn for their flight south, and close by is Ceann Chapill (the Horse's Head Rock). Cuas Innill – 'safe inlet' – provided security for boats and southwest towards Eastern Point is a blowhole – Poll a' Talaimh' located below the Crooked Ditch, a well-known mark for fishing. Préachán or Prehane, the Crow's Point, comes into view after rounding Eastern Point.

These are a small sample of the names in Irish spoken among the native people outside the town that were common up to the end of the nineteenth century. Ironically, the locations most associated with the use of Irish names were those surrounding British military installations, the garrison at Charles Fort and the coastguard at the Old Head. *Translations,* a play by Brian Friel, highlights issues where foreign military occupation impacts on the native Irish-speaking community. Lines from the play make reference to how the language impacted on the impoverished natives: 'A rich language. A rich literature. You'll find, Sir, that certain cultures expend on their vocabularies and syntax acquisitive energies and ostentations entirely lacking in their material lives. I suppose you could call us a spiritual people.'

A spiritual dimension was significant in the lives of people living close to the sea, where the prospect of death from drowning or shipwreck was a constant reality. The Church of the Holy Trinity was situated on Fort Hill overlooking the harbour and Charles Fort. As the proximity of the ancient church was seen as a serious defence weakness to the new fortification it was decided to move the church to a new site at Ardbrack and dedicate the rebuilt structure to Saint Catherine. Nevertheless the burial ground and the holy well, 'Tobar an Tríonóide' (the Well of the Trinity), on the old site continued in use. Annually on the Feast of the Holy Trinity the Pattern was celebrated. This was the practice where pilgrims gathered to pray and undertake the 'rounds', a spiritual exercise of walking in circles around the well. Boats full of people came from different points on the coast – Nohoval Cove, Oysterhaven, the Old Head and Sandy Cove – landing at Sallyport. Having completed the spiritual exercises the pilgrims then engaged in some riotous socialising, consisting of drinking accompanied by singing and dancing. These activities were disapproved of by the official Church which was also critical of the pre-Christian origins associated with the rituals of the Pattern. The objections eventually led to the demise of the practice in the late nineteenth century.

The close connection of the seaboard community on the eastern side of the harbour with religious practice was maintained into the early twentieth century. Twice a year a priest visited the isolated community at the Lower Cove to say the Station Mass, which was the opportunity for the Catholic clergy to conduct pastoral visitation and collect dues. Days prior to the visit were taken up with the preparation of a four-oared yawl used to ferry the priest from Kinsale and smartly row him to the remote cove. Great attention was paid to making the trip comfortable by avoiding the sea while crossing the Bar. As the bow grounded on the shingle a young lad was detailed to place a chair at the edge of the water so that the priest would remain dry when stepping ashore. Sean Keating's painting *Slán Leat, a Athair* (Goodbye, Father), which depicts a similar scene on the Aran Islands, evokes the strong belief in the spiritual that pervaded seaboard communities.

Cuirtaphorteen, meaning 'the church of the little port', was the burial place of families in the area and the site of a harbour south of Sandy Cove before the ravages of the sea destroyed the shelter and eroded the land, exposing the skeletal remains of the monks and the people who lived in the now-deserted village nearby. The weathering of the earth under the church is a noted example of a wave-cut platform.[25] While a beautiful place, a strange ominous feeling of dislocation, which many people experience while in the area, is expressed by the Kinsale poet Jerome Kiely:[26]

> knowing the waves
> ossiverous
> would prospect through the buttress rocks for graves
> and carry undersea the seasoned bones ...

At Kinsale, the need to provide for the spiritual dimension in the lives of mariners is continued in modern times by the work of the Mission to Seamen which also provides support and practical assistance when required.

The man-made amenities that were constructed and the natural qualities of the harbour that had attracted the earliest settlers were the basis for development by each influx of subsequent inhabitants. They added more facilities, making Kinsale port a safe haven for its seafaring community and a welcoming harbour for the sailors and fishermen who entered it. As a port of growing importance the harbour required landing facilities on the waterfront and a range of services to cater for ocean-going shipping which in turn generated even further maritime activity and demands. From the beginning, Kinsale was recognised as one of Ireland's premier harbours and inevitably its potential was realised in different ways.

Evidence of early settlement in the Kinsale area was uncovered by excavations undertaken by S.P. O'Riordan in the 1940s at Ballycatten, a ring fort near Ballinspittle, and at Garrans north of Innishannon. They indicated trade connections with southern Europe as early as the sixth and seventh centuries as shown by the discovery of beads, pottery, pins and bronze. Fragments of amphorae at Garrans suggest that oil and spices from the eastern Mediterranean were transported and that this trade came through Kinsale.[27]

Viking invaders from Scandinavia plied the south coast of Ireland in the ninth century and took control of the Munster rivers. They struck terror in the inhabitants as they arrived at the entrance to harbours in their 70-foot-long double-ended open vessels with carved dragons on high prows. The large single square sail bent to the timber yard was furled and with the rhythmic splash of up to seventy oars, the intrepid seafarers entered Kinsale and found a suitable place to winter, taking a respite from ravaging and plundering. Richard Caulfield, in the introduction to the *Annals of Kinsale*, suggests that these settlers may have given the name 'World's End' to the southwestern section of the town by the edge of the river. 'Engleworth' instead of Kinsale was the name used on the early town arms. The term has been interpreted as meaning a 'further harbour' or 'world's end', which it is reasonable to imply may have been the perception of the Norsemen when they arrived initially.[28]

Later the Vikings established small settlements, and after a period began to cooperate and integrate with the earlier inhabitants. The Scandinavian connection opened up trade from Kinsale with the

Baltic and the Hanseatic League which continued to the thirteenth century. The Vikings influenced boatbuilding techniques in Ireland, by introducing the use of overlapping timber planking in construction. The system, more commonly referred to as clinker construction, required large quantities of timber which produced extremely well 'found' boats.[29]

After the Vikings, the next phase in Kinsale's development as a port begins with the arrival of the Normans in Ireland in the twelfth century and ends with the death of the 15th Earl of Desmond in 1583. Henry II, who ordered the invasion, was the Plantagenet King not only of England but also much of western France through marriage with Eleanor of Aquitaine. The connection expanded trading contacts, particularly with the Bordeaux wine-producing area. The Norman Fitzgeralds, Earls of Desmond, who were ambitious and entrepreneurial had their manor house at Askeaton, County Limerick and were granted a million acres of land in south Munster in the thirteenth century. As feudal overlords they made land in the Cork area available to the de Cogans who in turn granted extensive tracts of property in Kinsale to the de Courcys of Ringrone, south of the Bandon River and to the de Barrys, who received lands on the eastern side of the harbour and at Oysterhaven. They had their seat at Rincurran which is now the site of Charles Fort. Among the other Norman families in the Kinsale area were the Roches, who built tower houses on the bends of the Bandon River and the Longs of Mountlong who held lands surrounding Oysterhaven creek. In the early years of Norman occupation, residual opposition from the old native Irish was overcome. Fineen McCarthy, encouraged by his victory at the Battle of Callen near Kenmare in 1261, advanced eastwards, reclaiming land taken by the invaders. He was eventually defeated and killed by de Courcy at Ringrone. With their property taken, the native families found their ancient rights disregarded. They were identified as 'the wild Irish' and described as 'cave dwellers living on rapine and pillage'.[30]

The Desmonds chose Kinsale as the harbour from which to trade the rich produce of the area and as an entry point for goods from abroad. Of significance in Kinsale were agricultural crops from the Bandon river basin and wool introduced by the Cistercians at nearby

Tracton Abbey in the twelfth century, which was exported through the harbour to destinations as far away as Lucca and Florence in Tuscany.

Trade links between Kinsale and the southwest of France grew in the early fourteenth century. Eighteen ships in 1308 transported wine from the Garonne at a period when the Irish were seafaring merchants as distinct from shipowners. The Irish traders used vessels owned by the Bretons from Cameret and Brest in northwest France and chartered at a rate of between one fifth and a half the value of the goods. The practice continued for many centuries, becoming even more common after the imposition of the Penal Laws on the Irish in the 1700s. The ships sailed close inshore, passing through the fast-flowing seas of the Raz de Bretagne and Quessant rather than making the longer passage in the open sea. Aboard these vessels the Irish merchant adventurers, taking nothing but a sea chest, made the voyage from Kinsale to the continental ports. The destination was often determined at the last moment, being dictated by the tide and wind or reports of market demand ashore. They were known to land on obscure beaches and remote sheltered inlets. The merchants never missed an opportunity, catching fish when outward bound to augment cargos of Irish-produced friezes, mantles, hides, furs, butter, woollens and leather already aboard. Ports regularly entered were Nantes, La Rochelle and Bordeaux, where firm trading links were established. The vessels returned with wine, honey, salt, brandy, plums, prunes, corn, iron and resin. At La Rochelle in 1559, Madeira wine was exchanged for salted herring and cod, using the barter form of exchange. Couraus, a blue dye, and alum from Italy were transported from Languedoc in the southeast of France and shipped from Bordeaux to Kinsale. Later, from the 1660s, the Canal du Midi, which linked Bordeaux to Sete, gave access to the Mediterranean and an even broader trading network. In the seventeenth century, Kinsale developed contact with the Spanish port towns of Seville and later Cadiz, which under the influence of King Phillip II in the latter half of the sixteenth century, became important centres through which the Irish traded with the extensive Spanish colonies. An English ship on a voyage to Andalusia and the Algerian port of Oran called to Kinsale

PLATE 1. Old Head of Kinsale looking north to the harbour mouth.
Courtesy John Collins

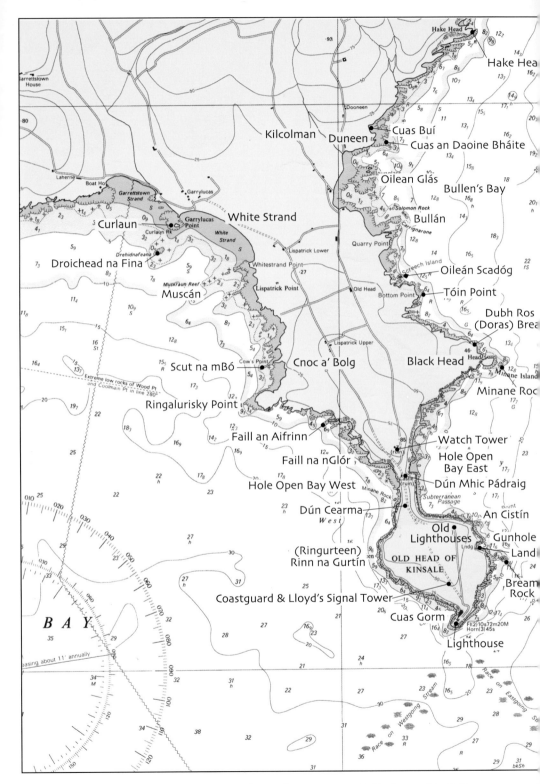

PLATE 2. Chart of Old Head of Kinsale. *Courtesy HM Hydrographic Office*

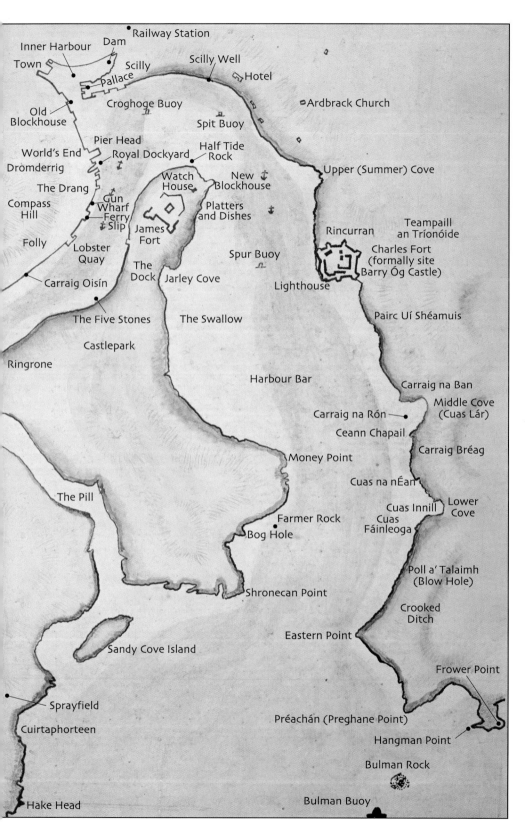

PLATE 3. Kinsale Harbour. *Courtesy John H. Thuillier*

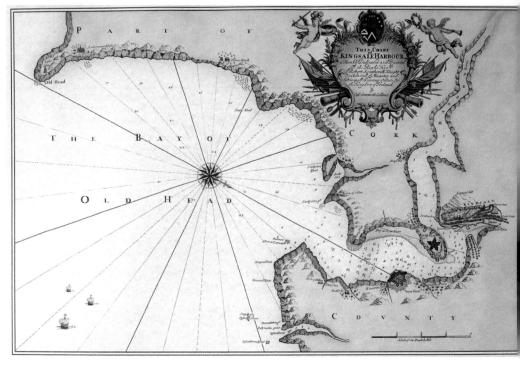

PLATE 4. Greenville Collins' chart of approaches and Kinsale Harbour, *c.*1690.
Courtesy Don Herlihy and Barry Maloney

PLATE 5. Pier Head under construction assisted with steam crane, 1888. *Courtesy Tony Bocking*

to recruit Irish sailors in 1481. Among the range of destinations for ships out of Kinsale are references to Bristol vessels bound for Iceland, calling to avail of services in the harbour.[31]

Bristol for many centuries with its wide and open channel, lying due east of Kinsale, was the port in Britain having most contact with the south coast of Ireland. After Waterford, Kinsale was recorded as being ahead of Wexford, Cork, Youghal and other harbours such as Dingle in terms of numbers and value of cargos. For the year 1504/5, of the 39 Irish-owned ships entering Bristol, 7 were from Kinsale and in the opposite direction imports to the town were carried in 7 vessels out of a total of 35 entrances. In addition, 126 English ships were involved in the Bristol trade, many calling to Kinsale. Ships were used to export quantities of hake, porpoise, salted fish, hides, corn and wood with products such as wine, alum, Breton linen and animals, including hawks and horses, landed at Kinsale and then re-exported. Ships returned with knives, aniseed, liquorice, salt, spices, iron, hemp, pitch, seeds, liquor and hops. Large quantities of fabric, cloth, dyes made from lichens, leather and silk ties for the fastening of bodices and jackets were brought into Kinsale.[32]

Exchequer customs returns for the sixteenth century confirm the extensive trade that took place. Unlike the ships used in trading with France, the vessels to Bristol were owned and skippered by the Kinsale merchants themselves. In 1516, *The Christofur of Kinsale* made at least five trips. On 8 March 1551, *The John of Kinsale* arrived in Bristol with porpoise, fish, train oil and meat. On 16 March, she left with silk, hops, saffron, orchil dye (a red or violet dye made from lichen) and knives. *The Richard of Kinsale* in 1576 returned to her home port with orchil, hemp, pitch, iron and 'cutts' (knives). In the same year *The Margaret*, captained by Richard Roche brought goods in for his brother Henry, a merchant. These accounts show the close economic ties that existed with England through Bristol, which continued until the Fitzgerald demise in Munster in the 1570s.[33]

Kinsale was not only a trading port but was also beginning to establish an important reputation for victualling and the provisioning of ships. In June of 1518 the Habsburg Archduke Ferdinand, brother of Charles V, King of Spain and the Holy Roman Emperor, on a stormy

eleven-day voyage from Santander bound for the Low Countries, was
blown off course and arrived in Kinsale. His fleet consisted of six large
ships. The chronicler reports that Ferdinand initially hid his identity by
removing the Hapsburg symbol of the Golden Fleece from around his
neck. He was recognised, however, and for three days was feted by the
locals who, it was reported, 'went on their knees to him'. He received
the representatives of the Desmonds, who presented him with gifts.
After loading with fresh water and food the fleet set sail for Antwerp
in a favourable westerly. In 1555, Ferdinand succeeded to the position
of Emperor, and as Spain's control of the Netherlands was threatened
and ports in Brittany were lost, it is conceivable that the hospitality
received and the services available at Kinsale were remembered and
initiated a pattern of contact with Spain that culminated in the Last
Armada to Kinsale in 1601–2.[34]

The harbour was the embarkation point for many travelling
abroad. Eleanor, Countess of Desmond took the route from Kinsale
to Bristol, when in January 1570 she sailed to visit her husband
Garrett, the 15th Earl. Because of rebellion and active resistance to
Elizabeth I's policies in Ireland he had been summoned to London.
His beautiful and dutiful wife, who wished to be at his side during his
imprisonment, spent a number of days in Kinsale in transit.[35] Many
Irish pilgrims going to Rome, the Holy Land and the Camino to
Santiago de Compostela in northern Spain, left through Kinsale. Irish
monks from the eighth century used the port on visitation to various
foundations, which had been established on the continent.

Expanding trade, growing prosperity, market tensions and
expressions of independence by the Norman settlers, which emerged
in the thirteenth century, alerted the authorities in London to the
need for regulation. This came in the form of a charter, the first
being granted to Kinsale in 1334 by King Edward III. In return
for a declaration of loyalty and contributions to the royal coffers,
the settlers were allowed to put administrative structures in place,
which established an elite self-perpetuating system of privilege
that continued in Kinsale to the middle of the nineteenth century.
Essentially the town was governed by a Corporation, consisting of
burgesses and freemen drawn from a restricted electorate. They had
the power to nominate a Sovereign annually from among their own.

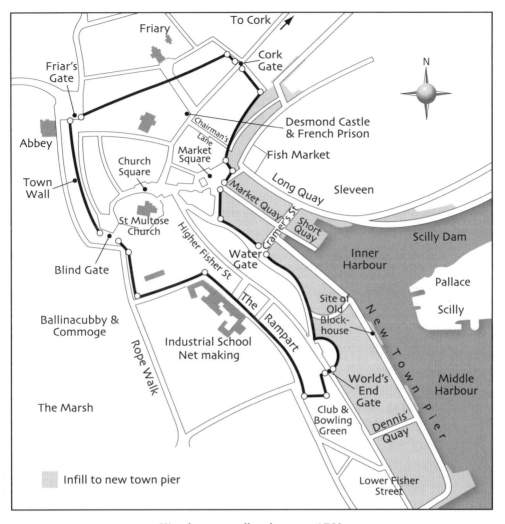

Kinsale town wall and gates, *c.*1750.

He had extensive authority and power, including jurisdiction over the harbour and port activities. The harbour arms adopted was the portcullis in the form of a gate made of grating with lifting chains attached. It symbolised defence and regulation of entry to the town.

The burgesses and freemen were given exclusive rights to trade and had private access to the piers, steps and slipways, many of which were constructed, owned and tolled by themselves.[36] As Corporation members, they granted licences and franchises for the development of lucrative port services. Within the town, trading dynasties emerged, shifting gradually from early feudal structures to the emergence of a business elite, in whom power was concentrated. They introduced market regulations and control to cope with the increasing complexity of expanding trade.[37] At various times, as the town prospered, the Charter was amended. In 1395 at Waterford, Richard II 'granted to the Provost of the Ville de Kinsale to take [the levies and tolls] for 5 years from saleable goods coming to said Ville or harbour'. The additional finance was used to complete the town wall.[38]

As the port's capacity to generate revenue increased, rival claims at the highest level within the administrative chain insisted on their share. In February 1563 the Earl of Ormond, the Lord Deputy, challenged the Earl of Desmond for his right to a 'prise' of imported wine (one cask from a ship's cargo or 'a pipe from every hulk') and also, on exports, a 'cocket' of hides was demanded. Desmond objected and the issue was referred to the Queen who eventually judged in favour of Ormond.[39] Royal intervention in this case demonstrated the authority of the monarch, which insured a constant stream of income to the royal coffers and the importance of maintaining discipline and loyalty, particularly in times of upheaval and threat. The opportunity of pledging fealty was taken whenever appropriate. Sir Richard Edgecombe in June 1488 arrived by ship to Kinsale and there took oaths of loyalty from the nobility. This in turn was acknowledged in the monarch's guarantee of support for the Kinsale authorities.[40]

References indicate that the Sovereign's authority of the harbour extended from Bulman Rock to Dursey Island off the Beara Peninsula.[41] This jurisdiction would seem to be confirmed in the 'fiant' granted by Elizabeth I in 1589, where the Corporation had customs responsibility for the coast from Bulman to the island of Dursey electing a searcher and gauger (i.e. customs officers who had the duty of uncovering cargo and determining size) annually. The often-quoted claim is disputed, though, by historians such as Father P. McSwiney, who said that authority was limited and only extended 'from the Bulman to the Dursees about 2 miles'. The ambiguity may be explained in that, while the name Dursee refers to the island off the west Cork coast, it may also, coming from the Irish 'dubh ros', refer to a black rock which is close to Black Head at the southern end of

Kinsale and Bandon Harbour Commissioners at Kilmacsimon in 1930 for their
regular meeting. Pictured aboard *Terry*, owned by Eamon O'Neill TD.

Bullen's Bay.[42] As with important ports such as Cork and Falmouth,
which have extended headlands giving shelter and protection, ships
awaiting orders while anchored in the lee of the Old Head of Kinsale,
inside the line from the Bulman to Black Head, were subject to the
authority of the town Sovereign. In 1870, with the growing sense of
democracy, control of the harbour and the river was transferred to
a Board of Harbour Commissioners by an Act of Parliament. Their
authority was further modified by the Harbour Act of 1947, which
fixed the harbour limits to a line extending from Preghane Point to
Sandy Cove Island and upriver to Innishannon.

The Sovereign was the searcher, inquisitor and gauger on the
sea and on land, but delegated the function to the Water Bailiff, 'one
honest man as collector of customs and subsidies to the Crown'.[43]
Apart from his role as revenue collector, the extensive responsibilities
of the Bailiff included the orderly functioning of the harbour from the
prevention of 'casting out of dirt, dung and waste which tended to

accumulate on the quays, slipways and above high water mark on the strands', to keeping access to the shore open. Thomas Chudleigh, the prominent shipbuilder remembered on a timber plaque in St Multose Church in Kinsale, was ordered by the Bailiff to remove 'a parcel of masts from interfering with the Kings highway as it was a hindrance to passengers'. Similar to the role of the modern Harbour Master, the Bailiff was the berthing master in the busy port. In 1684 'the Kings Old Quay near the [old] Blockhouse is reserved for ships, boats and barques so that they can land goods and merchandise'.[44] The official had his own insignia in the form of a silver oar which he displayed on boarding a ship. Presentments of the Grand Jury for September 1696 state that the Bailiff, in this case William Hammett, 'may have an oar made for him for 40/= [shillings] at ye charge of ye corporation with its arms thereon'. The silver oar is on display in Kinsale Museum.

The importance of Kinsale for the Norman settlers is still evident in the fine structure of Desmond Castle on Cork Street, which was built as a custom house in the fourteenth century (see plate 7). Situated 300 feet inside Cork Gate, the main exit in the wall, it was here that goods were held before distribution throughout Munster. A significant part of the trade consisted of wine and because of this link, the Castle became the location of Ireland's Wine Museum in 2003.[45] Located at the top of Chairman's Lane, it was used to hold goods that were landed at the water's edge. It is said that 'chairmen' with sedan chairs queued on the lane, not unlike a modern taxi rank, for hire to carry the wealthy merchants as they came ashore. The impressive three-storeyed Castle building, with its vine-leaf emblems, was the centre of the Desmond association with Kinsale.

At the foot of Cork Street the first town marketplace was located near St Multose Church, another Norman structure. Typically, in medieval times the commercial and ecclesiastical life of the community existed in close proximity. At a remove from the marketplace, the administrative hub was the Mansion House near the first Blockhouse overlooking the Inner Harbour, which was located close to where the monuments to Kinsale seamen are located today.

By the fifteenth century, the Normans or the 'Old English', had in some respects found common cause with the native Irish. Both groups gave adherence to the Roman Church and joined in opposition to the more aggressive plantation and conquest policies of the 'New English' settlers that emerged in the latter part of the sixteenth century. In Munster, a confederation of landowners rose in a rebellion that was ruthlessly put down by the English authorities, culminating in the killing of the Earl of Desmond in 1583. His lands were declared forfeit and made available for plantation, marking the end of the dominant influence of the Anglo-Normans in Kinsale, which had lasted for 400 years. The new regime moved quickly to establish itself, particularly in areas surrounding the leading port towns. Walter Raleigh received extensive lands at Youghal, later purchased by the Boyle family (Earls of Cork) and the Southwells, who were granted lands in the Kinsale area, where they had a major impact on the town and harbour for the next 150 years.

The following chapters trace how Kinsale became a maritime transport hub of significance to the colonies in the seventeenth and eighteenth centuries and a well-known fishing station in the nineteenth. In more recent years, after a period of economic depression, the town created a unique niche in Irish tourism that can again be traced to its qualities as a port and its connection with the sea.

2

The Golden Age of Shipping

After the defeat of the Desmonds, control in the town was quickly appropriated by the 'New English' settlers who secured their position in a number of ways. In the early 1600s the native Irish and the 'Old English' were removed from authority. The new settlers referred to the older inhabitants as 'Irish enemies and English rebels' or collectively as 'foreigners'. Catholics were legally prevented from trading and holding official positions in the town. A hundred years later, this policy was pursued even more vigorously. Presentments adopted by the Kinsale Grand Jury in 1702 and subsequent years ordered 'that no Papist be made a freeman or keep open a shop nor retail any goods'.[1]

An emphasis on individual entrepreneurship and capitalising on the harbour's natural qualities, which characterised the attitude of the new settlers, opened opportunities for the development of services for shipping en route to the new colonies overseas. In the sixteenth century Henry VIII recognised the importance of the seas and the critical necessity of control in response to Spanish expansion and colonisation.[2] Early in the seventeenth century, the English themselves began the process of establishing settlements in the West Indies, Barbados, Bermuda and on the American mainland at Virginia, Pennsylvania, the Carolinas and New England. Large plantations were made available to English occupiers who grew rich through the production of tobacco, sugar, cotton, tea, rum and coffee for which there was a demand in England. At the same time, the English, French and Dutch recognised opportunities emerging in the east. In England, a private company of 200 London merchants was licensed under charter, issued by Queen Elizabeth I, to found the East India Company. Consisting initially of 130 ships, the company established depots in Indonesia to trade in spices such as pepper and nutmeg. Cotton, silk, indigo, opium and saltpetre were brought from India and tea from China. For the investors the trading was profitable, capable of turning over profits of 200 per cent on a round trip that could take up to four years. In 1857 the East India Company handed over its worldwide network to the London government, which provided the economic platform for the emergence of the British Empire. Kinsale's natural attributes and its growing reputation as a victualling centre and provider of maritime services made the harbour an important hub in this trade which reached into the furthest corners of the known world. Positioned as the most westerly of the 'home' ports, the Old Head of Kinsale was the landfall on the approaches for ships seeking to replenish supplies after long voyages. For outward-bound vessels, the harbour was the last opportunity to stock up with fresh food and water. A very accommodating corporation, jealous of its links with the London and Bristol nuclei, created a focus for shipping until 1750 and it can truly be said that this was the golden age of shipping in the harbour. Kinsale was referred to as 'teeming with ships' and described rather extravagantly but with some validity as 'the road stead of world commerce'.[3]

The new English settlers displayed a capacity to accommodate changing political situations and to resist Irish insurgency in the seventeenth and eighteenth centuries. Outside Ireland, the burgeoning naval importance of the Netherlands, stimulated by commercial rivalry, led to a series of wars with England from 1653 to 1675. Later, the prolonged conflicts that England engaged in with the French and Spanish in European waters and against America in the War of Independence brought increased shipping activity to Kinsale. Through strategic positioning and political astuteness, the New English in Kinsale survived and even prospered in this period of instability.

Physically the town expanded, catering for the increase in shipping by encroaching deeper into the water. Quays were extended and the shoreline constructed to accommodate the necessary facilities. The Glen, the Long and Short Quays and focal areas such as the new Market Square, which became the commercial centre, were built on the mud and the strands. From this town focus, six streets, still evident in the modern street pattern, radiate off to the town's gates, to the earlier linear development on the hills and to the harbour. Developed in the late sixteenth century, the new centre was known as the Holy Stone, due perhaps to a stone bollard through which a boat could tie a painter at the top of steps off the Short Quay or more probably because of a stone cross, which was a feature of medieval town centres. The reclaimed portions, on which much of the modern town is built, are today still subject to flooding in exceptional tides and weather conditions.

At Market Square, citizens with power, authority and wealth tended to convene. In the adjacent coffee houses, taverns and exchange, deals were made, influence dispensed and networks established. Captains of ships received orders from owners or agents, collected their commissions and paid their dues. The local merchants, many of whom were also the burgesses and freemen, with their finger on the town's pulse, made decisions and had them formalised by the Corporation which sat in the nearby Market House from 1700. The culture of prestige and power was maintained by the privileged burghers and the traders who formed close relationships, which worked to their mutual benefit and enabled them to put policies in place exclusively in their own favour. A particular example was the presentment adopted in October 1692 which allowed a 'Mr Borrows have liberty to run out a quay as far as the old Blockhouse under a lease'. In return 'all the burgesses and freemen shall have liberty of landing and shipping any goods they think fit to land or ship off from said quay without paying any consideration'.[4]

The high level of networking and control was also maintained in more informal ways. Apart from the frequent incidence of marriage, relations were strengthened through membership of the quasi-religious Kinsale Knot of the Friendly Brothers of St Patrick, which was established in the early eighteenth century. The Club at the

Assembly Rooms, now the Municipal Hall, offered opportunities for socialising.[5] Informal contact was continued in the imposing weather-slated, bow-windowed houses built on the reclaimed land of the Long Quay and Fisher (O'Connell) St. In the gardens that existed behind, the remains of gazebos are evidence of a lifestyle where afternoon tea was taken and the exotic taste and smell of imported coffee, just landed direct from the plantations, was enjoyed. Kinsale was the largest import centre for coffee and tobacco in seventeenth-century Ireland.

From the patchy records, it is possible to show the importance of the town and how far its contacts extended in the seventeenth- and eighteenth-century maritime world. Apart from its role as a victualling port, it assumed other important functions, becoming the leading centre of naval operations in Ireland. King James I, having secured the throne in 1603, granted a new Charter to Kinsale in which it is described as 'a place of great resort for his majesty's ships of war'. The Navy Board designated Kinsale as its main provisioning harbour in 1630, a status which was established by the Southwells and supported by the Earl of Orrery, Lord President of Munster, who regarded Kinsale very highly as a port.[6] As the official provider, the Southwells were engaged in the complex logistical operation of building networks with producers and local merchants to provide supplies when required. The servicing of ships, complicated by the contingencies of wind and tides, required sophisticated management to plan and project quantity needs and storage in the warehouses that were built between 1637 and 1655.[7]

A review of some of the shipping that called to Kinsale over a short period of forty years will illustrate how busy the port was in the latter half of the seventeenth century. Beginning in May 1667 the *St Lewis*, a Portuguese ship taken as a prize, was brought to the harbour. In June Sir Jeremy Smith arrived with 8 ships of war, 2 bomb ketches and 2 fire ships which made up the convoy accompanying one 800-ton Dutch East Indiaman (ship) richly laden with 13 chests of silver worth £23,000. While cruising on the coast Captain O'Brien, son of the Earl of Inchiquin, captured a further 2 Dutch prizes, which were the result of privateering operations conducted during the Dutch wars. At the same time 130 vessels arrived from the West Indies. Soon afterwards,

English East India ships, the *St George* and *Constantinople*, arrived with £300,000 in cargo which was not declared.[8] Moving to July 1673, the *Saint David* with 20 East Indiamen and 40 other rich merchant ships entered Kinsale to await a convoy to England.[9] In August 1678, the English and Dutch, at peace since 1675, formed an alliance to fight the French. A Dutch man-of-war, the *Prince William*, brought several French prizes to the harbour and Dutch ships that had been won back from the French. The ships were loaded with sugar from the West Indies, tea and spices from the East and oil and whalebone from Greenland.

Even the French, despite being at war with England, were welcomed in the harbour when James II landed in 1689. Having been deposed as King of England by Parliament and replaced by William of Orange he sought the aid of Louis XIV of France, not just to secure his Irish kingdom but to begin the process of winning back the English throne. Victuals for the French fleet were procured by the loyal citizens, comprising '50 fat oxen and 400 fat weathers [wethers] as a small acknowledgement of the universal thanks due to them [the French fleet] for transporting his Majesty thither'. Typical of Kinsale pragmatism, appreciation of the French effort was short-lived after James was defeated at the Battle of the Boyne and, without qualms, the town declared for William after the Duke of Marlborough overcame the residue of support for James that remained in Kinsale.

Cargos from the Far East did not always make the long voyage to Kinsale via the Cape of Good Hope. In July 1691, English and Dutch fleets lay in Kinsale Harbour, having come from Smyrna (modern Izmir) in Turkey loaded with spices, which had been transported overland. Later in the same year, a fleet of seventy-two ships from Virginia and Barbados took shelter in the harbour to await the protection of the warships *Experience* and *Wolf* for the final stage of the passage to Bristol. Throughout the eighteenth century, the navy in Kinsale participated in the war against the French and shared in the benefits from the prize ships taken off the coast. The captured French sailors were imprisoned in the old Desmond Custom House on Cork Street and because of this association the building is sometimes referred to as the 'French Prison'.[10]

Following the Williamite Wars, letters to the Southwell family, then living at Kings Weston near Bristol, give further accounts of shipping through Kinsale.[11] On 23 August 1696, 'the Virginia trade of sixty sail convoyed by the Harwich and Weymouth arrived in this Harbour'. In a review of the records available, an outward-bound fleet of twenty-two West Indiamen in the company of the *Swan* and *Thunderbolt* arrived in the harbour bound for Barbados, Virginia and New England. In 1703, Alderman Hoare, Southwell's representative in Kinsale, reported that 'eleven sail of Jamaica men bound for Bristol arrived in Kinsale to await a convoy'. He was about to apply to the Lord Deputy for the use of the *Feversham* and *Arundell* anchored in the Harbour. On 17 August the arrival of a fleet of thirty merchant ships bound for Newfoundland and the West Indies, convoyed by nine men-of-war under the command of Admiral Dilkes, was announced. Fleets of this size were frequently delayed in the harbour. The reason in this case, as Hoare explains, was difficulty in acquiring ship supplies. The fleet sailed eventually on 14 November, a delay of three months. Such a large fleet in the harbour caused Hoare some anxiety, as by September he had reported difficulties in supplying 'provisions for 2,000 men for a month at short notice'. Another letter in September 1705 highlights the convoy system, which was required for protecting the valuable cargos of a large fleet of 'sail' from Virginia, which arrived in the harbour on 13 September. A fortnight later, five ships of the line convoying nine East Indiamen carrying china wear, silks and saltpetre came in. More evidence of shipping from the East was reported in October 1707, when three fourth-rate frigates accompanying six richly laden ships from Bengal entered the port.[12] Charles Vallancey, in a similar list, reporting for the period 1667 to 1756, described Kinsale as the harbour where ships seeking 'a secure sanctuary' awaited a convoy to England.[13]

Whenever the English East India Company vessels arrived in Kinsale they created a stir. The ships were noted for their elegance and were always in the best of trim with ornately carved gold-plated sterns glistening in the still water. They were fitted with the most sophisticated rigging, which enabled the use of sails high aloft on masts. The masters of these vessels were held in great standing, chosen for their seafaring experience and proven ability. Signing on as crew aboard an East India Company vessel was the preferred option for seamen of the day and carried the added bonus of being able to engage in a little private trading. Returning with small supplies of easily carried but valuable goods, such as spice, china, cotton and silks, the sailors would sell privately. A substantial black market economy was generated by the activity, in which harbour officials did not interfere. It developed to the point that there was a threat of a 'breakdown in revenue control', and purchases were such that cash became noticeably scarce. In 1748, it is reported that 'women of fashion went off to Kinsale in search of bargains' from the ships. After calling to Kinsale, the vessels were provisioned and in convoy, sailed to Bristol where they unloaded the manifest cargo.[14]

For the majority of sailors and voyagers, long outward-bound trips were anticipated with trepidation, as they were fraught with danger, overcrowding and the constant threat of harsh punishment or worse for the crew. At the beginning of a trip, fresh meat was provided by animals slaughtered aboard and – when supplemented by rations of cereal, butter, cheese and beer – provided a balanced diet. As the voyage progressed, food became scarce and the men were reduced to 'hard tack', surviving on ship's biscuit often infested by weevils, tiny beetle-like insects. Corrupt procurement practices, common among suppliers and buyers, meant that ships often departed harbour lacking supplies and poorly serviced. Lack of hygiene, the crew living in close quarters, with water turning putrid in the warmer latitudes, propagated the spread of fever, typhus and dysentery, with fatal consequences for a number of sailors. Human and animal waste found its way to the bilge of the ship. The foul environment, in which rodent infestation was common, generated the conditions in which contagion spread in the crew. On arrival in port, vessels flew the yellow Q signal flag requesting 'clean pratique', a statement that a ship was disease free and requesting clearance to land and conduct business. In the case of a ship with infection, when it arrived in Kinsale it was put in quarantine, isolated from other ships and the community ashore.[15]

Conditions aboard some ships were so intolerable that crews at times reacted by spreading dissent or mutinying, which occasionally ended in violence. An example of this occurred aboard the *Cinque Ports,* a ship that arrived in Kinsale in August of 1703. She joined the

Saint George, another vessel in the harbour, to provision and prepare for a privateering expedition to the West Indies and the Pacific. The sailing master aboard the 130-ton, 20-gun vessel was Alexander Selkirk. After three weeks in the harbour they set sail under the command of a Captain Thomas Stradling. From the beginning it was evident that this was not a happy ship, with the ninety-man crew complaining about overcrowding. Selkirk was the most vocal among the dissenters. Stradling accused him of encouraging and fomenting the quarrelsome atmosphere. Passing close to the island of Juan Fernandez off the coast of Chile, the captain decided to rid the ship of the main troublemaker and abandoned Selkirk on the isolated island. He was left to his own devices and managed to survive, being eventually rescued after four years by a passing ship. Later, the story became the basis of Daniel Defoe's novel *Robinson Crusoe.*[16]

In Kinsale, catering for this level of shipping required a complex range of services and facilities, which emerged close to the quays. Smoke-filled blacksmiths' shops turned out the fairleads, chainplates and mast hounds which were fitted to the vessels as sailmakers sewed in bolt ropes, cringles and reef points in lofts or flat open spaces. The makers of multi-purchase blocks and deadeyes provided standing and running rigging. Clambering up ratlines, the sailors bent on sails to yards on masts and bowsprits overhanging the quaysides. The vessels careened on strands listing on bilges, high and dry on the gridiron at the Dockyard or hove down at quay walls, had damaged bottoms, garboards and rudder pintles surveyed and repaired. Block and tackle slung out on derricks were used to discharge cargo or load supplies from handcarts and horse-drawn drays which trundled over the cobbled sets (the cut stone blocks laid to give a smooth surface) on the bustling waterfront. At deck level, the shipwrights and riggers with rope, sail and block makers worked under the watchful eye of the ship's bo'sun, who in turn was pressed by the ship's master, pacing the poop deck, anxious perhaps to make the tide or link up with a departing convoy. The activity on the quay walls overflowed onto the water to the larger ships anchored in the middle or outer harbours that were tended by flat-bottomed barges and lighters from the shore.

The supply of provisions and services to hundreds of ships had a large impact on the town's economy. In May 1686 the cost of feeding one man for a week amounted to 3 shillings and 6 pence. The Commissioners of Revenue, in September 1693 in attempting to quantify the economic impact on the town, estimated the duration of voyages out of Kinsale as follows: 'to the West Indies 8 months, to Portugal and Spain without the Straits and also the Canaries, 3 months, to Holland and Flanders 2 months'. They also estimated that the food required per person per day at sea was 2 lb beef or pork, 1 lb bread, and a gallon of beer. In addition, 1 lb butter or cheese was provided for each week.[17]

The complement of men aboard ships varied considerably. Vessels engaged in privateering, for instance, were overcrowded at the start of an expedition as extra men were needed to crew the prize ships which they hoped to capture. From the naval perspective, the largest ship capable of entering Kinsale in 1700 was the fifth-rate frigate, which was approximately 120 foot in length and on average had a complement of 80 men and armed with between 32 and 50 guns.

Other lists give some idea of the range of goods supplied by the merchants. Alexander Selkirk aboard the *Cinque Ports* at Kinsale in 1703 records that bread, biscuit, dried peas, meat, cheese and a gallon of beer per man per day were required. Before leaving the harbour 4 barrels of beef, 4 hogsheads of salt pork, 82 firkins butter, 12 barrels of oatmeal, and horsehides, hammocks, rugs and coats were put aboard. Bellowing bullocks, bleating sheep and pigs, goats, hens and geese in pens were tethered aboard ship to provide freshly butchered meat during the voyage.[18] Victualling was an enormous logistical task, for which the prosperous Kinsale burgesses had built a reputation in being able to satisfy. The tavern owners, shopkeepers and retailers sold the goods and also in many cases manufactured them. John Heard, who had a boot and leather shop, also cut and made leather-handled buckets. Companies of craftsmen were formed to control access and maintain standards in the trade. Similarly, sail and rope makers were regulated. Important suppliers – butchers, victuallers, bakers, shipwrights, smiths, textile makers and coopers – followed strict rules and were bound by certain codes of practice. In the case of the coopers: 'we present that the master of the company of coopers be every year required to use all diligence and care that all beef barrels, beer barrels, hogsheads and butts be made exactly to the usual and accustomed gauge both those made in the Corporation and those brought in'.[19]

Alderman Hoare of Kinsale reported on the procurement process and provides information on the quality, price and difficulties he had in sourcing the victuals and provisions that were required. In October 1693 with regard to beef, he wrote 'that of the seven or eight hundred cattle bought for the West India trade he called on an extra hundred choice oxen for the service, which must now be salted with the rest'. When the season was over 'the jack cattle [bulls] cannot be had, but at extraordinary rates'. Apart from the difficulties in regard to procurement he complained about the difficulty of debt collection and in particular the tardiness of the Admiralty to pay.[20]

Beer was consumed at sea instead of water, which after a period in the casks became undrinkable. The beer was produced in large quantities at a number of breweries in Kinsale in the eighteenth century. At the foot of Barrack Hill in the town, the Brewery Corner continues to identify the location of one of the manufacturers. Alderman Hoare alone from 1692 produced 20,000 barrels per year. As late as 1818, with shipping in decline, George Dunne's brewery was valued at £12,000, one of the highest outside Cork city. Many tavern keepers also made a product of dubious quality, being accused of using contaminated water in the brewing process. The authorities, obviously concerned, were forced to enact laws against the use of 'gutter water' collected from the streets.[21]

The extensive range of facilities and services that were available in the town and harbour attracted more and more shipping. The cachet for Kinsale, which marked it out from other busy ports such as Waterford, Youghal and Cork, was its location as the Royal Naval Dockyard, which provided protection and maintenance facilities for ships. It also had the distinction of being a designated prize court at which the spoils of war were officially apportioned.

Ships arriving in Kinsale were often detained in the harbour due to weather, wind direction or difficulties with the supply of food or services. The enforced sojourn, perhaps a regret for the owners and merchants, provided a welcome break for sailors after a long voyage. Francis Rogers, a London merchant sailing from the West Indies, put into the harbour on 3 October 1703 in heavy weather. With his vessel riding snugly at anchor amid other merchantmen and men-of-war, he went ashore and in his diary gives an account of the hospitality he experienced: 'The town lyeth on the River Bandon which runs far up where there is very good salmon … I remember we bought here a fine salmon for 8d … we thought ourselves in the land of the plenty and just come off a long tedious starving drink water voyage we did not a little indulge ourselves. Very good claret we drank in the taverns at an English shilling the bottle ditto at 3/6 and 4/= [shillings] per gallon.'[22]

Coming ashore, landing at the slipways or quay walls near the Old Blockhouse, the crews frequented taverns such as The Jolly Mariners, The Red Lion, The Peacock and the Kinsale Arms. They drank beer, gin or aqua vitae, sometimes adulterated by unscrupulous innkeepers. The inns were frequented by women who were willing to make themselves available to the men, who had been deprived of female company for weeks or even months, in return for drink or a small financial consideration. In scenes not unlike those depicted in Hogarth's etchings, sailors freely spent their allowance or share of a prize in wanton indulgence. In 1654, the period of Cromwell's Commonwealth and puritanism, Kinsale inhabitants and innkeepers were accused of taking advantage by 'allowing drunkenness in their houses, and enticing seamen, servants and soldiers to debauchery whereby the Lord is highly displeased and the Commonwealth exceedingly prejudiced'. For Rogers, his arrival in Kinsale was a welcome relief initially but after four weeks, the merchant and the ship's crew 'much to their satisfaction' weighed anchor and joined a convoy of three men-of-war under the command of Admiral Dilkes and left the harbour.

The revenue generated for the port was considerable. Corporation records for 1796, at the end of Kinsale's golden age, show that dues were based on keelage and ballast. Vessels were levied at the rate of 4d per vessel. Dues on some cargos were paid in kind as shown on the toll board at the Market House, now the Museum. For example: 'one barrel of coal, salt, meal and malt for every twenty barrels [of these products] bourn [carried by ship]'. Ballast, which is extra weight in the form of iron or stone required to keep a boat stable when light, was charged at the rate of 2d if unloaded by the ship's master at his own expense and in a location decided by the bailiff, 8d if the work

Kinsale waterfront, Royal Dockyard and Scilly from Castlepark, Drawing *c.*1750.

was undertaken by the harbour authorities. To avoid obstruction for shipping created by dumping ballast overboard, it was ordered to be placed above the high-water mark. 'No ship or sloop or boat whatever shall throw any ballast off their ships into the sea on the penalty of paying 20/= [shillings] for every offence … '. To ensure prompt payment of penalties crews would have their rudders, sails and yards confiscated. Dealing with ballast remained a contentious problem for the authorities until the beginning of the twentieth century, as indicated in Harbour Board minutes. Not a problem, however, was the Portland stone used in the building of Charles Fort in the 1670s that was carried as ballast on ships arriving empty.

Conspicuous consumption was part of the opulent lifestyle enjoyed and paid for directly from port revenue. Corporation vouchers show the finance expended in celebrating the coronation of George I in October 1714 and the sumptuous hospitality that was provided on the occasion of the Lord Lieutenant's visit in 1722.[23] Lavish expenditure was not confined to special occasions and political junkets occurred frequently. For centuries, members of the harbour authority and fishery inspectors enjoyed the perks of public service as they 'gaily spent a fair proportion of harbour revenue in periodical junketing to Kilmacsimon Quay ... where on the sylvan sward they regaled themselves with enormous lunches of roast and boiled, washed down in healths five fathoms deep by copious libations of "Billy Wise" returning to Kinsale at dewy eve'.

The regal style and excess, despite some efforts to curb the exuberance, persisted at least till 1879 when the Harbour Board continued to ensure that the members would be amply fortified with food and drink for their meetings held regularly at Kilmacsimon Quay.[24]

Two families, the Boyles and Southwells, personified the spirit of entrepreneurship, based on early Enlightenment principles and Protestant individualism which characterised port activity in the seventeenth and eighteenth centuries. They established an extensive network of contacts extending beyond Kinsale and drawing on influence in Dublin, London and other centres throughout Europe.

As a new settler, Richard Boyle, the first Earl of Cork, bought the estates of Walter Raleigh near Youghal in the early 1600s. Coming from a relatively modest background he capitalised on and successfully exploited opportunities to engage in trade. Boyle gained power and influence by presiding over the grants of lands to new planter settlers and opening markets for timber, fish, beef and butter throughout the 'nascent British empire'.[25] Recognising the importance of education, he encouraged his sons to take the grand European tour and engage with the new ideas of the seventeenth century. His son Robert was a founder member of the Royal Society and is known for the discovery of Boyle's Law and the emergence of chemistry as a scientific discipline. Of more significance to Kinsale was Roger who as a young man received the title Lord Broghill and later became the Earl of Orrery and Lord President of Munster. He fell within the orbit of Charles II as a playwright and was the recipient of royal affirmation. Throughout the major upheavals of the seventeenth century the Boyles were deft diplomats, surviving the purges when others were transported, jailed or executed. As the Earl of Orrery, Roger placed great importance on the defence of Kinsale, describing it in 1666 'as one of the noblest harbours in Europe'.[26]

The Southwells, coming from a similar background to that of the Boyles, dominated Kinsale town and harbour affairs in the seventeenth century and for much of the eighteenth. They had extensive interests in trade, victualling and fishing and were closely associated with the naval establishment and harbour administration. They cultivated contacts and nurtured networks, gaining prestige and influence among the most important people of the time. In Ireland they had close relationships with the Butlers, Earls of Ormond, who on a number of occasions held the position of Lord Lieutenant. The older Robert Southwell was made collector of customs for Kinsale in 1631 and what was immediately apparent was the family's determination to develop the port of Kinsale, building on its natural qualities. He wrote to Ormond in 1637 saying that Kinsale had 'fit places ... to build and erect wharfs, cranes and custom houses for the conveyancing of trade and securing of customs'. He proposed 'a dock for receiving and repairing of ships together with victualling and shore houses to be employed upon that coast'.[27] In another incident Prince Rupert, nephew of the executed King Charles I, while blockaded with the Royalist fleet in the harbour in 1649, was adequately supplied with victualling by Southwell. While this association in the tense conclusion of the English Civil War could have been interpreted as treachery, Southwell later received the contract of supplying the Parliamentary fleet in Ireland. This was authorised by the Commissioners of the Commonwealth.[28] In addition he managed to augment his property portfolio after Kinsale submitted to Oliver Cromwell. Then, following the restoration of the monarchy in 1660, Southwell was not only forgiven by the new regime but appointed Vice Admiral for the province of Munster. While this was a voluntary posting, it furnished the Kinsale supremo with information on shipping and trade.

It was, however, with the emergence of the younger Robert that the fortunes of the family really flourished. As a young man he left Kinsale to study at Oxford and subsequently travelled widely, visiting France, Italy and the Netherlands. He had an eclectic range of interests, which included membership of the Royal Society, having been proposed by fellow Corkman Robert Boyle. Southwell was to become President of that august body and among his acquaintances were Isaac Newton, the poet John Dryden and Sir William Petty who, having surveyed the country for Cromwell, had extensive knowledge of Kinsale property which he undoubtedly made available to the Kinsale man.

Robert Southwell's curious mind absorbed many ideas, building contacts which were used to introduce innovation and promote family interests in trade, fishing and the provisioning of ships. His Dutch travels may account for the introduction of the iconic tumblehome or rounded sides of the Kinsale hooker, a traditional feature of boats in the Low Countries. In London, the young and ambitious Southwell had entrée to the highest echelons of society. Prince Rupert, who had received assistance from the family while blockaded in Kinsale Harbour in 1649, was godfather to Robert's son and vouched for the loyalty of the family to the King in 1664 by reminding the authorities that they had 'furnished very reasonably the said navy [Royalist] with such provisions as enabled them to leave that country then revolting on every side to the usurper [Cromwell's] Government'.[29] He became a Member of Parliament, ambassador to Portugal and envoy to Brussels and Berlin where he had discussions with the Elector of Brandenburg concerning 'those affronts it daily receives from France'. In 1664 Robert assumed the position of secretary to the commission on prizes and used his position to establish a prize court in Kinsale for the purpose of regulating the distribution of the valuables from enemy ships taken outside the harbour. The ships, captured by licensed privateers, were brought to Kinsale where their valuable cargos were apportioned by the court with a share lodged to the coffers of the local corporation.

He succeeded to his father's property and offices in 1677. By 1700, the Southwell properties in Kinsale were yielding £1,218 per annum, an enormous sum, which provided the resources to promote the family's other interests. The Kinsale Manorial Records give an account of the extent of Robert's estate. Around the harbour, liberties and adjoining baronies Southwell had a total of 5,560 acres. In the town his cellars, lofts and Custom House were leased, generating valuable income. There were also 'a mill, a malt house, a brew house and other conveniences necessary for those who victual the Kings ships which in time of war yields £200 in rent'. Southwell also had 'land next to the sea fit for the building of houses, wharfs and quays'. Fifty tenants in Scilly were involved in the pilchard fishery. He held 'large woodland within a mile of the town and a wood of rising oaks two miles upriver'. The report concludes by saying that finances varied from year to year and 'cannot be reduced to a certainty'. Yet 'one may reasonably judge they make it a growing estate ... and rents are never lessened [even] in times of war which are occasions for the more plenty and expense'.[30]

Apart from important properties in the town, Southwell held '50 plantation acres' at Rincurran which had been confiscated from 'the traitor' Barry Óg following the 1641 rebellion. In relieving the Earl of Orrery's anxiety concerning the defence of the harbour, Southwell made a portion of this land available for the site of Charles Fort for which he was well rewarded, receiving £1,041. He also benefited from the advowson that went with the parish in return for land at Ardbrack given for the relocation of the old church that had existed at Rincurran as it was considered too close to the fort. Whether by design or accident the tower of the church in its new position provides an important clearing line, giving a safe passage into the harbour.

The ability to capitalise on situations and exploit opportunity was a constant factor in Southwell dealings. A letter from Robert to his agent in Kinsale in June 1695 illustrates how every decision had an ulterior motive. He wished to make his house at the bottom of Cock Hill, now St John's Hill, available to a Mr Timewell who was about to take up the position of the King's Commissioner at the Dockyard 'to make his sojourn in Kinsale both easy and welcome'. Southwell's letter clearly indicates that this gesture was not just an act of kindness but an incentive to encourage Timewell to use his influence with the Admiralty and the Navy Board to 'erect a dock which must draw a constant resort of shipping'. The effort, however, may not have had the desired outcome as Timewell was not impressed by the 'dilapidated, soiled and dirty' state of the accommodation.[31]

Among his London acquaintances were many who held influential positions, and who could encourage and direct shipping through Kinsale. Samuel Pepys, the noted diarist, was a senior officer in the Navy Board with particular responsibility for the victualling of ships. Procurement was a major task and, on account of its western location,

Pepys designated Kinsale as a provisioning port principally for fleets bound for the West Indies.

Southwell's relationship with Pepys was a good example of networking in operation, favours granted and payback called in when required. Towards the end of the 1670s Pepys became embroiled in a web of intrigue, which included accusations of involvement in murder and treason. Southwell, however, through contacts with a Nicholas Reeve in the Netherlands, discovered that Pepys' accuser was himself a criminal and involved in a range of nefarious activities in the Low Countries. This information undermined the prosecution case and Pepys was released from the Tower of London and the possibility of execution. Reeve was the expert whom Southwell invited to Kinsale to promote the fishing industry at the Pallace in Scilly and may have been the Dutch link that influenced the iconic design shape of the early fishing hooker.[32]

Among the many traders and merchants who called to Kinsale for victualling were the Earls of Shaftsbury, based at Bristol, who with extensive plantations in the Caribbean were engaged in the slave trade. They also moved within the Southwell circle.

In the 1690s Robert and his son Edward took up residence at Kings Weston, close to Bristol, which was the main port to the Atlantic handling the majority of goods landed in England. Contact with Kinsale in a favourable breeze was possible under sail in twenty-four hours and close links were maintained through their steward Alderman Edward Hoare, whose constant stream of reports was a source of shipping news at Kinsale and of commerce generated ashore.[33]

In 1676 Robert was nominated a Kinsale burgess for 'good services done for the advantage of this corporation'. His contribution extended to concern for the Protestant poor in the community, which is still evident in the 'Gift' houses at the Mall in Kinsale (see map of Town Walls and Gates, p. 27.) They were built 'for some hapless and decayed old people that might be in shelter and might have some conveniences towards ending their days in rest'.[34]

After Robert's death in 1702, Edward, his son, continued to oversee the family's interests in Kinsale, exercising discretion and astute diplomacy at a time when Kinsale's maritime status was being

questioned. By the end of the eighteenth century the old influence and
prestige of families such as the Southwells were reduced, due in part
to the growing assertiveness of the native Irish population, a decline
in the effectiveness of the Penal Laws and improvement to the port
facilities in Cork Harbour. Through marriage the family assumed the
title Lord de Clifford, and continued to hold property at Scilly until
the middle of the nineteenth century when the Pallace was sold off to
the Dawson Williams fishing interests. It was at this time that the cut-
stone quay walls were constructed at Scilly Point.[35]

Apart from the elite group holding sway in Kinsale, the indigenous
majority population scavenged an existence outside the walls in abject
conditions, finding shelter in mud huts, stuck precariously to stone
fences and ruined walls. Dispossessed and denied rights of citizenship,
they lived in penury and disadvantage with no access to the levers of
power or the benefits and prosperity generated by the shipping activity
in the harbour. Described as the 'vulgar Irish', they were allowed to
enter the town only when extra manpower was required for lifting,
bearing and undertaking menial tasks. Poorly clothed and on inadequate diets, the people suffered high levels of illness and disease, with
a life expectancy of no more than forty years. The condition of the
people was commented on by Cosimo de' Medici, the Grand Duke
of Tuscany, at Kinsale in March 1669. While de' Medici, whose influence was extensive in Europe, was lavishly entertained, he nevertheless
criticised the discrimination against Catholics in relation to trade,
religion, language and custom. He was highly disparaging of the
poverty and living conditions of the 'rustic native people who have
no other resting place than the bare earth. Moved by curiosity, he saw
that inside [the huts], people lived like wild animals'.[36] Census returns
for as late as 1841 show that over 70 per cent of the population
continued to live in single-roomed mud cabins.

Poverty and famine, to a lesser extent, were also features of life
for some of the population within the town. Mr Vasey, the town's
representative in Parliament, found it necessary in May 1766 to write
to the Lord Lieutenant appealing for a grant to purchase provisions
and that 'they be sold out to the poor inhabitants of this town at such
prices as they can afford'. By October of that year, hunger was such
that the sloop *Ceres* bound for Gibraltar, laden with potatoes and

other goods, was 'boarded by a disorderly and riotous mob composed of fishermen' and 'discharged potatoes out of the sloop which they had taken possession of'. It was necessary for the Commanding Officer of the barracks to take control of the situation and restore order. Later, in 1800, a presentment directs that 'in view of the prevailing distress and of exorbitant prices, a sum of £1000 be provided for the lying in a supply of rice and Indian meal to be sold at a cheap rate to the poor'.[37]

Among the native population exclusion created disadvantage and marginalisation, which encouraged clandestine activity and attempts to subvert the law. The order to seal off access to ships anchored in the harbour proved impossible to enforce. Grand Jury presentments, 'banning of hucksters, bummers and hawkers from swarming and trading aboard ships as they arrived in the harbour', were largely ignored. The activity continued even after the captains of the ships were made accountable for the illicit trade aboard their vessels. Women with a predominance of Irish names – Elenor McCarthy, Elizabeth Dineen, Kathleen Donovan and others – were in 1700 accused of causing 'great prejudice to the shop keepers of this Corporation. Such persons so offending their goods to be seized and disposed of as the Sovereign shall think fit'.

In addition, the regulations were couched in terms that reflected the Puritan ethos and religious strictures that prevailed. It was obvious in many cases that the 'trading of wears' was a euphemism for prostitution as on occasions women 'were found lying aboard ships', and described as 'being persons of bad fame [who] occupied lewd houses of entertainment'.[38]

Many crews were detained in harbour, sometimes for periods of months, as ships awaited convoys, needed repairs or were on standby for a favourable breeze. The men with time on their hands frequently became intoxicated and on occasions rushed into quickly arranged marriage contracts in ceremonies conducted by clergymen of dubious status. When they left the harbour, 'their' women, if not already abandoned, faced the prospect of poverty, hunger and destitution. No option remained but to place themselves at the mercy of the Corporation. Several presentments show that assistance would be provided if the unfortunate took herself and her family out of the town. 'We present a strong woman with two children living in one of the turrets upon the rampart – constables to see her out of the town.'[39]

For the less compliant, a ducking stool was put in place at the Mill Hill 'for punishing scolds and disorderly women'. It was sometimes referred as the 'cuckolding stool' with its obvious reference to the punishment of 'fallen women'.[40] The scale of public retribution ranged from the whipping of vagrants to execution on the scaffold, which was reserved for men. An example of an extreme instance of deterrent was the hanging of six coal heavers in 1732 for defying the Corporation's price control rules on fuel being taken from ships.[41]

The diet of people was limited, at best, to potato and fish. Every possible patch of ground was utilised, as indicated by ridges still evident on the slopes of Sandy Cove Island and the inclines inside Money Point. The French consul Coquebert de Montbret, visiting the area in 1790 gave an insight into conditions for people living at Middle Cove. He wrote that he had a 'meal in a cabin of potatoes and fairly good fish caught by children from the rocks at Cove Llaer [Middle Cove]'. Moving to Garrettstown he commented that the living conditions of the people were primitive. Basic protection from the elements was in hovels which clung to the walls that extended from Dún Mhic Pádraig, and were impregnated with the smell of salt from the gale-blown spray. They survived on fish caught in dragnets by men standing up to their waists in water at Garrettstown beach and by growing potatoes in little plots of arable ground cleared between the rocks. Smuggling and the gathering of bounty from wrecks was common and gave much sought-after relief from the threat of starvation.[42] During the Famine, in the period from 1845 to 1852, the limited food source was reduced to turnips, black bread and fish.

The new colonies emerging in Virginia, Carolina, Maryland and islands in the Caribbean were occupied by English trading companies from 1609 and were seen as an opportunity to utilise the surplus of labour available in Ireland. Barbados was settled by the English in 1625. Initially, slaves were taken from Africa to harvest the tobacco plant and later sugar cane, the cash crops of these newly acquired territories. In Ireland for those left landless, including a large number of women and children whose menfolk had been killed in the sixteenth-century rebellions or who had left to join European armies as swordsmen and soldiers, transportation to the West Indies offered an alternative to the dismal prospects at home. As an inducement, a contract or 'denture' was signed, which tied the servant to a proprietor for seven years and afterwards receive a piece of land 'where they may support themselves by their labour'. The concept of the indentured servant was planned to deal with the dispossessed in Ireland and to assist in building white settlements in the new colonies. The policy quickly degenerated into a system of forced transportation when, after conducting a severe military campaign, Cromwell adopted a policy of confiscation of land in the period 1652 to 1657. It is estimated that 50,000 Irish from whom land was taken were shipped to Barbados, many through Kinsale.

Records exist of a Captain Joseph West who arrived in Kinsale in April 1636 expecting to embark with a cargo of 120 Irish 'servants' for Virginia. Much to West's frustration the group had already sailed aboard 'a Flemish ship of 140 tonnes'. Undaunted, he set about acquiring a replacement group. He sent agents into the countryside to seek and, if necessary, kidnap men and women when persuasion failed. His instruction was to gather young people from their mid-teens to thirties with 'lusty and strong' bodies. While waiting to fill the complement, which took six months, the unfortunates already captured were incarcerated in Kinsale in conditions similar to the 'baracoons' in which Africans were corralled before embarkation on slave ships. While the concept of human dignity in the seventeenth century was not as valued as today, they were kept penned like animals in huts. The treatment was only a foretaste of the horror to come. At the end of November 1636, with a 'cargo' of 102 people aboard, West set sail from Kinsale into the teeth of Atlantic winter gales. The captives were kept below deck and fed a form of gruel, which was lowered to them in buckets. The ship was not well found and began to leak badly in the poor weather, forcing West to bear away for Barbados. When the vessel finally docked at the end of January 1637 eight 'servants' had died and the others were ill and in poor condition.

In 1672 Sir William Petty, who had had a major input into land survey in Ireland (the Down Survey used in conjunction with the Cromwellian settlement), highlighted the irony inherent in the expression 'indentured servant'. He described these people as 'the widows and orphans, the deserted wives and families of swordsmen, who were captured and transported by the slave trading merchants of Bristol which their previous experience enabled them to organise'. In essence, they were white slaves prized even more than the 'black gold' which in earlier times had been brought in manacles from Africa.[43] When ashore, they were led to the marketplace at Bridgetown in Barbados, examined like cattle and handed over to the plantation owners. They were forced to work long hours in sweltering heat, cultivating and harvesting tobacco and sugar. Any faltering or hesitation warranted automatic punishment with the use of the lash and, as public warning, hangings occurred frequently. Brutish practices were not confined to dispensing punishment, as it was not unknown for young girls to be forced to engage sexually with 'the bosses'.[44] Reading the official accounts, the impression conveyed was that these 'servants' were willing transportees. In March 1679, it was reported that a 'Bryant Connor personally appeared before me to acknowledge himself free and willing to stand by the covenants of his indentures which were that he should serve said Josias Persivall, as an apprentice for 7 years and after the expiration of his term to have 10 li [livre, the equivalent of £1] according to the custom of the country and during said term to be supplied with clothes, meat, drink, washing and lodging'. There is no mention of the brutal conditions that forced young Bryant to 'freely and willingly' agree.[45]

It is estimated that 20 per cent of the indentured servants got to the stage of working the property promised in the contract. The majority became outcasts living in ghettos, ostracised by the white masters and equally unacceptable to a native population already accustomed to a culture of discrimination. Due to their fair complexion, they were sensitive to the burning effect of hot sun, a condition that persists in their descendants. Consequently, they became known collectively as 'red legs'. For the most part, they remain a deprived and disadvantaged group within the population of Barbados. A number of these displaced Irish were transferred to other islands in the Caribbean, and may account for the name of the capital of Montserrat in the Leeward Islands being Kinsale.[46]

For his 'cargo' in 1637, Captain West was paid off in sugar from which he made a handsome profit when he returned to London. Soon afterwards, he received further orders to sail for Kinsale to procure another group of 'indentured servants'. West's career in the trade extended over a long period. Thirty-two years later, on 31 August 1669, Robert Southwell in Kinsale wrote to Lord Ashley Shaftesbury responding to a request 'to procure servants to serve the Lords Proprietors of Carolina at Port Royal' and that Captain West aboard his ship had arrived in Kinsale the night before. Southwell expresses some reservations about the procurement of these 'servants', saying that despite poor living conditions at home, they were reluctant to go, 'as they have been so terrified with ill practice of them to the Caribbean Islands where they are sold as slaves'. Lord Broghill (Boyle), on the other hand, responded positively to the Bristol merchants in 1654, assuring them that he could provide 250 women above the age of twelve in a very short time. However, he expressed a word of caution, not for reasons of humanity but that the policy of ethnic cleansing was depriving the new planters in Ireland of a supply of labourers and tenants needed to work the land. Yet he also saw that the policy of transportation was a means of building up Protestant centres in Ireland not contaminated by Papists.[47]

From the early years of the seventeenth century, Kinsale's significance as a port was based on its ability to supply victuals, provisioning and marine services to large fleets. Trading, in the sense of handling imports and exports, became a minor aspect of activity in the harbour after the end of the Desmond era in 1583. Part of the reason for the reduction was to protect British manufacturing. Constraints were imposed under various Navigation Acts introduced from 1651, which meant that all goods from or to Ireland were required to pass through English ports. The restriction on Irish exports was extended in the 1660s to include agricultural products such as lamb, beef, pork, butter and cheese. The Irish tried to sell directly to America but this too was cut off in 1670 and in 1698 the export of woollens was prohibited. These regulations had a devastating effect and retarded the development of Irish agriculture and industrial manufacturing.

The laws applied equally to the new settlers but they did benefit in periods of crisis, such as war, when food was scarce and the rules were relaxed. Butter with the Kinsale mark was taken to Cork in fishing hookers and exported throughout the world from the Butter Exchange. Cured pilchard from the pallaces at Scilly, World's End and Lower Cove were sold to the West Indies and to the 'Lenten' markets of Spain and Italy.[48] As the rules were relaxed in the eighteenth century, quantities of spirits, fruit, sugar, spices and weapons were landed at Kinsale. Wine, though, remained a constant feature of trade in the town when the Irish 'Wine Geese' families, forced to leave after the Williamite Wars, established vineyards in the Bordeaux area of France. The Bartons, producers from 1722, Lawtons from 1739, Kirwins from 1715 and Lynchs from 1691 sent wine to Ireland through Kinsale.[49]

Efforts to lift the trading restrictions in the harbour were made by Robert Southwell in 1675. Through contacts in London he promoted the idea of 'free port' status for Kinsale, arguing that it would be 'of benefit to the loyal citizens and in its many apparent advantages superior to any port in Kingdom'.[50] The Earl of Orrery lent support to the idea and to the proposal of having Kinsale recognised as a 'home port' through which imports and exports could pass freely. The proposals, however, did not progress as, ironically, they were opposed by vested interests in Kinsale, consisting of the custom and toll collectors who perceived these developments as a threat to their revenue-generating capacity.[51]

Kinsale, because of its location, shelter and other natural attributes, was a bustling port in the seventeenth and eighteenth centuries capable of providing services to shipping with all the romance and adventure of timber ships and lofty billowing sails. It was geographically positioned to capitalise on the new sea routes opening up to the Americas and to the East. It is also true that living in the port town was harsh for some, where there was scant regard for life or liberty, and where commerce and profit were paramount.

Despite its many natural qualities as a harbour and its significance as a port, signs of decline began to emerge at the end of the seventeenth century and by 1750 they were fully acknowledged. The lack of an adequate depth of water for the larger vessels then afloat could no longer be denied.

3

Naval Presence – A Monitor of Rise and Fall

Nothing identified the importance of Kinsale as a port more than its designation as a naval base. Its success and decline were reflected in the navy presence. A powerful sea force was central to Britain's desire for economic expansion and empire building. Coinciding with Kinsale's successful period of shipping, a dockyard was developed and a naval facility was established in the harbour. It was also the era when piracy and privateering on the high seas were rampant, and protection was essential for the mercantile fleets and their valuable cargos as they converged on their ports of destination in Britain. In the restricted approaches they became easy prey to the Dutch and later French privateers of the seventeenth century. Protection was required and Kinsale was chosen as the base from which the convoying systems would be coordinated.

Henry VIII was the first English monarch in the sixteenth century to recognise the importance of fighting ships, specifically designed to carry guns. The Navy (Admiralty) Board was established in 1546, which focused on the development of ship design evolving from

PLATE 6. Ornate stern on the model of HMS *Kinsale. Courtesy John Collins*

PLATE 7. Desmond Custom House, later the French Prison and now the Wine Museum. *Courtesy John Collins*

PLATE 8. Fish shed with Casey's sail loft on the right, *c.*1900. *Courtesy Tony Bocking*

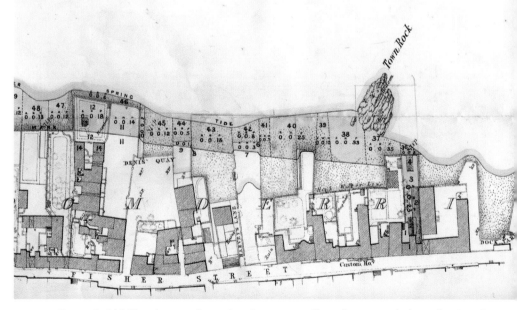

PLATE 9. Old Kinsale waterfront showing quay walls and town rock, later the site of Pier Head. *Courtesy Ordnance Survey, Kinsale Harbour Commissioners, June 1883*

PLATE 10. Part of modern fishing fleet at Kinsale. *Courtesy John Collins*

PLATE 11. Ringrone Castle looking
towards Ballinacurra and White
Castle. *Courtesy John Collins*

PLATE 12. A 2006 aerial photograph of the lower reaches of the Bandon River flowing into Kinsale Harbour. *Courtesy John Collins*

the carrack to the galleon. By 1600 a system of rating ships was introduced, ranging from the first in the line, the large battleship bearing 100 guns, to the fast sixth-rate frigates which had twenty-five guns and were designed to act as the eyes of the fleet. During Queen Elizabeth's reign, from the middle of the sixteenth century, world trade expanded and the colonisation process opened many new sea routes, which in turn required regulation and further protection. The Hawkins brothers, formerly English privateers who were noted for their seafaring exploits, developed a recruitment system that trained sailors in the use of swords and guns as fighting men. The Admiralty Board continued to function until 1832 when the Royal Navy was established.

In the early seventeenth century, Kinsale was described as a 'place of great resort for his Majesty's ships of war'.[1] A naval dockyard facility existed in the harbour at Castlepark during the period of the Battle of Kinsale in 1601. On the sandy isthmus between the river and the beach, boats were careened on the gridiron, part of which was uncovered in the 1960s. The surrounding area, known as The Dock, still carries associations with the shipyard.

Later in the seventeenth century the docking facility was trans-ferred to the other side of the river at the foot of Dromderrig, on part of which the Trident Hotel is now located. Some of the original dockyard and quay walls were filled in during the 1960s to create car-parking facilities but left the 'knuckles' or the outside section of the quays still prominent on the waterfront.[2] The Kinsale Dockyard for a period was the single naval presence on the Irish coast and in 1686 King James II was advised that, in considering sending a 'squadron of men of war to the Irish Coast, it should be allowed by all men who understand sea affairs that Kinsale is the best and safest harbour ... ships of the greatest burden may ride within less than a half cable's length and that His Majesty had a victualling office and has been at great expense in fortifying the Harbour'.[3] It was a large complex operation working closely with traders and suppliers, and contributed significantly to the town's prosperity in the seventeenth and eighteenth centuries. In 1725, a list of senior personnel and the level of remuneration illustrates the importance of the yard. The commissioner was in receipt of £500 per annum, the clerk of

A 1920s photograph of World's End with the site of the Royal Dockyard at the foot of Dromderrig, now the Trident Hotel (right) and the Thuillier Boatyard and family houses on the 'Drang' (centre). *Author's Collection*

the cheque £100, master builder £100, clerk of the survey £60, storekeeper £60, boatswain and master caulker each received £50. Each of these was a head of department carrying a large staff.

There is also a report that: 'The Harbour teemed with English, Dutch and Danish fleets riding at anchor or plying off the coast haling prizes in their wake or convoying merchantmen to Kinsale from Bristol, London, the West Indies, Barbados, Virginia, Tuscany and Genoa'.[4] The statement highlights Kinsale's main naval functions: first as the coordination centre for convoying operations and secondly the harbour to which captured prize ships were brought.

As English merchantmen approached home waters they were particularly vulnerable to preying privateers who cruised off the coast waiting to bear down on the valuable cargos. The main threat came from the Dutch in the period 1656 to 1675 and afterwards from Spain. The French were constantly lurking and remained a threat until Napoleon's defeat at Waterloo in 1815.

Privateering was a strategy of war, the objective being to damage the enemy's economy by capturing its shipping. Companies were licensed to recruit prize crews and prowl the approaches in fast luggers ready to pounce on ships that were isolated from the convoys.[5] Approaching England, shipping enters the narrower, more confined sea space of the English and Bristol Channels. In the case of Bristol, ships were constrained by the massive range of tide in the funnel-shaped approach of which Kinsale was an outer port of entry and the Irish south coast part of its extended limit. A map of County Cork inscribed by Charles Smith in 1750 names the Cork coast as St George's Channel which in modern times is associated only with the narrow stretch of water between County Wexford and Pembrokeshire in Wales. In the confined waters many vessels were captured. A French prize crew, bristling with arms, would board an incoming English ship and force the captured crew to sail to a port in the Bay of Biscay where the proceeds of the ship and cargo were divided on a share basis. A similar reprisal strategy was employed by the English against French, American and Spanish shipping. The Americans allied with the French in the War of Independence, having suffered a major defeat at the Battle of Quebec in 1760, and were by 1775 active off the Cork coast, engaged in privateering against the English.[6]

Two English gentlemen touring Ireland in 1751 gave a first-hand account of encountering privateers on a fishing trip out of Kinsale Harbour. They were overcome with anxiety when a Spaniard was spotted rounding the Old Head. Rather than attempting to escape, the skipper wisely remained in position. On coming alongside, the privateers put two pilots aboard the Kinsale boat and enquired as to what ships were in the harbour. The fishermen informed them that two vessels laden with provisions had left that morning for the West Indies. Satisfied, the Spaniards departed, having exchanged wine for fish; they informed the local men that they were out of St Sebastian carrying 30 guns and a complement of 400 men which included not just Spaniards but also English, Irish and Scots in the crew.[7]

For protection against the enemy, the English adopted a number of counter-strategies. One was to place patrols on the coast. On instructions from Dublin the fifth-rate man-of-war, the *Dolphin*, was ordered to cruise between the Old Head and the Saltees.[8] She was part of an integrated approach where the London Parliament in 1694 allocated a total of 43 ships, 'cruisers and convoys to protect the great trade'. The Welsh coast was coordinated from Bristol, while the western approaches were controlled from Kinsale.[9]

A second strategy was to convoy ships in large fleets, protected by fast fifth-rate frigates. Swift and armed, they scouted for enemy privateers, which they matched for speed and manoeuvrability. After long voyages, individual merchant ships arrived in Kinsale and waited until a viable number had gathered. They would then receive the security of a convoy to Britain for the final and most vulnerable part of the trip.

Apart from preventative strategies, the English authorities went on the offensive by promoting their own privateering expeditions. Companies were formed and issued with a 'letter of marque', which was a licence to cruise the oceans and capture ships of nations at war with England. Unlike the normal naval practice of forcing men to go to sea, crews on privateering vessels were willing recruits, being aware of the potential rewards available from the shared spoils of captured vessels. Privateering was a relatively humane practice, as it aimed to minimise damage to enemy ships at a time when conflict at sea was characterised by severe violence and bloodletting. The objective was to capture the cargo, the ship and the crew who were needed to sail the vessel. Instead of using cannon in attacking a vessel, grappling hooks were heaved, fouling gunwales to draw the ships together and in the process reduced damage to masts, spars and rigging. Often this was followed by hand-to-hand combat until the crew of the captured vessel surrendered.

A sample list of ships brought to Kinsale in the latter half of the seventeenth century shows the incidence of privateering occurring off the harbour.[10] In August 1678, vessels earlier taken by the French were recaptured by the *Prince William*, which in addition brought in other prizes. The frigates *Montaque* and *Dover* in February 1691 captured a large, heavily armed privateer from Saint-Malo. The *Dover* was again in the harbour on 6 December 1693 and on that occasion succeeded in selling a prize ship of three guns to the Admiralty.

The success of privateering expeditions out of Kinsale was recognised in 1745 by the presentation of a silver cup to acknowledge the range and value of the captures and of one expedition in particular. The piece is held at the headquarters of the Honourable Company of Master Mariners, which has its headquarters aboard the HQS *Wellington*, permanently moored on the River Thames at the Victoria

Embankment, London. In *The Honourable Company – A History,*
Maurice Disney (1950) gives an account of how the privateers
Prince Frederick and *Duke* under the command of Captain Talbot
intercepted three French ships – *Marquis d'Antin, Lewis* and *Notre
Dame de Deliverance*. After 'they entertained each other smartly for
three hours', two of the ships lost their masts but the *Notre Dame de
Deliverance* escaped. With difficulty, the disabled vessels were towed
to Kinsale. The effort was worthwhile because as prizes they realised
'over two and a half million dollars in spices, pistols, doubloons, gold
bars, wrought plate besides 800 tonnes of cocoa and other valuable
effects'. The 'proprietors', who were the captains, officers and the
owners of the capturing ships, received £700,000 as their share. 'Every
common seaman got £850 for his dividend' a vast sum in the middle
of the eighteenth century. The euphoria of the backers at their London
clubs and the scenes on the piers of Kinsale and later at Bristol as the
treasures were landed can be imagined.

The practice of privateering, driven by self-interest, was viewed
with some ambivalence as it was argued that it was an excuse for
piracy. Inevitably, in times of peace, when it could not be justified as
part of the war effort and letters of marque were withdrawn, the skills
acquired by the sailors frequently found an outlet in piracy on the high
seas. The reverse was also true: the poacher became the gamekeeper.
When appointed Governor of Jamaica in 1718, Woodes Rogers, a
frequent caller to Kinsale, recruited pirates to act as privateers to hunt
down the Spanish.[11]

Privateering gave rise to duplicitous practices and opportunities
for embezzlement. Frequently ships' captains and officers hived off
valuables before they declared their prizes in ports such as Kinsale.
To curb the incidence of fraud and regulate the practice, Admiralty
Courts were established in the late seventeenth century at Dublin and
Kinsale and other ports on the coast. As a formal instrument of state,
the courts were mandated to judge on the legitimacy of the prize,
assess its value and supervise the share-out after state levies were
taken. Ten to twenty per cent of the total, 'the tenths', was reserved
for the Crown. Two thirds of the remainder was generally allocated to
the private companies who had financed the expedition and one third
to the officers and men of the vessel, distributed according to rank.

In terms of personal wealth, this was a rare bonanza for seamen of the eighteenth century. Banned by the courts were goods having any connection with smuggling or the capture of allied shipping, which were considered capital offences. The prize court sitting at Kinsale brought extra demand for victualling and increased market activity, cash flow and provided employment for lighter men and porters.[12]

The captured ships usually included a number of prisoners when they arrived in the harbour. In 1665 Robert Southwell was obliged to quarter forty-six Dutch captives of the *Bonaventure* in private houses as the sheriff refused to keep them in jail, presumably because of overcrowding. Southwell was reimbursed out of the 'success of the prizes that will far exceed all such charges'. In fact, the prize sale was celebrated with a dinner for merchants and appraisers in William Swan's inn after the business was complete.[13] Other prisoners were not as fortunate as they were incarcerated in what came to be called the French Prison on Cork Street (see plate 7). It had been the Custom House of the Desmonds until 1583 and in 1601 used by the Spaniards as a magazine during the siege of Kinsale.[14] The atrocious conditions under which the prisoners were held were vividly described in the following report. 'Meat in great scarcity and not half boiled ... no proper facilities for the sick and the sick and well lay promiscuously together crowded in dirty rat infested cellars, which were hardly cleaned out.'[15] The prisoners scavenged for sustenance. Tradition has it that they carved models from animal bones which they exchanged through the bars of the jail with the local people for food. The unhygienic conditions, squatting or lying on damp straw, led to a high incidence of infection and death.

The 'shameful irregularity' and ill treatment meted out came to a disastrous head on the night of 29 January 1749, when fire broke out in the prison and was fanned by a gale. In a terrible tragedy, 54 out of 600 inmates died in the flames. The survivors were herded together and driven like cattle to Charles Fort where they were confined in the dungeons of the casemented bastions. On the following day they 'were called into an open field where they were kept for some hours to air them'.

There were many attempts made by the prisoners to escape. An exchange arrangement, though, existed between the English and

French, which offered hope of relief. On 25 December 1710, 567 French were shipped to Saint-Malo.[16] In 1763 the *Black Prince* carried 200 to Brest and the *Pitville* transported almost 500 to Bordeaux. John Howe, agent for the prisoners in Kinsale, sought tenders for vessels to transport 250 Spanish in 1781 and the same ships were used to bring 350 English to Plymouth.[17]

American prisoners, captured during the War of Independence, were also held in Kinsale. In 1775 the war against Britain saw action off the Irish coast. Suffering similarly to the French, the Americans' plight was highlighted by the Rev. W. Hazlitt, a clergyman in Bandon and father of the noted essayist, William. As part of his Christian concern he set out his objective 'to expose in public print, the cruelties inflicted on them and air their grievances to the effectual improvement of their condition'.[18]

Nevertheless, in Kinsale the arrangements required for convoying and regulating the activities of the privateers were additional harbour operations under naval administration which brought further prestige and wealth to the Corporation and the town burghers.

Privateering as a seafaring enterprise was exceptional in that it held out the prospect of wealth for many who sailed on expeditions to track down and capture enemy ships. But generally, life at sea was difficult, uncomfortable and particularly cruel aboard fighting ships. Under reforms introduced during the reign of Elizabeth I, sailors aboard naval vessels were trained in the use of arms. The effect was that the functions of fighting and seafaring were combined, laying the basis of the modern navy.[19] England's involvement in the sixteenth- and seventeenth-century colonisation process and the need to protect shipping and sea routes created a demand for seamen to crew the ships. Each captain was responsible for filling his own complement with little inducement to entice men to sea.

For the uninitiated, the first encounter with shipboard life were the nauseous conditions, poor food and scant attention to hygiene that pervaded the vessel. The crews were subjected to severe discipline with punishment meted out frequently by means of flogging at the end of a cat-o'-nine-tails or the ultimate sanction of execution by hanging from a fore yard arm.

Such prospects naturally curtailed the numbers of recruits voluntarily signing up. At the end of the eighteenth century the full muster for the English navy stood at 100,000 men, which represented the largest number among the seafaring nations. It was, however, insufficient, particularly during the period of the French wars when there was a constant threat to England itself and English interests in America.[20] Of the total it is estimated that one third were Irish and 50 per cent were reluctant seafarers, who had been forced or press-ganged into service.

Enforced recruitment was undertaken in many ports, enlisting men from the surrounding areas. The image often depicted of recruits dragged off in front of family and loved ones was a reality. On occasions, the local innkeeper, in what was referred to as 'crimping', would identify some drunken down-and-out to the press gang, who having sobered up would find himself deep in the bowels of a ship under a deck grating, stricken by horror and cowering in fear.[21] Press gangs were active in Kinsale in the eighteenth century. A 'voucher', or pay order, issued to Kinsale Corporation in July 1739 for £1-17-0 was the bill for expenses incurred in 'subsisting nine impressed seamen for his Majesty'. In the same month the naval authorities paid 8 shillings for a further five seamen. When they got to sea, many suffered weeks of sickening empty retching, and were often the first aboard ship to succumb to disease, illness and death.

Certain categories of seamen at Kinsale were exempt from impressment, including fishermen and pilots who, being skilled seamen, would have been eminently suitable for service in the navy. The importance of fish as food and the need for efficient port operations excused them. Their special position was highlighted in correspondence of Sir Robert Southwell in May 1697 concerning the threat posed by a naval ship.[22]

> One Capt. Clark who commands the 'Humber' lay between this [Kinsale] and Cork harbour for two days and sent his boat into the road where fishermen were catching fish and took several men out of their boats to the utter ruin of their families which doth also terrify others that they dare not go to sea for fear of being so served. Unless

the men are restored and protected we shall have no more fish brought here which will raise our provision being now very dear ... but until there is an order from the Lords of the Admiralty commanding the Captains of HM ships not to disturb fishermen, there will be danger.

Nevertheless, despite the protests, tradition has it that a fisherman by the name of Arnopp, from a well-known Kinsale family, was seized while at sea, albeit by the French. Fortunately for him, as part of a prisoner exchange, he was repatriated to Kinsale.[23] A second account involved the Daly family, consisting of a father and three sons who were longlining off the Old Head of Kinsale. When they saw a boat being launched from a navy frigate, they immediately abandoned fishing and rowed furiously for shore, pursued by the navy press gang. In the fine weather, neighbours of the Dalys gathered on the cliff top to view the pursuit and by the time the family got ashore a large number of people had come together, enabling the men to mingle and scatter in the crowd and they were lost to the press gang. The story concludes with the navy leaving without their quarry, much to the relief of the community.

Another group exempt from impressment were the pilots who provided an essential service for visiting ships. Samuel Lewis, writing in 1839, said that Kinsale pilots '... have been noted for the goodness of their boats and their excellent seamanship, their services in supplying the markets of Cork and other neighbouring towns and their skills as pilots procured for them exemption from impressment during the last war [the Napoleonic War].'[24]

These incidents were a continuous feature of life for the seafaring community who, apart from coping with difficult weather and eking out a meagre living from the sea, were under constant threat of being carried off and forced to fight on distant seas.

It was the strong naval presence and the town's role in victualling the westbound fleets that gave Kinsale its importance in the seventeenth and eighteenth centuries. In terms of trade in exports and imports, Kinsale was very much in third place on the Cork coast, after Cork and Youghal. This was clear from the custom receipts of products such as wool, hides and livestock, which were the basis of

Irish exports. For the 100-year period from 1699 to 1798, figures show that Cork had 87 per cent of the customs' revenue, which rose to 99 per cent by the end of the eighteenth century.[25] Easy access and the short distance to the open sea at Kinsale, which had built its reputation as a victualling port, were no longer advantages, as ships got bigger and were unable to enter the harbour. By 1765, an Admiralty house had been constructed at Cove (Cobh) in the Port of Cork and harbour usage at Kinsale declined, many of its naval functions having been transferred to Cork by 1800.

After the Napoleonic Wars in 1815, the end of the golden age of shipping in Kinsale was a reality. Physically the street pattern of the modern town was in place but on the waterfront the old quay walls were slowly becoming derelict. In contrast, at Cork increased shipping activity followed the dredging of the River Lee and the construction of quay walls which narrowed the channels to create deep-water berths. This in turn facilitated the bridging of the river that gave access to a large agricultural hinterland north of the city. Quantity and turnover were the critical factors in Cork's rising economic fortunes, which came to dominate the butter, meat and brewing industries exclusively supplying the colonies. The export of grain and hides was also significant. Its superiority over Kinsale as a shipping port was affirmed in 1849 when it was designated a supply base for the Royal Navy Atlantic Fleet.

The larger harbour had the capacity to build the critical mass which inevitably required the transfer of victualling, chandlery and other services from Kinsale. Cork trade was further encouraged by the emergence of banking in the city, established by the Quaker community from the 1750s.[26] Doubts about Kinsale's ability to take the growing size of ships had already been referred to in correspondence between the Southwells and their agent, Alderman Hoare, as early as 1693. Hoare argued that Kinsale could take vessels up to the size of fifth-rate frigates, approximately 120 feet length overall, and that it should focus on the needs of the smaller vessel. The inadequacy of the harbour was confirmed for the Navy Board in 1694 when fourth-rate ships, of which six were allocated to the south coast of Ireland, had difficulty in entering Kinsale and it was no longer considered suitable for development.[27]

The East Indian fleet engaged in the growing China trade, which had victualled at Kinsale from the beginning of the seventeenth century, no longer called. Instead the fleets gathered at Spithead in the English Channel, sailing directly in convoy to the Cape of Good Hope. This was a further, significant blow to Kinsale's mercantile aspirations.[28]

There was natural reluctance to cede business to Cork. Hoare, as the man on the ground, saw the inevitability of losing some of the victualling services, but was severely reprimanded by members of the Kinsale Corporation. The record subsequently proves that his position was correct. In letting some business transfer, Kinsale could have focused on more specialised markets associated with brewing, baking and slaughtering in which Hoare had made a major investment in the 1690s.[29] He wrote to Edward Robertson in August 1703 arguing that Kinsale could continue as a victualling base ahead of Cork, using the old argument that 'victualling from Cork of men of war or merchantmen was too difficult owing to the long river and estuary of the Lee'. This was a long shot as the position in Cork was being remedied but in any case, his effort was not helped by the inflexible attitude of the Kinsale authorities.

To improve the service on offer at Kinsale, he initiated a drive for cooperation among Kinsale merchants. Jointly they raised £2,000 capital as 'no single person is able to have a stock of goods by them to furnish shipping as they come in'. The investment was planned to improve facilities to compete with Cork's growing reputation and at least hold Kinsale as an alternative to the growing assertion that all ships 'must go to Cork'.[30]

In naval terms, it was abundantly clear that Kinsale was inadequate after 1750, despite the fact it could still report that 'the Royal Naval Dockyard worked well into the eighteenth century'.[31] The decline was arrested during periods of conflict in Europe and America. A report dispatched to London in 1759 said that the HMS *Newark*, an eighty-gun vessel with a complement of 650 men under the command of Admiral Francis Holburne, arrived in Kinsale having completed a cruise in the Bay of Biscay during the Seven Years' War. 'She lay here in safety from the 3rd to the 14th of December when she sailed for England. Her draught was 22 feet and at low springs she

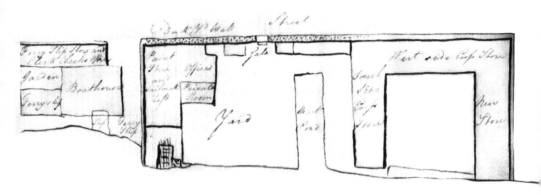

Charles Vallancey's rough sketch of the Royal Dockyard, showing mast pond, sail lofts, nail and paint store. *Courtesy English Heritage Archive*

still had 8 feet of water more than she drew'.[31] Bearing so many guns this was a large vessel and it is obvious that the report was designed to promote the harbour. While she must have lain outside the bar, it shows the continuing significance of Kinsale for the fleet, which had just defeated the French at the Battle of Quiberon, halting a significant threat of an invasion of England.[32] In the following year, a French squadron under M. Thurot, which had attacked Carrigfergus, was intercepted off the Isle of Man by a fleet under the command of Captains Elliot, Clement and Logue. The fleet had been dispatched from Kinsale.[33]

The days of Kinsale as a naval station were numbered. Colonel Charles Vallancey, a military engineer, surveyed the 'defensive capabilities' of the coast in 1777 and confirmed that while 'Kinsale was suitable in former years it could not [now] cater for our ships of war which draw more water than formally'. In conclusion he stated that 'the notable eighteenth century progress in boat building and marine engineering together with the general expansion of shipping had rendered the old Dock and Harbour of Kinsale inadequate for any considerable maritime accommodation or enterprise ... '. In 1788 from the shipping perspective, Kinsale had thirty-nine small vessels, many no bigger than the local forty-foot hookers with a total tonnage of just 1,500 tons. These engaged in local coastal trade within a limit that included the harbour, Oysterhaven, Cork, the Old Head of Kinsale and Courtmacsherry. Reflecting its reduced status Kinsale was placed fourteenth in importance on a list of twenty-six Irish harbours.[34] Samuel Lewis in the immediate pre-Famine period, described Kinsale's shipping trade as confined to agriculture products. Imports consisted of timber, coal, iron and salt and in 1835 only five deep-sea vessels arrived in the port, averaging 200 tons.[35]

Cork, on the other hand, was a thriving centre. In a survey of ports in the United Kingdom in 1881, Cork received 40 per cent of all shipping calling 'for orders'. This was more than double the number entering Falmouth, which was the leading 'call' port on the British coast. The vessels, while anchored, required services such as repair, victualling, towage, fuel and facilities for crew change, all of which had a spin-off economic benefit for Cork.[36]

Apart from the constraints imposed by the limited depth of water in the harbour, Kinsale had no locally owned large vessel sailing out of the harbour, and as a result was unable to avail of opportunities presented when the restrictive navigation acts were repealed following the Act of Union in 1800. The town was incapable of responding to the changed circumstances without an indigenous shipping fleet, which it never had and would struggle to acquire due to a lack of entrepreneurial spirit in the native population. John Mitchel, the Young Irelander, attributed the apathy to previous neglect. He said that people living in communities such as Kinsale had no access to capital, experience of management or ownership, which made them incapable of compensating for the deficit in 'commercial marine ... and mechanical skills'.

Yet as the nineteenth century progressed, the extension of the democratic franchise sparked an emerging mercantile class in the town. They became active in local politics after 1840 when the Town Commissioners replaced the Corporation, the old bastion of privilege. Later some were appointed Commissioners of the Harbour Board, which was established in 1870. While not having access to the privately owned quays or slipways, they nevertheless saw the potential in establishing a shipping company. According to Basil Petterson, writing on the emergence of companies at the time, 'the fleets consisted of a variety of schooners, brigantines and smacks built for the coastal trade'.[37]

Consisting of a fleet of small ships between 100 and 200 tons, the Kinsale Shipping Company was established in 1881. The major shareholders were members of the O'Neill, Acton and Crowley families who had become prominent in the commercial life of the town. Among the better-known vessels in the fleet, with the name of the skipper in brackets, were *Sidney* (Sheat), *Marion* (Cummins), *T. Crowley* (Parker), *Esmeralda* (Greenway), *Harlequin*, *The George Brown*, *Ellen Dawson* and *Hannah*. The *James O'Neill* (O'Donovan) was described as a beautiful three-masted schooner of 140 tons built at Connah Quay, near Liverpool, in 1903.[38] By 1920, many of these ships had auxiliary engines fitted, which improved their efficiency and profitability. The Crowley ledgers show that on average each vessel made between fifteen and twenty trips per year trading out of Kinsale and between ports on the Irish, English and French coasts. Regular ports of call were Appledore, Cardiff, Guernsey, Jersey, Newport, Padstow, Bordeaux, Dieppe, Nantes, St Brieuc, and Santander in Spain. Cargos varied, with coal, iron, cement, clay, paving and salt inwards, and hay, barley, pit props and fish the main exports.

Profits generated by each vessel were distributed annually on the basis of sixteen shares with a half allocated to the running costs of the ship. The *George Brown*, which made eleven trips in 1873, produced a dividend of £147-15-00 for its two owners from transporting pit wood, corn and coal. The calculations were based on a fixed rate for coal at 9/6 per ton. Other information gleaned from the company's records show that the ship, the *T. Crowley*, brought a supply of iron for the new Bandon River Bridge from Gloucester on 24 July 1877. She was a profitable ship for the Company but on 10 March 1917, she was torpedoed by a German submarine, 15 miles south of Hook Head. All hands were rescued. Justification for the sinking was that a number of the Company's ships were being chartered by the British government for the war effort. For an eight-month period in 1918, the *Sidney* was in fact on contract to the Admiralty, earning £1-12-6 per day which paid the ship's way and helped the Company to survive.

The records provide an insight to the dangers to which Kinsale seamen were exposed when sailing aboard these vessels. On 22 May 1897 the *Marion* lost her sails in a severe storm in the Bristol Channel. For twelve days she was laid up for repairs at Newport in South Wales. Reflecting the harsh working conditions of the time, the crew had to argue for wages and expenses to cover food costs while the repairs were being undertaken when they later returned to Kinsale. The mean-minded attitude of the Company may be attributable to annoyance at the crew because, soon after returning to sea, the *Marion* collided with a French vessel to which the Company was required to pay eight days' demurrage (this was a charge payable to the owner of a damaged ship when it could not fulfil its contract agreements).

Having received extensive repairs at Appledore, another ship, *Colleen*, was stranded at Padstow, remaining hard fast for the months of October and November 1917. She was an unlucky ship as on a cross-channel trip from Padstow to St Brieuc, she carried away her foremast and became unmanageable. Blown into Mounts Bay in Cornwall she was driven off course and onto the rocks near Mullion, north of the Lizard. All hands were saved but the vessel broke up in the stormy conditions. The terse language of the report hides the terror which must have been experienced by the crew, who scrambled to safety amid the tangle of fallen rigging and torn sails, as the scraping hull crunched on the surf-covered rocks.

Back in Kinsale, vessels were in constant need of repairs after trips, which brought business to the shipwrights who were con-tinuously engaged in caulking and replacing broken spars to facilitate a quick turnaround. Casey's sail loft at the end of the Short Quay repaired the heavy-duty canvas sails and Murphys, the blacksmiths at the bottom of St John's Hill, hammered out a myriad of iron fittings.

By 1900, the days of sailing ships were coming to the end, with engines being fitted to the Kinsale Shipping Company fleet. The last Irish sailing schooner built by Tyrrells of Arklow in 1921, *Invermore*, had a connection with Kinsale: she made the passage from Kinsale to Plymouth in a record time of twenty-four hours, running under spinnaker in a following gale. On reaching the Seven Stones, the strong wind backed westerly giving a fast passage up the Channel for the bluff-bowed vessel.[39]

The war years in particular were difficult for Kinsale Shipping. Dick Scott, maritime historian, wrote that the Company went into liquidation in 1917 resulting in many of the ships being sold to a company in Guernsey.[40] A local observer noted in 1921 that the fleet was 'worn out, others lost in collision while others were torpedoed in the German War and at that time there was not a single schooner belonging to the town', which amply reflects the low level of shipping activity at the time.[41]

The same source recalled other efforts to engage in shipping which ended in failure. The 600-ton *Lord Sandown*, a barque which traded to St John's in Newfoundland, taking passengers and general cargo and returning with timber, was owned by the McDaniel family who were active in town politics. The vessel unfortunately ended her days in Kinsale Harbour as a flaming hulk, burned out at the Half Tide rock, having drifted onto the Castlepark shore.

The *Emilie*, a small coaster owned by the Thuillier family, also came to an unfortunate end. The *Cork County Eagle* in 1901 headlined the 'Loss of Kinsale Schooner – The Crew Saved' on Saturday 28 December. With a cargo of coal, a crew of four and two passengers under Captain P. Colman, she ran aground in foggy weather and poor visibility in the Mersey. Severely damaged, she was declared a hazard and, with explosive charges put aboard by the authorities, was blown up. The crew and the passengers were saved but the ship was a total loss to the owners.

The Kinsale men who had sailed aboard these ships were readily accepted on vessels sailing under foreign flags. Others engaged in fishing locally or in the cod fishery in the North Sea out of Hull. Many, before Irish independence in 1921, joined the Royal Naval Reserve and with their seafaring experience, they received the call-up soon after the declaration of the Great War in 1914. Travel vouchers were collected at the Kinsale Custom House where the new recruits were informed of the base to which they were assigned in the UK. Subsequently, a number of these men became casualties of war, leaving families at home fatherless and in difficult circumstances. One such was Denis Gimblett, who was forty-six years of age when his ship was sunk by a German U–boat off Wexford just before the declaration of the armistice in 1918. He left a wife and a large young family, which was not an uncommon experience for families in Kinsale.[42]

The Custom House and its royal coat of arms, emblazoned with lion, unicorn and crown over the doorway, was the last remaining symbol of the old naval establishment in the town. After national independence in 1921, the Custom House continued to provide an important function where wives went to collect the 'half pay' sent home by husbands on voyages in the far-flung parts of the world. The arms, though, were unceremoniously dumped in the harbour when the Free State took control of the town in 1922.

The Bristol Channel was the part of the British coast most closely associated with Kinsale. Apart from Bristol at the apex of the wedge-shaped channel, other ports frequently called to were Barnstable, Appledore and Padstow on the south side. On the Welsh side Milford Haven became significant when fish caught off Kinsale were landed directly by steam drifter for rail distribution throughout Britain. In the nineteenth and twentieth centuries, Barry Dock, which was a major Welsh trading coal port, became the hub for men to sign on aboard foreign-owned ships.

Men, some mere boys, left the security of a close-knit family to begin a seafaring career. For the first trip the young lad would travel steerage from Cork to Fishguard under the watchful eye of a relative or experienced neighbour returning to sea. On arrival he was accommodated in a boarding house until a berth aboard a ship was found through the 'pool' system, which was a essentially a hiring hall. Sometimes he waited weeks for owners and ship's masters to employ him under Ship's Articles. Often lonely, homesick and extremely vulnerable, he needed to buy a 'donkey's breakfast'. It was a bag full of straw, which was used as a mattress for sleeping on the tiered timber bunks in the fo'c'sle of the ship. The accommodation, smelling of old straw, echoed loudly to the clanking of the anchor chain in the hawse pipe when at sea. Kitted out in oilskins, sou'westers and wellington boots the youngster, 'deep sea' for the first time, soon had the opportunity to test the adequacy of the waterproofing when wettings from breaking seas and gale-driven rain were encountered.

Accommodating to the avalanche of experiences in adapting to shipboard life and overcoming seasickness, the young sailor set about the various tasks. Settling into the pecking order among his shipmates, he was taken through the various safety drills, introduced to different shipboard procedures and the watch system. In ships under sail the young man went aloft, learning to furl and set sails on yards which swayed high above a yawing deck. As he 'learned the ropes', he became skilled working over the side on platforms or being hoisted in a bo'sun's chair, painting, chipping, learning to splice, and deal with hatches, berthing and helming. With the introduction of steam in the engine room below deck the critical work of machinery maintenance, which involved oiling, greasing and stoking steam boilers, never ceased. The initial encounter with a hurricane or a storm was recalled vividly. Descriptions of the vessel dropping low into the sea as water crashed over the bridge and then slowly emerging in a twisting roll as green torrents cascaded through scupper holes in feather-white seas were retold around the family hearth in later years.

Kinsale men worked the tall ships – requiring seamanship skills and physical courage that enabled them to undertake tasks on deck and aloft. Conditions varied from the tedious boredom of the doldrums to the wet and terror of the 'roaring forties' around Cape Horn, bound for Chile and the South Pacific. Others aboard vessels travelled to Australia, 'running their easting down' as they benefited from the trade winds in the southern hemisphere. Many sailed on 'home trade' coasters and tramp steamers carrying grain from Odessa and coal from Newcastle or aboard magnificent passenger liners and on great warships.

Gerald Gimblett as a young man went to sea in 1923 and later recalled the fumigation process on the grain ships. Poison was poured into the holds to kill the rats and vermin after the grain cargo was unloaded. Then birds were lowered into the hold and if they survived it was considered safe to put men down, who had the task of shovelling the rats into bags and dumping them overboard to float away, belly up on the tide.[43]

The seafaring life was not all bleak as it also provided the opportunity to see the world and return home with many stories of escapades ashore in foreign ports. Voyages could last up to two years or more before men would get leave and have the opportunity to renew family connections.

At sea the sailors developed marine skills and qualified as able seamen, perhaps rising to the exalted position of bo'sun. Most Kinsale sailors received certificates in 'efficiency' as lifeboat men, judged on their ability to launch and handle small boats when afloat. Additional skills were acquired during times of war. Many vessels had small guns mounted on the deck forward and it was necessary for sailors to train in gunnery and proficiency in maintaining such weapons as Hotchkiss or Lewis and Merlin. These skills were recorded in discharge books.

On leaving a ship, the seaman was issued with a Continuous Certificate of discharge book. Completed by the ship's master, it gave information on the duration of the voyage and the seaman's rating and character in relation to ability and conduct. When he signed on again the book was passed to the captain of the new vessel. The men were paid off, receiving the balance of earnings less deductions for tobacco, advances given when going ashore in foreign ports and the half pay allocations already sent to families at home. In 1940, the monthly pay was £24-0-0 (€30 approximately) for an able seaman. A number of Kinsale men went to sea as deck and engineering apprentices, qualifying eventually as ships' captains and master mariners. They had command of some of the world's largest oil tankers, iron ore and grain carriers at sea, managing and navigating ships to ports in every corner of the world.[44]

In later years, after lifetimes at sea, retired sailors and fishermen gathered daily on the Low Road in Scilly looking to the harbour mouth, casting wistful eyes on the horizon. Pacing backwards and forwards, they recalled events and discussed them with others walking in the opposite direction over a short communicating distance. This form of shared conversation was instilled by the habit of taking exercise at sea, pacing the width of a ship's bridge or in the lee of a wheelhouse.[45]

In modern times although greatly reduced, Kinsale continues as a shipping port, catering for approximately fifty vessels per year, of up to 120 feet and cargos of 3,000 tons, mostly importing animal feed for Henry Good Ltd, the local milling company. These provide casual employment opportunities and substantial dues used to maintain the port. It is a welcome activity despite criticism of the dust and noise generated in the discharging process, which is seen as inconsistent with the town's prominence as a tourism centre.[46] Access to the upper reaches of the Bandon River was cut off to shipping by the construction of the Duggan Bridge in 1977.

After a glorious period of shipping that made Kinsale an important harbour in the seventeenth and eighteenth centuries, its position was greatly reduced after 1750. The presence of the navy had originally followed on from the successful development of the port but declined as Kinsale's significance decreased and various aspects of the services provided by the naval authorities were removed to Cork.

The physical development that produced the quay wall and sea frontage of the modern town emerged not from shipping activities but from the harbour's growing importance as a fishing station in the nineteenth century. Fishing was always part of the town's economy but for a period from 1860 to 1900, up to 500 vessels annually thronged the harbour to fish for the spring mackerel and autumn herring to feed the growing concentrations of population in the industrial centres of Great Britain. The expansion of the fisheries was another example of how the town capitalised on the potential of the harbour and the sudden arrival of large shoals of fish off the harbour.

4

Fishing

Fishing has been a significant element of Kinsale's economy from the earliest times. John de Courcy Ireland said that the port had a foremost place in fifteenth-century Ireland, exporting fish to Bristol, Brittany, La Rochelle and Bordeaux. 'Fish was undoubtedly the most important product in Ireland in which Kinsale figures prominently.' So plentiful were stocks in the 1640s that Charles I allowed the Dutch under licence to fish off the south coast of Ireland for which they produced a chart to assist their fleets.[1] The earliest written evidence of the industry in Kinsale was in 1611. Robert Cogan, who had been appointed fishery inspector for Ireland by James I, described Kinsale as a 'poor town destroyed in the last rebellion [a reference to the siege of Kinsale, 1601], but one of the best harbours in the Kingdom ... It depends on the fishing of pilchard, herring and hake which are taken in the harbour.'[2] So important was the pilchard catch that Sir Thomas Button, who was delegated to protect the coast in 1631, highlighted the importance of James Fort in defending the fishery.[3]

Hake, which followed the pilchard shoals, were caught on long lines of 100 fathoms (600 feet) sometimes called spillers, using pilchard or mussels as bait. In a skilled operation involving numerous hooks, the lines were shot in foul ground for pollack, coalfish, bream and wrasse. Hake, cod, ling, halibut, haddock and other bottom-feeding white fish were caught in clear sandy areas. Up to the middle of the nineteenth century, these were caught in the Kinsale hooker which fished up to 50 miles offshore. The position of the spillers was marked by using sewn-up air-filled dog skins, an example of which may be seen in Kinsale's museum. Known as 'watchmen' they supported the lines with 200 hooks attached.[4]

Longline fishing was also practised inshore, in small open yawls, using oars and spritsail, by old-timers with a lifetime of seagoing etched on weatherbeaten faces that gave witness to the expression of being 'wrung out of the sea'. They were continuing the custom of heading for Hole Open to the east of the Old Head of Kinsale on an ebb tide to catch hake, whiting, mackerel and pollack. After a day's fishing they returned on the incoming flood, assisted by the breeze filling the sail on a short mast stepped forward in the boat. Sitting astern with an arm resting on the sculling oar for steering, the boat was sailed to the calm in the lee of the Blockhouse. The sail was simple, loose footed, easily handled and stretched up and outwards from the tack to the peak with the sprit (or pole) to give effective wind power. It was a common sight until the 1950s.[5]

As boats went further out to sea, the Kinsale hooker emerged as the craft most associated with fishing. The term 'hooker' derives clearly from the idea of line fishing. R.J. Scott, in his book *The Galway Hooker*, says that it may come from the Dutch, who used such terms as *howker* or *holker*, which were small, easily handled cargo vessels, a function for which both the Kinsale and Galway boats were used when not fishing. The Dutch connection is further highlighted by the bulge-shaped hull when viewed from directly ahead or astern. This feature or 'tumblehome' is similar to that of the flat-bottomed barge-style vessel used on the shoal waters around and off the Dutch coast. The origin of the hooker and the evolution of its distinctive shape are not known but have been the subject of much speculation. A letter from Robert Southwell to the Lord Deputy in 1671 records that sixty of these boats, each crewed by three men and a boy, worked out of Kinsale. Townsend, in 1815, reports that apart from fishing they were also used as pilot cutters and as small merchant ships supplying the

Cork market 'constantly and copiously' with goods.[6] By 1836 the fleet had grown to ninety and were described as a very fine class of boat and varied in size from 15 to 25 tons. The cost of producing one provided with mackerel nets, longlines, hand lines and herring nets for deep sea was set at £8 per ton. In 1859 fewer than thirty-five boats were reported and the decline was attributed to a number of factors, including difficulty of finding bait for the longlines and the efficiency of other craft from the Cornish coast that were appearing off Kinsale.[7]

From the early seventeenth century, nets were employed for seine fishing. Two boats worked together; the larger, up to 30 feet in length, was accompanied by a smaller boat known as the 'faller' or follower. The direction of an approaching shoal, which could be pilchard, mackerel or sprat, was signalled by a 'huer' or lookout scanning the surface of the water standing forward in the boat. Sometimes directions were taken from someone ashore, looking out from Sandy Cove Island, Hake Head or Preghane Point, whose keen eye recognised the presence of fish in the darkening water or a break on the surface. By various forms of visual signs to the crew in the boats, the location of the school was indicated. The scene is described by a visitor to Kinsale in 1695: 'Up a steep hill of which Preghane begins they actually walk to observe the shoals of pilchards and from thence give direction to those below in the boats how so to manage their nets for the looking of them.'[8]

At night the frenetic activity of the captured fish produced glowing phosphorescence. The ends of the seine, which had been shot from the larger boat, were drawn together with the assistance of the smaller boat, encircling the trapped fish. Stones thrown from the boats or the surface slapped with oar blades attempted to reverse the slewing bid for escape of the glinting fish. To finally trap the catch a ring rope at the bottom of the net was pulled to make a purse, sealing off any possibility of freedom. Amid frantic splashing on the surface, the fish were gathered into wicker hampers on listing boats.

The hake and the pilchard, which are noted for their oil, were landed at different points in the harbour where the bustling activity continued. As the catch was brought ashore, the whole community including women and children were involved. An observer reported in 1695 that at 'Scilly Point and around that place … their boats had newly come in. They were all on the rock setting out their catch which was chiefly of very large hake which they had [caught] overnight.'[9]

Ashore at Scilly, the World's End and Lower Cove, the sites of prototype processing operations, the fish were counted, cleaned, salted, smoked for preservation, or pressed to extract valuable oil. The slippery fish were gathered in groups of three, which two hands can grasp. After twenty, the count continued 'one and twenty' up to 'twenty and twenty' and finished with the expression 'cast and tally' which involved a final six fish, giving a total of 126. This was called 'a hundred' and was the unit on which payment was made. Another feature of these sites, known as pallaces, was a large barrel to which the catch was transferred. A flat plate, the 'buckler', attached to a weighted beam hinged on the adjacent wall, was lowered on top. The 'buckler' squeezed down on the fish, extracting the liquid, which dripped into a sump. The lower-density oil rose to the top, separating it from the water and blood that had been pressed from the fish. After a period of settling the waste liquid was drained off by removing a wooden plug at the bottom of the barrel. To refine the oil further, fresh water was added and the process repeated. A stone drain which took away the waste liquid is still visible at Scilly.

The oil obtained in this way was used in the preparation of leather and as a fuel source for lighting. In 1672, because of large catches of pilchard, Kinsale contributed significantly to the total of 109 tons of oil produced in the country.[10] In terms of food the high oil content of the pilchard did not suit the Irish palate. When cured or smoked they were exported to Cornwall, where there was an appetite, to the extent that Dover fishermen even complained of the market being oversupplied by Kinsale fish.[11]

Herring were often confused with pilchard. In terms of price, herring were more valuable and it was necessary to distinguish them from the pilchard. This was achieved by applying the test of floating a dead fish in water. Pilchard floated horizontally and herring tended to sink by the head, an early example of quality control in practice.

The preservation of fish was an important aspect of the shore-based activity. It was an essential process for transporting the catch and for local consumption when fresh fish were not available. Kinsale

Scottish girls cleaning fish at the Short Quay, 1896. *Courtesy Tim O'Donovan*

fish were consumed in great quantities in what were known as the Lenten countries, a term associated with southern Europe and the practice of abstaining from meat during periods of the Catholic Church's liturgical year. The process had a major impact on the town's economy. Before refrigeration or the availability of ice, the only preservation methods possible were curing or smoking. Both required copious quantities of salt, imported from France and Portugal, and water, of which there was an ample supply at Scilly.

The process of curing, which continued into the twentieth century, involved groups of three people working together, two gutting and one packing. When landed ashore the fish were transferred to troughs, close to benches where the work took place. The fish was cut at the gills with a sharp knife held between the forefinger and thumb and the guts were drawn in one swift movement. Graded into different containers, they were then packed into barrels, head to tail with bellies up and covered in salt. The next layer was angled to the previous one and so on until the barrel was filled.

The salt had the effect of drawing the blood and water from the fish, which were drained off after a number of days. The extra space created was then filled by fish from another barrel and covered in pickle. An apple floating on the surface was the density test for the effectiveness of the briny mixture. After curing for eight to ten days, the pickle was again removed and more 'filling-up' of the barrel if required. A final quality control check was undertaken by the buyers who would crudely kick over a sample barrel and examine the spilled contents. If satisfied, the coopers were brought in to tack down and label the barrels, which were stacked three tiers high to await transport by ship or train to Cork, Dublin or to further destinations in England, Germany, America and Russia.

Almost 100 per cent of the workers ashore were girls who in busy periods worked up to sixteen hours a day, continuing until the last fish was packed. A team of three managed on average to pack 100 fish per minute, filling a barrel with approximately 850 fish, with the guts placed in containers at the side of the trestle benches for disposal. The work was restricted to the stretch of the quay south of a line from the Middle Slip to Scilly because of the all-pervading smell. During the fishing boom after 1862, the buyers organised the girls, most of whom were Scottish and who had followed the fishing fleets down the east and west coasts of the United Kingdom, finishing the season at Kinsale. Some, as young as fifteen years of age, stayed in boarding houses in the town and were known for their cheerfulness and singing as they walked the Short Quay in their colourful headscarves. Like the fishermen, they were contracted to a particular buyer after they had received an allowance, known as 'bounty money', to purchase aprons and leg gear for protection from the cold spring weather. In Kinsale they were roused each morning to get ready for the early boats with the call 'get up and tie your fingers'. Prior to the availability of rubber gloves, the girls put binding on each finger for protection against the stinging effect of the brine and salt and to prevent damage to their hands from the sharp knives. On occasions, while awaiting the arrival

THE PIER. KINSALE. 37333 JV.

The village of Scilly from Compass Hill with Kipper House (*middle left*), 1896.
Courtesy Lawrence Collection

of another catch, the industrious women spent the time knitting for their menfolk. Financially the season was quite rewarding. In the 1880s, the girls earned between £17 and £20 for the season, which was not much less than the average earned by the fishermen.[12]

Smoke, generated from smouldering oak dust, was used as another means of preserving fish at the 'Kipper House' in Scilly, applying both hot and cold techniques. The cleaned fish were placed in salt for a period of three weeks, again to draw off unwanted liquid and residual blood in the flesh. They were then skewered or hung on narrow poles for a number of days in a smoke-filled room.

Apart from fish preservation, there was an additional need to protect nets made from cotton, hemp or flax and also sails cut from calico and later Egyptian cotton. The fabrics were susceptible to attack from mildew and rot caused by damp and exposure to salt water. Beeswax, egg yolk, alum and linseed were rubbed into the sails for protection but the most common material used was the bark from trees, usually oak, cut into small pieces and stewed in water-filled barking kettles boiled over fires. The mixture produced was a reddish brown liquid, which gave the tan colour to the sails and nets when applied by brush or swabs. The backerals or sheds in which the barking took place, were stained from the smoke as were the fences and ground on which sails and nets were spread for drying after tanning. Nets were drawn through the mixture in the kettles or large pans in sunken troughs which gave off a distinctive odour that wafted through the waterfront area.

The raw material taken by the removal of the bark from trees had a detrimental effect on the forests in the area, leading to a ban in 1775 on 'the villainous practice of stripping trees merely for the bark'. Later, oil and tar were used as substitutes. In the nineteenth century a new substance known as 'burma cutch', supplied in large rectangular blocks from J.B. Woodword of Liverpool, was prepared. It arrived in a pressed-leaf form and was then hacked into small pieces. The practice of barking died out in the 1950s as new synthetic fibres, made from the petrochemical industry, became available, reducing the maintenance required on nets and gear.

Access for fishermen to the town market was through the Water Gate during the seventeenth and eighteenth centuries. This was located in the wall at Main Street, close to the foot of the Stony Steps, which was then adjacent to the water. The market was essential as a means of selling the fish and it provided the Corporation with a system of regulating supply and a method of collecting tolls. Severe penalties were imposed if fishermen attempted to deal directly with joulters and bypass the system 'until the town's needs were first served'. Joulters, belonging mostly to the native Irish community, lived outside the walls, and were essentially engaged in selling fish on the black market. The name derives from the jolting of carts which were horse-drawn or hand-pulled as they rumbled through the rough lanes, hawking fish to the population in the surrounding countryside. For the fisherman, dealing directly with the joulter was a more attractive proposition than having to wait for the traders in the market to decide whether a particular catch was required or not. Apart from tying up in line for hours outside the Water Gate, the fisherman paid tolls which were collected by the market clerk. Complaints by 'poor' fishermen to the Lord Deputy in 1619 led to a modification of the rules and a reduction in penalties for fishing offences. The water bailiff, who controlled access through the gate to the market, was directed to blow a horn when a boat with fish arrived 'for giving notice to the town [market] and after one hour to be timed by the running of an hour glass – the water bailiff shall blow his horn again and then the joulters are to have free liberty to buy and carry away fish without interruption'. The new rule improved the situation for the fishermen who now had access to the market but were free to do business with the joulters after a certain period. [13]

It was in the nature of the joulters to live on the edge of the law, and they were constantly in conflict with the officials. On 29 June 1674, a complaint was recorded in the Kinsale Court Book 'that fish joulters frequenting this town and the creeks and harbours adjacent, do daily ingress all sorts of fish and carry them off to Cork and other places which are served by a greater choice of fish and often times at easier rates then what the locals can take. This is contrary to the law and a great damage to the inhabitants, which practices cause a scarcity.'

The joulters also traded in shellfish from the river. To regulate and preserve this fishery, in October 1726, the Corporation ordered 'that no joulter presume to carry any oysters dredged in this Harbour to Cork or elsewhere before the town is first served on a penalty of 10/= [shillings]'. Despite attempts to curb their activities, the enterprising traders remained active to 1836, at least. As the structural condition of the town walls and gates deteriorated, landings took place on the quays 'along the sides of the Harbour downward to the ocean – kept in repair by proprietors of their sites'.[14] Father P. McSwiney, writing of Kinsale in the eighteenth century, said that the waterfront extended from Lower Fisher (O'Connell) Street, close to where the town park is located today and north to Newman's Mall. After landing, the catch was brought to the fish market opposite the Courthouse 'underneath the town wall at Glenbeg' which was established under a Grand Jury presentment of 1723.[15] Facilities were further improved by the building of a new fish shambles in 1784, where the Blue Haven Hotel is now located, at a cost of £178.

Prominent among the fishing community were the residents of Scilly, 'an English colony who had settled on this point close to the water when the Southwells were granted lands after the Battle of Kinsale. They were a close-knit community who never marry outside of the village'.[16] Robert Southwell (Senior) who had direct access to the Lord Deputy, the Earl of Ormond, in 1635 wrote on behalf of the 'poor fishermen on Scilly point ... showing the grievous molestation of the Sovereign of Kinsale, David Roche ... who doth force your supplicants to give unto him at his own price the prime of all your supplicants' fish ... Yet upon denial he doth imprison them and send out bailiffs and takes away their rudders and sails to the utter ruin of your poor petitioners, their wives and small children'.[17] Even though these were loyal citizens, they suffered the disadvantage of living outside the walls and consequently, under the rules that governed the market, they could not trade freely. Southwell's contact with the Lord Deputy, though, ensured that the dispute was resolved quickly. The Sovereign was required to fix a price with the fishermen in advance and could not act arbitrarily.

The Southwell influence was evident again in 1671, when Sir Robert (Junior) complained about the incursions of French fishermen into Irish waters, 'who by means of their long and unlawful nets do utterly break and destroy the great shoals of fish ever coming upon the coast'. Southwell received the following response from Samuel Pepys, then holding an important post with the Admiralty Board. 'I have laid your letter and petition from the fishermen of Kinsale before my Lords, Commissioners of the Admiralty and they have sent orders to the Captains of the frigates stationed upon the coast of Ireland to protect His Majesty's subjects of that Kingdom in their fishery from any injury or interruption from the French.'

The incursions of the French persisted into the eighteenth century. They were accused of using trawls which 'raked the bottom' and driftnets that had the effect of splitting the shoals for the seiners. The report goes on to say that from 1733, 200 to 300 sail came close to the shore, each with nets of up to a league (3¼ nautical miles) in length, 'breaking the shoal and driving the fish from the coast'.[18] It would appear, however, that it was not just a problem created by the French as the local fishermen were apathetic and were criticised for doing little to counter the success of the French by persisting in the use of traditional methods and refusing to adapt to newer techniques, such as working with trammel nets and trawling.[19]

The fishermen themselves had been severely reprimanded by the Grand Jury in 1731 for not obeying conservation practices. The Corporation were ordered to make 'proper laws for restraining unfair practices in fishing and to prevent [the use of] illegal nets. The Sovereign would appoint sub admirals to inspect abuses committed by fishermen and make laws for the conservation of salmon and no person to use nets within the limits of this Corporation for taking any fish the mesh where of shall not be [less than] one and a quarter inches square. Herring can only be taken from the 20th of September to the 1st of January.'

An unexpected reason offered to explain the reduced fish catches was the shock caused 'by the firing of great guns' on state and ceremonial occasions at the Fort and courtesy cannonades which reverberated through the water on the arrival and departure of His Majesty's ships with ensigns dipped. They 'disturb the said fish and destroy the spawn and drive the shoals out of the harbour'.[20]

No support at all existed for the 'wild Irish' fishermen who, because of adherence to the 'popish' religion were subject to the Penal Laws, which prohibited the ownership of boats. The only opportunity to gain from the bountiful sea was to operate illegally using clandestine methods. Generations of second-class treatment created dependency and a certain feckless attitude. In 1772 the fishermen 'were accused of being half their time idle and greatly prone to drunkenness'. Unfortunately, it was a perception that was to persist and was actually presented as an excuse for the authorities not to give assistance. In 1856 it was suggested that the lack of progress in the industry was due to 'the indolent nature of the Celt'.[21] With the decline of the Southwell influence in the late eighteenth century, the malaise, which had been associated only with the 'native Irish', spread to all involved in fishing in the harbour. The image of lacking enterprise and skill was picked up by Thomas Davis in his poem 'The Boatman of Kinsale'. While Davis was sympathetic to the plight of the Kinsale fisherman, Myles O'Hara, he implies a degree of indolence:

His hookers in the Scilly van
When seines are in the foam
But money never made a man
Nor wealth a happy home.

Davis, who died in 1845, advocated the development of the 'Resources of Ireland' in his paper, *The Nation*. He attributed the lack of motivation in the Irish peasant to the fact that the individual had no incentive as any initiative or improvement undertaken was automatically penalised by increased rent paid to the landlord. 'Toil as they may they only labour to increase the rent.'[22]

Yet the irony was that whenever support was offered, no matter how minimal, there was an immediate and positive response. During the period of Grattan's Parliament (1783–1800) large exports of herring were reported because tax on salt was reduced. Later Kinsale fishermen benefited when English boats were withdrawn from the coast during the Napoleonic Wars. Afterwards, in 1819, a House of Commons Bill 'for the encouragement and improvement of Irish Fisheries' was passed, making a nationwide grant of £5,000 available to repair and build new piers, assist fishermen in the purchase of gear and provide a bounty based on catch. This was supplemented by contributions from charitable and private sources which amounted to almost a quarter of a million pounds over a ten-year period.[23] After just three years the Irish Fisheries Commission Report for 1822 showed that in Kinsale the number of men engaged directly in fishing had increased to 2,822 which was still less than half the number fishing out of Galway, then the most successful fishing port in Ireland. By 1829, the Tenth Report showed a dramatic improvement for Kinsale with a total of 4,612 employed, an increase to two thirds of the Galway numbers.[24] Ancillary services ashore provided work for 120 coopers, 13 sailmakers and 500 net makers who were 'poor females in the town', putting the total number ashore and afloat involved in the industry at 6,527. While the numbers appear large, a closer analysis will show that much of the cleaning and gutting was undertaken in lean-tos that were attached to the gables of the fishermens' huts, which dotted the seashore. This suggests that much of the fishing was for family consumption and not on a commercial scale. In 1836, the Fishery Report indicated that many of the fishermen 'were partly employed as small farmers'.[25] The reports show that the industry on the whole was a part-time subsistence activity and the vast majority of the boats, 73 per cent in 1836, were small row or open sail boats. This level of engagement did not have the capacity to generate the impetus required for the development of a viable indigenous industry. Nevertheless, the number of small boats was maintained throughout the Famine period which, together with Kinsale being designated a hub for the distribution of imported Indian meal and also known as a potato-growing area, mitigated the worst effects of the starvation from 1845 to 1852 for the population in the immediate area of the town.[26]

Similar surveys of the fishing industry for Scotland, Cornwall and the Isle of Man show that they had a greater number of larger boats. From 1840, the fishermen in these areas were actively encouraged to purchase boats, develop a 'capitalist' ethic and build an enterprise momentum that would maintain the industry in periods of depression.[27] Commenting on the state of Irish Fisheries in 1857, Robert Worthington said that the fish were there and specifically that the people were not indolent but that the native industry required assistance in the provision of instruction and targeted aid if it was to be as productive as the industry in Scotland or Cornwall.[28]

From 1862, for a period of approximately thirty years, Kinsale flourished, not from the development of the native industry but from the large fishing fleets that arrived annually in the harbour from the Isle of Man, Cornwall, Scotland and France. The catch potential off the coast was recognised by the British fishermen. At the height of Kinsale's prominence in the industry, London newspaper *The Mail* in January 1876 reported that 'Isle of Man curers quadruple the quantity of what Ireland does, most if not all were fish taken from Irish waters'. Speaking of Kinsale in 1888, Thomas Quilliam, skipper of a Manx drifter said, 'It [the fish] is there on their coast and yet we can go on their coast and take it home from them.'[29]

As with shipping in the seventeenth and eighteenth centuries, Kinsale became economically prosperous because of the services it provided. It was estimated that, in 1864, 150 boats from the Isle of Man, which was half the Manx fleet, and 1,400 men had arrived in Kinsale by St Patrick's Day. In 1874, close on 300 boats fished out of Kinsale with 68 per cent of the fleet coming from the Isle of Man alone.[30] The number doubled in 1880 to 700, two thirds of which were foreign and the remainder Irish from Ardglass, Howth and Kilkeel. Only fifty of the massive fleet, 7 per cent, were Kinsale-owned. While known for their migratory habits, mackerel shoals appeared off Kinsale consistently each year from mid-March to mid-June, identifying the harbour as the primary mackerel station in these islands, landing more than the collective catches of all the other fishing ports on the Irish coast.[31]

Apart from the natural qualities of the harbour and the regularity of the mackerel shoals, a number of other factors came together to create conditions for the success of the fishery. With the extension of the democratic franchise in the 1830s, a new entrepreneurial class emerged in the town who responded to the business opportunities presented by the fishing fleets, establishing the services required for the annual influx.

In addition there was a growing demand for fish in the industrial manufacturing centres of Britain with large urban populations. Liverpool and Billingsgate in London were the destinations for much of the Kinsale catch, which was transported through Milford Haven in South Wales.

The arrival of the railway in 1862 to Kinsale, a spur of the West Cork line, enabled the transport of the freshly landed fish to Cork and from there to Dublin and cross channel for distribution through the various rail networks in Britain. Steam power was also adapted for use aboard the boats themselves. 'Donkey' engines and boilers were installed to power the winches and capstans in hauling the long trains of nets. Later, as sail was replaced by steam power, the catch was collected from the boats, allowing them to remain longer at the fishing grounds. The Robertson family, whose fish business was located where the Shearwater apartments are today, had three of these efficient vessels, *Unique, Atlanta* and *Maryland.*

Availability of ice was a major contributor to the success of the mackerel fishery. The arrival of gleaming Norwegian schooners in early March filled with Arctic ice heralded the start of the spring fishery. The ice in blocks was transferred to 'hulks', old redundant

Lug-rigged drievers heading to sea, 1896. *Courtesy Tony Bocking*

sailing vessels moored permanently in the harbour. After a night at sea the fish-laden drievers came alongside the black-sided ice hulks, jostling for the inside berths to receive their quota chipped off the large, frozen blocks with picks worked by the men below. The ice ensured that the fish could be transferred to Britain, consumed fresh and receive premium prices. Lawrence photographs (*c*.1911) show these hulks in the harbour with masts and spars removed, sad relics of once-great sailing ships. One such vessel was the barque *Stirlingshire,* a 365-ton vessel built in New Zealand in 1841 and from 1865 owned by a Youghal company, which traded regularly between Cork and Quebec. In 1887 she was deregistered and ended in Kinsale as an ice hulk.[32]

Counted in hundreds, the fish carried in rope-handled boxes and wicker creels covered in ice were brought ashore in lighters or craned onto quayside walls. If not already sold they were auctioned and then drawn by horse or in handcarts up the steep Barrack Hill or Feather Bed Lane to the train station.

The Manxmen in their lug-rigged boats known as nickies, or the larger nobbies, and collectively referred to as drievers or drifters, were the major catalysts of the fishing boom in Kinsale.

John Morley, an enterprising retired coastguard from Peel in the Isle of Man, was the first to recognise the potential. At the end of 1862, his first year of fishing in Kinsale, he brought in driftnets purchased from Robert Corrin, a Manx net maker. The introduction of these nets was a major change, relegating spiller and seine fishing to a minor place as the long trains of driftnets proved more effective. Both men, revealing a keen entrepreneurship, encouraged fish buyers and agents to set up in Kinsale which in turn brought more fishermen.

The Manx boats were swift and could make up to 10 knots under way. The lug sail, with the tack attached to the stem, proved efficient, outsailing other boats when going to windward. They were capable of going 50 miles off shore, and returning quickly to port to land their catch in pristine condition. Another factor that contributed to the success of the fishery was the Manx cotton nets that replaced the older hemp. Made of lighter material, the fishermen were able to carry and shoot longer trains. At the beginning of the boom period, each boat worked fifteen to twenty nets, each 15 fathoms (90 feet) in length, 5 fathoms deep and of 2-inch mesh. By 1900 this had increased to fifty nets, which were hauled using steam-powered capstans.[33]

Initially the Manxmen encountered some scepticism and even hostility. After a short time their initiative, productivity and the commercial activity they were generating were recognised by the local merchants and providers. The town became prosperous in catering for the boats, the crews, repairs to sails and gear, and the supply of provisions. Teams of women mended nets and for thirty years there was work for every man, woman and child in the town during the season. In the harbour, tenders moved between the tightly moored drievers with nets spread between masts, drying in the wind like cormorants' wings. Small boats queued for fresh water at different springs. Buyers, auctioneers and the Scottish girls after a busy morning on the pier returned to the boarding houses and ate in eating rooms which enterprising local women established in their own homes. On the quayside amid the bustling activity of the gutters and the coopers, the cart and barrow pushers shunted nets piled high like domes and moved boxes and barrels about the pier.

After three months of fishing the spring mackerel, the Manxmen returned to their crofter holdings to save the hay in June. Economically it was quite similar to the practice adopted by Irish lobstermen who fished the waters off Kinsale, returning to their Heir Island homes for the hay and later to save the harvest in the autumn. After the spring mackerel season at Kinsale, the full-time Manx fishermen sailed north for the herring season which began off Stornoway in the Isle of Lewis or Lerwick in the Shetland Islands. Then following the shoals that moved south down the Irish Sea, they could end up in Kinsale for a second period in any year.[34] As the town's reputation grew, boats from other parts of the United Kingdom, such as Lowestoft, Grimsby, Hull, Penzance and Milford, arrived in the harbour.

A special affinity existed between the fishermen of the Isle of Man and Kinsale. Their boats, nets and technical approach were more advanced. Of the Methodist tradition, their demeanour was characteristically modest, sober and provident. Preparations for the trip to Kinsale were undertaken with care. Boats were launched, masts stepped, sails bent on, standing and running rigging checked and gaffs hitched to halyards. Nets, ropes and fishing gear were wheeled to the quaysides. For personal comfort, fishermen had black leather knee boots hand-sewn by cobblers and tailor-made suits of oilskin. Crews were signed up and each member was expected to contribute to the vessel's stores. Beef, sides of bacon, tins of milk, flour and sugar were the basic staples.[35]

As the day of departure approached, which would separate husbands from wives and children, sons from mothers and young fishermen from their lovers, religious services were held at Castletown, Port St Mary, Peel, Ramsey and Douglas for their safe return. At night, music was played as extended families gathered in the homes to exchange farewells. Invariably there was the unspoken foreboding that a number of the departing men would not be part of the joyful return in mid-June. There is a delightful, if a little romanticised, word picture by Hall Caine of the boats setting sail from Peel to Kinsale about to head into the harsh cold March weather of the Irish Sea.[36]

Manx boats leaving Peel for the spring mackerel fishing off Kinsale, 1880.
Courtesy Leece Museum, Peel, Isle of Man

One hundred and fifty boats each with a light in its binnacle, its sails half set at the turn of the tide, began to drop down the harbour. Then there was a rush of women, children and old men to the end of the Pier. The last of the boats was out in the bay by this time. She could be seen plainly in the moonlight with the green blade of a wave breaking on her quarter. There were shouts and answers across the splashing water. Then, a fresh young voice on the boat began to sing 'Lovely Mona, fare thee well'.

Depending on wind direction and strength, the boats would expect to be on the Irish coast by dawn the following morning. The overall trip to Kinsale could take two to five days. Known to have made a quick passage was the *Swift* of Port St Mary who from the Calf of Man got to Kinsale in thirty-seven hours, averaging 6 knots. In less than a week the whole fleet had gathered in the harbour to begin the season's mackerel fishing.

Skippers, who in many cases were also owners, took pride in their boats, paying attention to rig, sail trim and tuning similar to the practice of improving performance on modern yachts. A Manx boat, the *Lively Polly*, was considered by the locals observing from the shore to be the swiftest in the fleet. Leaving the harbour after midday, the boats got to the fishing grounds, often in a prevailing southerly breeze with a cold, grey sea breaking over the windward rail.

Having decided on location, fifty nets floating on canvas buoys were shot on the starboard side as the vessel, with the wind abeam, drifted to leeward. The driver was tied to the head of the last net by a rope known as the 'swan', passing through the fairlead on the stem. With the mainmast lowered, resting on crutches, and the mizzensail set astern to keep the boat head to wind, the drifting vessel rode to the nets stretched in a line to windward. At night, viewed from a distance, the carbide lights mounted forward on each of the boats created the impression of a town illuminated by gas lamps. The crews occupied their time hand-lining and any fish caught in this way were known as 'scran'. These fish belonged to the fisherman himself and were sold ashore to buy tobacco or supplement the 'share' from the night's catch. The share was determined after the boat's expenses were paid and the remainder generally divided into twenty parts. Ten were allocated to the owner and the remainder to the crew, with an extra share for the skipper. At the height of the industry in the 1870s, the average payment to each fisherman was £25 annually, which was considered a fair return for the season's work. Crews were contracted when 'bounty money' was paid by the owners at Christmas to purchase foul-weather gear and acceptance of the bounty money was a commitment by the crewman to a particular owner.

The skipper, who had gained his position aboard a vessel after years of experience, carried much responsibility and had many decisions to make. On reaching the grounds, the shooting of nets was guided by the activity of the 'fowl', perhaps gannets with folded wings diving, rocket-like, into the sea. Apart from watching the flight of birds or perhaps the movement of porpoise or dolphins, physical features on the land ashore provided marks or locations where specific species were caught. The expression 'the light just under' alludes to the flash of the loom of the lighthouse on the Old Head and when just visible on the horizon at night gave a bearing to a known point and confirmed that the vessel was 25 miles off, far enough to catch the early spring mackerel. Another location well known for line fishing was the Ling Rocks. Before echo sounders and navigation systems such as Decca or GPS, the precise position of the rocks, 9 miles southeast of Kinsale, was identified in good visibility by two transits. Looking north, the cave at Ballymacus open (visible) on the smaller of the Sovereign Islands and west, the 'dip in the Westland' appearing just south of the Old Head gave the necessary transits. The term 'Westland' used by the fishermen referred to the Seven Heads promontory and the 'dip', to a depression in the land near Lislee, which is 2 miles north of the headland. Closer to the Old Head itself, marks for fishing were indicated by the sea arches at water level cutting through the 200-foot-high cliffs in the narrow isthmus under de Courcy Castle. When daylight from one side to the other can be seen, the holes are said to be open and when aligned in different ways provide the marks for locating different species of fish. These natural phenomena, created by weathering and erosion over thousands of years, have given the names Hole Open Bay East and West to each side of the headland.

Apart from deciding on where to fish, an experienced skipper was acutely aware of weather, constantly watching the sky to windward for indications of deterioration or a change in wind direction or strength. Imbued with weather lore passed down through generations, he was required to make critical decisions on when to haul nets and run for shelter or remain fishing when a boat under sail could be exposed in a strengthening breeze. Holds full of fish lost value if landed late in the harbour when the price on offer could be greatly reduced. Before hauling the nets, the size of the catch was estimated by noting a section of the net that was sinking or hauling a few fathoms as a sample. Too small a catch would not be viable economically and too large would make handling difficult or even unmanageable.

The larger boats had a crew of seven men and a boy with all hands on deck for the net hauling, which was a long and strength-

Fishing fleet, ice hulks and shipping in the harbour, 1896.
Courtesy Lawrence Collection

sapping task taking up to three hours as the fish were 'picked' from the net coming aboard. The tough conditions are vividly described by Conchúr Ó Síocháin in an account of his life as a fisherman: 'There wasn't a shred of skin on my fingers and what should cause that but the high sea tugging and tearing them through my gripping fingers as I was trying to hold them [the nets] knowing not at what minute I would be swept over'.[37]

Then the heavy mast was stepped in the 'tabernacle', a difficult and dangerous operation when a sea was running. As the early signs of dawn appeared in the eastern sky, the crew made way for Kinsale. There they tied alongside the hulks for ice and landed the fish ashore for sale to the buyers.

Across the harbour at Castlepark, boats grounded at high water on the strands and heeled over on their bilges had repairs undertaken

97

below the waterline. Fishermen hauled aloft in bo'sun's chairs replaced standing rigging or rove new halyards through sheaves on the masts. For many years during the boom period, the land around the ivy-clad walls of the Old (James) Fort was leased by the harbour authorities to provide space for the drying and mending of nets. A barking kettle was available at the quay in the Dock and a pumped well for fresh water was provided which the Harbour Board and the fishermen jointly funded.[38]

When not fishing at weekends, the focus of the fishermen's activity was church related. Lennox Robinson, son of the local Church of Ireland curate, gives a glimpse of life aboard the fishing boats when accompanying his father undertaking pastoral visits on Saturdays. In a small punt they 'paddled a few strokes from one smack to the next and hung alongside until he [his father] returned. Afterwards towards the end of the afternoon he was taken down below and given tea. Very occasionally his host would remember the boy in the punt ... The tea was drunk in large mugs of very thick delft. It was coloured with tinned milk and a large slice of very fresh bread liberally spread with salt butter.'[39]

The majority of the Manx and Cornish fishermen had a deep and sincere faith expressed in singing at morning service and could be heard throughout the town from the Methodist church at the Short Quay. To avoid the temptation of drink in Kinsale's numerous public houses, the men in the evening gathered in the Fishermen's Hall. Here they participated in informal religious services and hymn singing, accompanied on the harmonium by ladies associated with the church. Normally sober, reserved and taciturn, some fishermen spontaneously burst into stuttering speech and in a quaint, unfamiliar language proclaimed their faith. An account is given as to how an old Manxman, so fervent in prayer that while kneeling in the aisle, with vigorous arm waving and chest beating, drove himself forward until he reached the top of the hall. The Fishermen's Hall was built, where Higher Fisher (O'Connell) and Main Streets merge, so that 'English and Manx fishermen may worship and Kinsale fishermen the sons of Huguenots and the English will meet together in Divine Service twice a week and the fisher lads will have a sound scriptural and secular education given them'.[40] In modern times the worthy work of ministering to fishermen continues under the Flying Angel Mission to Seamen, coordinated by the Rector of St Multose Parish.

The success of the fishing brought the buyers to capitalise on 'the large catches of splendid mackerel and the prices higher than ever before'. A record from the time described how 'the fish buyers were quite a curiosity to the [local] fishermen as they dressed in the latest fashion, lived in the best hotels and lodgings, had ready money on all occasions and large bank accounts'.[41] In marketing terms, as the classic middlemen, they valued the fish trade in terms of their percentage commission. Wielding control each buyer, in a rowing yawl crewed by six oarsmen, went to meet the incoming fleet in the morning. Prices were negotiated and often fixed on the water. Each day demand was indicated by how far the yawls would row to initiate the bargaining process. News of the night's catch was quickly conveyed back to the harbour and preparations for the arrival of the boats swung into action. Fish not already sold were brought ashore for auction where buyers, fishermen and interested public gathered around the auctioneer in semicircles. The introduction of the telegraph in the 1860s brought information on market demand at important centres such as Dublin, Liverpool and London. All eyes were fixed on the auctioneer as bidding switched from buyer to buyer, gradually tailing off until the final offer was accepted.

The buyers and their agents were hard-nosed businessmen who had a reputation for arrogance. To maximise profit the buyers formed syndicates, acting collectively and were often referred to as capitalists. They were viewed with some suspicion and concern was expressed when they became boat owners while still engaged in auctioneering. In classic Marxist terms, the cartels achieved control and ownership of the means of production. They had the power to fix prices to the disadvantage of the fishermen and squeeze the small independent buyer out of the market.[42]

A particular incident in April 1873 illustrates the tense relationship that existed between buyers and fishermen when the industry was at its most successful. The buyers unilaterally decided to levy six pence in the pound on all catches. In protest the fishermen gathered at Scilly and marched to the house of Edwin Lawrence, a buyer living at Fisher (O'Connell) Street who had refused even to consider the grievance.

After some stone throwing and window breaking, Lawrence confronted the men and fearful for his family's safety fired a shot in the air which created a mini-riot. The local Royal Irish Constabulary were called and found the situation difficult to control. In the ensuing melee they fired a number of rounds in which James Corry, a Manx fisherman, was fatally wounded. The shock generated by the killing quelled the riot and subsequently produced a positive outcome for the fishermen. They received general local support and their cause was acknowledged and highlighted in a number of editorials in the *Cork Examiner*. Lawerence, his wife and a number of other buyers required police protection for a short period but eventually 'unconditionally abandoned' efforts to collect the levy.

On the following wet and gloomy Saturday, James Corry was laid to rest in St Multose Churchyard at a service attended by 7,000 people. Many local Catholics lined the route of the funeral in solidarity, which, in those pre-ecumenical days, was a rare occurrence. In a press report of the funeral in *Mona's Herald* on the Isle of Man, the hymn singing of the men following the 'highly polished and expensive coffin' was noted. For the Corry family, who returned to fish in subsequent years, the church services were occasions to remember their brother. Calloused and heavily bearded, dressed in undersized best jackets, they recalled the killing that occurred within a 100 yards of where they were worshipping.

The tension between fishermen and buyers remained a feature of the fish trade. Good catches were recorded during the early season of 1886 and as fish were plentiful the price dropped. However, subsequent bad weather for a number of weeks prevented the fishermen getting to sea and fish became scarce, which should have resulted in an increase in the price. The buyers' cartel conspired to keep the price low. On 19 April, 5,000 men did not go to sea and called a protest meeting at Scilly and requested all workers engaged in the fishing trade to lay down their tools. They proposed an alternative purchasing system which the buyers recognised as a threat to their dominant position, forcing them to relent and increase the price.

Some of the better-known buyers who established bases in Kinsale were the Kelsalls of the Isle of Man who had a store on Crowley's Quay opposite Scilly. Davidson and Perry's of Leith had an establishment at

Drievers tied up 'stern on' to rings at Scilly, 1896. *Courtesy Lawrence Collection*

Fryer's Quay close to where the Tourist Information office is currently located. Incidentally, both these quays were capped off when the Pier road was constructed in the 1880s. Dawson Williams was based at Scilly where the South of Ireland Fish Company was located.[43] Among the other families involved in the fishing industry as merchants and boat owners were the Robertson family, Roger Murphy of the Short Quay, and the O'Sheas on Fisher (O'Connell) Street.

A leading buyer was Hugo Flinn from Liverpool, who had a base at the old dockyard from 1893 to 1919, and continued in business even when the fishing was in decline.[44] As a member of the Harbour Board he was a strong advocate on behalf of the fishing interest, constantly seeking a reduction of dues on fishing craft. In July and December 1904, he complained about commercial shipping which was obstructing access to the Pier by the storage of timber and ballast. Flinn's intervention reflected the cut and thrust of debate, which characterised much of the Board's business and continued until its demise at the end of 2011.

Thomas Johnson who came to Kinsale at the age of twenty in 1892 worked on the Pier as a buyer's clerk. Described as a big-browed man with thick pompadour-grey hair, he was known for his ability to organise and as an energetic worker robustly engaged in all aspects of the trade. From observing the industry at close quarters in Kinsale he developed an understanding of and an appreciation for the lot of workers, becoming interested in labour politics and the cooperative movement. This led him eventually to Dublin and involvement in trade unionism in the early years of the Free State. He became leader of the Labour Party in Dáil Éireann, which was followed by a number of terms as a senator. In 1927 he published a pamphlet *Labour and Ireland's Sea Fisheries,* which proposed the organisation of cooperatives run by the fishermen themselves and a system of representation where fishermen would advise the Minister on policies for the development, protection, research and marketing of the fisheries. It was a bottom-up approach, with fishermen taking responsibility for their industry. No doubt these ideas were informed by his experience in Kinsale.[45]

During the early years of the boom period it became apparent that Kinsale did not have the physical infrastructure of piers, slipways and quay walls adequate to cater for the increased fishing. In the crowded harbour there were constant calls for mooring rings at Scilly to which the fishing vessels could tie stern on. The lack of suitable landing facilities made it necessary to transfer catches from the fishing boats to flat-bottomed lighters which were then punted or rowed ashore. Fish handling was inefficient, time consuming, costly and affected the freshness and quality of the product by the time it got to market. Efforts to improve the facilities were not helped by the attitude of the private foreshore owners who objected strongly to the rings. From the same quarter even the provision of public conveniences on the proposed pier for the use of fishermen became a contentious issue.

Earlier requests for assistance, in 1844, produced a minimal response from the authorities. They 'granted a sum of thirty pounds towards the erection of a pier for the fishery', a paltry sum at the onset of the Famine. The perception was that Kinsale did not require assistance following the success of the industry in the 1819–1830 period. On the positive side the extension of the franchise in the 1830s had begun to stir a latent confidence in an emerging mercantile class. In the 1840s the Corporation was abolished and replaced by Kinsale

Town Commissioners whose membership was more representative and where religious beliefs, at least in theory, were no longer a barrier to participation.[46] In addition, seaboard communities, if given the opportunity, tended to have a natural aptitude for ownership and responsibility to take on the duties associated with the industry. As Father Charles Davis, parish priest of Baltimore in west Cork, who influenced the development of fisheries in the 1890s, said, fishermen were the 'peasant proprietors of the sea'.[47] Kinsale men were further encouraged by contact with the Manx and Cornish fishermen, who supported the demand for improved piers and quays. Frustration at the lack of progress and the long delays surfaced periodically. In 1879, fish merchants and boat owners at a meeting in the Kinsale Arms Hotel demanded improved facilities for the 'proper carrying out of the fish trade and the protection of life and property'. Representations were made by numerous delegations with a particular focus on the local Members of Parliament.

One of the first initiatives privately undertaken was the formation of the South of Ireland Fish Company in the 1860s at the old Pallace site in Scilly, having nominal capital of £20,000 and under the direction of Robert Lander. It was he who initiated the project of building the stone wall and graving dock at Scilly Point, which provides a view of the harbour that identifies Kinsale. By 1868 the company had sixteen boats landing enormous catches of mackerel at prices that gave a return of up to £70 per boat for a night's fishing. For a period, the firm took over the old dockyard at the World's End for extra wharf space, storage and icehouses.

The momentum generated by the practical demands of catering for the burgeoning fishing industry eventually led to establishing the Kinsale Harbour Board, a specific authority with responsibility for the harbour. It was set up under statute of the Pier and Harbour Order Act in 1870 with specific terms of reference to dredge and deepen the harbour, provide buoys, navigation aids, collect tolls and dues and, most urgently, improve landing facilities.

The Board drew up memoranda in July 1871 for the purpose of acquiring treasury funding for a new pier. It stated that the port catered for 500 fishing vessels annually, each boat having a crew of eight, and generated £100,000 in turnover. The document goes on to highlight the inconvenience and danger of lying off and the difficulty of handling fish boxes, gear and ice from hulks moored in the harbour. The practice gave rise to inefficient auctioneering and led to price fixing. The new pier would also provide lighting from the gasworks and water could be taken aboard directly. An added justification was that the pier would be used by fishermen from around the British and Irish coasts and not confined to local boats. At the June meeting in 1872 the minutes reported 'the want of which [pier] is very seriously felt by all concerned in catching, buying and disposing of fish in this increasing important fishing station'.[48]

The Harbour Board's first task was to decide on the location for the new pier. The choice lay between Scilly, the World's End and the eventual site at the Town Rock close to the Custom Quay. Each was examined in relation to the possible extension of the rail line to the pier. The site chosen was the Town Rock location as it was close to deep water and was sheltered from the prevailing weather by the high ground at Dromderrig and could be accessed by rail, albeit with difficulty. Construction would partially cover the rock which was an ever-present obstruction highlighted in 1855, when the 368-ton SS *Glasgow* went aground. Originally access to the proposed pier was planned from Lower Fisher (O'Connell) Street but the project engineer, Robert Warner, decided that a new causeway constructed from the Short Quay would be more suitable. This radically changed the waterfront by cutting off the older quays, and produced the Pier roadway as it is today (see plate 9).

Requests for financial assistance received the classic Adam Smith response as can be seen in the debate on the Irish Sea Fisheries Bill which took place in the House of Commons in July 1880. Eugene Collins and Col. Colthurst, Members of Parliament for the Kinsale area, proposed support for fisheries on the basis that they produced a 'wholesome and valuable supply of food' and that engagement in fishing trained men in seamanship skills 'to meet the requirements of the [British] mercantile marine', an argument which surfaced regularly. In response, the Chief Secretary for Ireland agreed that Ireland was at a disadvantage because the bigger boats from Cornwall and the Isle of Man carried off catches to the extent that Dublin itself was supplied with fish not caught in Irish boats but by the Manxmen.

104

He nevertheless argued against the use of state capital for Kinsale, because it contravened laissez-faire economic principles, all of which delayed assistance.

Eventually, after much pressure a grant and loan were sanctioned for the Pier Head and causeway at Kinsale in 1880. The estimated cost was put at £14,000, funded by a treasury grant of £7,500 and the remainder through a loan raised by the Harbour Board over twenty-five years at 5 per cent and bonded jointly by the Town Commissioners. Unfortunately, however, on completion of the project in 1889, costs had escalated to £21,800. Harbour Board minutes of a meeting held in June 1888 show that the extra expenses were attributable to the unexpected level of compensation paid to the owners for the rights of way to the old quays and the intervening strands. Another reason for the extra costs was the disruption caused by a change of contractors during construction. These matters were eventually settled at levels of compensation which all but bankrupted the Harbour Board (see plate 5).

The Pier became operational at various stages and was eventually completed in 1890. From the beginning, relations between the Board of Works, who had been appointed to oversee the project, and the Harbour Board were fraught. It is generally accepted that as a body the Board of Works, established in 1842 with responsibility for fisheries in Ireland, was over bureaucratised.[49] Accusations of incompetence and bad faith were made by both sides. Relations deteriorated further when, in the 1890s, fishing activity suddenly declined and the Harbour Board found that it was unable to repay the loan within the agreed schedule. It was particularly ironic that, following the effort to have the much sought-after facilities provided, many boats left the harbour to fish out of Baltimore when the mackerel shoals migrated further west. The consequence was that harbour revenue available to fund the massive and escalating debt was greatly reduced. The Board of Works was uncompromising, refusing to recognise the problem or accommodate the new circumstances that were emerging.

The very existence of the Harbour Board was threatened as the lack of cooperation with the funding authorities persisted following the Anglo-Irish Treaty and Irish independence. After submissions to the Free State government in June 1924, the official response, which was to enforce the bond, was described as 'Shylock like'. At the time the loan outstanding stood at £1,176, with £19,000 repaid since 1882. The small balance was eventually cleared.[50]

The inefficient Board of Works is often contrasted with the effectiveness of the Congested Districts Board which was established in 1892 and was responsible for improving infrastructure at locations such as Baltimore and Dingle. Kinsale did not qualify for these funds as it fell outside the rateable valuation criteria for inclusion as a congested area.

The Pier Head and Road (Causeway) are today the focal features of the harbour. After completion, the strands between each of the old piers, which were tidal, were gradually filled in to create the town parks, hotel gardens and act as the interface between town and harbour, which identify Kinsale's waterfront. The causeway made extra berthing space and slipways available, completing the final physical step in the emergence of the modern town.

The road and pier bear levels of traffic and loads far in excess of what were originally envisaged. The structure is a monument to the vision and achievement of the first Harbour Commissioners. Part of the original Town Rock remained exposed on the eastern face of the Head, which made it a foul berth. This was finally made safe when the Pier was extended in 2001.

Even before the long-awaited pier facility was fully operational, some ominous signs of decline in the industry were evident. From a position of being recognised as the primary mackerel fishery station in these islands, landing 92 per cent of the national catch, Kinsale port activity went into a spiral of decline from 1890 to utter depression in the 1920s. In 1880, records show that almost 240,000 hundredweight of fish were caught in 569 vessels, giving a total value of £130,000. Ten years later figures submitted by the coastguard show that the number of vessels was reduced to 126, crewed by 419 men, and only 44 men on a full-time basis. The catch of spring mackerel for the period from early April to the end of June had declined to 9,260 hundredweight, giving a return of £5,171, a small fraction of what was caught twenty years earlier.[51]

Other evidence confirmed the trend. Harbour income from fishing vessels was £837 in 1884 but reduced to £467 by 1890.[52] Halving of revenue in just six years was more than would be expected by the drop in boat numbers. The discrepancy may be accounted for by the fact that the Harbour Board was attempting to convince the Board of Works of their straitened circumstances. The difference may also be explained by noncompliance in the payment of dues for which receipts would not have been issued and therefore no record kept, whereas the function of the coastguard, responsible for the official returns, was to count actual traffic in the harbour, having no function in regard to revenue collection.

The immediate cause for the decline at Kinsale was the unpredictable movement of the mackerel shoals in the late 1880s, making it easier to fish out of Baltimore. The pragmatic response of those in the business forced the Manx, Cornish, French and Irish fleets together with the buyers and their entourages to move where the fish were and by 1890 Baltimore had surpassed Kinsale in terms of catch.[53]

The location of the railway station at Kinsale was another factor in the decline. It was established in 1862, but was a mile from the waterfront up a steep incline overlooking the town, which added to the cost and delay of getting the fish to market. By contrast, in Baltimore the train connection was extended to the pier itself, enabling the transfer of fish directly from the boats. The unsatisfactory situation in Kinsale was never resolved as the finance required and the engineering involved were not available, despite the express desire of the shareholders of the Cork, Bandon and South Coast Railway 'to carry the line to the deep water if money can be got at a cheap rate'.[54]

Steam power to propel the drifters gradually replaced sail in the fishing fleets. Boats were able to return to British ports and unload directly at railheads which provided fast links to markets in the large urban areas. At sea the men were no longer constrained by the capricious wind and tide. They landed frequently at Milford Haven and other west coast ports on the British mainland and thus bypassed harbours such as Kinsale.[55]

Joseph Thuillier, who as a prominent Kinsale shipwright, boat owner and chairman of the Harbour Board, was well placed to comment on the decline, which in part he attributed to the advent of steam power. 'The English Capitalist owners sent in steam trawlers which soon exhausted the fishing grounds. Not content with that they

Complete Pier Head and Causeway, 1896. *Courtesy Lawrence Collection*

built a class of steam drifter which fished off our Irish coast and took the fish direct to the English buyer, cutting the people of this country off.'[56]

The installation of engines and the mechanisation of the local fleet would have increased efficiency but was only slowly introduced. It was not until the 1930s that TVO (Tractor Vaporising Oil) engines were fitted to the few boats operating out of Kinsale. These engines were started using high-octane petrol and then transferred to the cheaper paraffin which produced a distinctive 'tunk–tunk' sound. The slow pace of change was due to apathy, a lack of capital, and little appreciation of engine efficiency and convenience.

Even at the height of Kinsale's prominence in the industry, London newspaper *The Mail* in January 1876 reported that 'Isle of Man curers quadruple the quantity of what Ireland does, most if not all were fish taken from Irish waters'.[57] In the broader context, a more developed industry would have been able to survive the downturn. Geographer Patrick O'Flanagan attributes the underdevelopment of fishing on the Cork coast to the fact that 'it never served as a long-term promoter of urban growth', in terms of developing a processing industry: 'Several short bursts of buoyancy were always marked by the arrival of foreign boats which transported the fish abroad for processing.' He continues: 'the variable demographic behaviour of the majority of fishing centres is a reflection of a range of unstable elements varying from fish supply to market demand. Small boats, meagre investment, scarcely any on a share processing capacity, basic technology and poor organisation were among the leading factors which arrested progress of this sector and hence its capacity to drive urban growth.'[58] The Kinsale experience at the end of the nineteenth century supports this analysis.

In a delayed response to the Economic Development Act of December 1903, Florence O'Sullivan, a local solicitor, put forward a list of reasons for the decline, which were shared by other commentators. At a public meeting in the Courthouse, Kinsale in 1911, attended by 256 people involved in the industry, he criticised the 'local capitalists who owned the boats and took half the profits in shares' with little benefit to the fishermen who were powerless. He argued strongly for grants directly to the fishermen so that 'when they are made owners of boats and nets they would not shamefully or scandalously neglect and abuse them'. He went on to say, 'that the more you increase his means and responsibility the more will his civic and domestic virtues shine out'. The argument was based on similar principles put forward by Father Charles Davis of Baltimore, and the benefits derived from the 'free [of interest] loans' provided to the fishermen of Cape Clear Island. The success of the Kinsale Fishermen's Benefit Society, established in 1900, indicated a growing level of thrift and providence. A membership of 265 men contributed two pence per week each to a loan fund, based on the idea of mutual support which helped to remove the feckless reputation that had attached to the fishermen.

Finally in his address, O'Sullivan invited Horace Plunkett, the founder of the cooperative movement in Ireland, to Kinsale, clearly indicating his preferred type of control structures, management and ownership of the fisheries in the port.[59]

While Kinsale maintained its official status as a fishery station into the 1920s, the decrease in activity had major implications for the town's economy and the debt-burdened Harbour Board. A great despondency enveloped the town and harbour, which persisted to the early 1960s. Many young people left to work abroad. Of the occupational groups working in Kinsale the proportion of fishermen (aged fifteen to forty-nine) declined from one in five in 1901 to one in twenty in 1911.[60] Census returns show that the total indigenous population fell from a high of 6,500 at the height of the boom in 1871 to just over 2,000 in 1946. Of the young men who left, many joined the merchant and Royal navies, serving at sea during the world wars. The town and harbour fabric was neglected, many buildings became derelict and the Harbour Board itself was under constant threat of dissolution.

In the period after 1911, Kinsale's status as a commercial fishing centre was well described: 'The boom lasted for years and years, then it died slowly lingering, however, with intermittent returns of vigour like a strong man stricken down in the day of his prime.' One of the revival periods came when the American market opened for cured mackerel and herring following the collapse of their own fisheries in 1886. This was a profitable enterprise for ports on the south coast in the autumn months, when the fish shoaled closer to the shore and were caught by local fishermen in small open boats. Exported through Liverpool, the fish required high standards of curing and coopering to ensure quality on arrival in America.

This market was threatened on a number of fronts: first of all, from a competition point of view, the quality of a similar Norwegian product was superior and secondly, a $2 tariff was levied on each barrel by the American government. In a resolution adopted by

Fish cleaning, 1927. Note the steam drifters in the background.
Courtesy Irish Examiner

Kinsale Harbour Board in May 1909, seeking to remove the tax, they appealed on the basis of 'providing good food for poor American citizens and helping Irish fishing without injury to the American industry'. Copies were sent to the chairman of the Ways and Means Committee in Washington, to the Chief Secretary of Ireland and John Redmond MP. The pleas ameliorated the situation for a period but pressures surfaced again in 1925 as protectionist policies, introduced prior to the economic crash of 1929, finally closed off the American market.

Cured fish were also exported to Russia and Germany directly aboard the SS *Weser* of Bremen, a 600-ton steamer, which called regularly to Kinsale. The barrels were stamped in German with the expression 'select herring', phonetically pronounced as 'select matches', which became a catchphrase among the local people at the time.[61]

Periods of war in the twentieth century created a demand for Irish-caught fish and landings increased in the harbour. Kinsale-owned boats were used again as the English fleet was commandeered for minesweeping duties in the dangerous work of keeping channels and fairways into harbours clear. Cork, which was a British Admiralty base during the First World War, was regularly checked.[62]

During the Second World War English and Belgian trawlers continued to use Kinsale for shelter, anchoring in the deep pools of the river off the Dock and undertaking mechanical repairs with Merricks of Cork. They frequently came in to land fishermen injured from strafing by German aircraft at sea. The boats themselves were distinctive looking with their narrow, straight stems, tall, raked funnels and high, slender wheelhouses amidships. Apart from provisioning, the trawlers required tendering services and ferrying to and from the shore, which gave income opportunities for boys who absented themselves from school while the vessels were in the harbour. Often the payment was in the form of much-appreciated coal.

For a short period in the 1960s a fleet of immaculately maintained Norwegian boats, with harpoons mounted on the fo'c'sles, arrived in the harbour in quest of the porbeagle shark. In the 1970s the interest shifted to Eastern Europe when large, 100-foot-plus, dark Romanian trawlers and accompanying factory ships availed of the harbour while fishing for herring. They made a significant contribution to the town's economy for a period.

The prospect of developing the indigenous fishing industry remained an aspiration. Various ways and means were debated by such bodies as the Kinsale Development Association. Similarly the Harbour Board, reflecting the depressed state of the town and harbour, discussed proposals for development. A motion at the March meeting in 1937 put by Commissioner Roger Murphy, who was a fish merchant, to extend the fishing limit to 15 miles received unanimous approval. The proposal, which included 'condemnation of [the foreign] steam trawlers in destroying immature fish, fishing inside the three-mile limit' was referred to constituency TDs Eamon O'Neill and Tom Hales, who took it to government, initiating a debate on national exclusive fishing zones.

Activity in the harbour during this depressed period was enlivened during the late spring and summer each year by the arrival of the 'western men', mostly from Heir Island, who came into Kinsale to land their week's catch of lobster and crayfish. After completing the sowing of crops, they set off from their island homes, in open boats of about 25 feet in length, fishing the coast as far east as Ardmore in County Waterford. Working up to twenty-four pots, 14 fathoms (84 feet) apart and baited with salted mackerel, they fished inshore in foul, weedy ground. Power was provided by sail and oars which required great skill and a detailed knowledge of tides, currents and the location of submerged reefs. Acutely aware of the weather, they often ran for shelter at Wood Point at the entrance to Courtmacsherry, Ballymacus near Oysterhaven or in the lee of Hole Open. The sources of fresh water ashore were well known and frequently visited.

The crew of three slept on straw under a towelsail rigged forward of the mast in the open boat. Cooking facilities were primitive using a fire on stones or an iron sheet in the bilge until primus stoves became available. Griddle cake baked daily, together with potatoes and fish cooked in one pot and washed down with tea, formed the staple diet. Cutlery consisted of timber-handled, all-purpose knives jammed into risings near the mast. A lobster fishermen in the 1930s and native of Heir Island, Danny Minihane, recalled that the boats built by the Pyburn family were known for their sailing ability off the wind, particularly pleasant when heading east in a westerly breeze. In comparison, the three-sailed boats built by Skinners of Baltimore performed better to windward.

Conditions aboard improved in the 1940s, when an additional top strake gave extra freeboard, safety and more space and a timber half deck replaced the towelsail that provided shelter for the crew in heavy weather and at night. Petro/paraffin 15-horsepower engines, usually Kelvins, were fitted under a bridge deck that made the boats more easily handled.

On arrival in Kinsale on Saturday afternoon or Sunday morning in time for attendance at Mass, the week's catch, kept in baskets submerged in the water, was brought ashore and sold by the dozen

Towelsail lobster yawls at the Pier Head slipway, 1934.
Courtesy Father Browne Collection

and later by weight to fish merchants: Loves of Cork, Con Burke of Heir Island and Francie Healy of the Old Head. Some of the regular lobstermen using Kinsale were the Hartes, Pyburns, O'Donovans and Dalys aboard boats such as *Valette, Ebinezer, Aileen, Colleen, Sally Brown* and the *Pride of Toe Head*.

Saturday and Sunday evenings were spent socialising in the Seaview, Bill Deasy's on the Pier or at Herlihy's in the Glen. The men, invariably courteous and pleasant, enjoyed their drink, in high-necked, buttoned-up jumpers and soft tweed caps, puffing on pipes filled with penknife-cut plug tobacco. On Monday morning, with pots freshly baited and weekly provisions aboard, they headed to sea. The lobster fishing continued generally until October, with 29 September, St Michael's feast day, marking the beginning of the end of the season. According to the Cape Clear men, '*téann an diabhal san fharraige tar éis lá Mhíchil*' – the devil goes on the sea after Michael's day.[63]

By 1952, the fishing and general activity in the harbour was so reduced that it was decided to transfer the Harbour Board's functions to the Urban District Council. Before this was formalised, however, port traffic increased marginally and an awareness of the potential for marine-based tourism began to emerge. It gave a spark of hope to the Board.

A major initiative came to fruition in 1959 when a fish cannery was built on the site now occupied by the Shearwater apartment complex. The project received local support and funding. Technical and financial assistance was provided by the Nantes Fishery Company from Brittany. It was a bold effort to establish fish processing on a sound commercial basis. Requiring a constant quota of catch, it was anticipated that this would provide opportunities for local men fishing in small boats. Unfortunately, the project was unsuccessful as it was not possible to maintain a continuous supply, resulting in intermittent operation which was not viable and led to the eventual closure of the plant. Problems with the supply of raw materials, price and some quality issues with the canned product itself were a demoralising blow to the possibility of developing an indigenous industry. It was a regrettable outcome, as the failure to establish added-value processing meant that Kinsale would simply continue, at most, to provide services to foreign boats, which had been its traditional role.[64]

Fishing continued as a low-level operation in the 1960s with a number of Bord Iascaigh Mhara 'béal' boats fishing out of the harbour, engaging in trawling, longlining, lobstering, driftnetting and catching a variety of species. On occasions in the 1970s when mackerel and herring shoals appeared in the harbour, two or three men aboard open yawls fished them. A verse of a poem by Desmond O'Grady, who lived in Scilly at the time, captures the atmosphere at the tail end of the night's work.[65]

Midsummer. Under the sun the sea as smooth as a dish.
Below on the quays the fishermen wind up the morning's business:
Stacking the fish boxes, scraping the scales from
their tackle and hands.

Many references acknowledge the ability and seamanship skills of Kinsale fishermen who were much sought after as pilots and as sailors in the merchant marine. Nevertheless, commentators constantly highlighted the need for education and training to improve marine-related work practices and break the cycle that tended to keep the industry depressed.[66] Kinsale played a particular role in initiating training in this area. In 1848 the Sisters of Mercy opened an industrial school which provided training in net making.[67] At the Technical School established under the Agricultural and Technical Education Act of 1899, training in net mending and navigation on year-long courses was provided. The minutes of the school board reveal that they were conducted during the winter months until fishing got under way in March and the pupils left to avail of work opportunities on the Pier. Adapting the timetable to the inevitable, the school scheduled navigation classes for Saturday evenings when the boats were in the harbour to observe the Sunday obligation.[68]

In the 1930s Master Murphy, a teacher at the primary school in Summer Cove, introduced voluntary classes in navigation. Conscious of the career prospects for young people in the seaboard community, he provided some preparation for life as a fisherman and at sea. His initiative is still remembered and appreciated.

In October 1977 a full-time programme in marine skills was approved by the Department of Education as a Pre-Employment Course for Kinsale. It was taught initially in the old Loan Office on Fisher (O'Connell) Street as an out-centre of the Vocational School. It then moved to the building on St John's Hill which had been vacated as a primary school. Extensive syllabi were devised at the school, providing instruction in fisheries, net mending, mussel farming, navigation, safety and seamanship ashore and afloat. Modules were developed in boatbuilding, maintenance, engineering and cooking. Teaching staff were drawn from practising and retired seamen, fishermen and engineers, selected for their experience and ability to communicate. The course was new at post-primary level, pitched at the standard set for the Rural Science Programme in Vocational Schools. The course coordinator, in proposing the plan to the Department of Education, said that 'what Rural Science did for agriculture, the Marine Skills Course would do for the maritime'. The course received the full support of Brendan O'Kelly, chairman of Bord Iascaigh Mhara, which was responsible for fisheries in Ireland, and

Kevin McLaverty, Principal of the National Fishery Training Centre, Greencastle, County Donegal. A system of credits was proposed that would be awarded to students attending the Kinsale course which would ease their entry to the National Centre. The course was acknowledged in both the public and educational press, boding well for its future.[69]

After 1981, Department policy shifted and funding became available for the promotion of recreation and sport, which changed the focus at Kinsale from the purely vocational to instructor training courses in marine-based leisure pursuits. These continue as programmes at the Kinsale Further Education College preparing young people for work in the marine environment, including fishing.

In recent years, despite the decommissioning of vessels, EU regulations, the imposition of fish quotas and the lack of facilities, commercial fishing continues in the harbour. While not in any way comparable to the boom period of the late nineteenth century, traditional families in the business have been joined by a number of energetic fishermen and together are stimulating a revival in the industry (see plate 10). Prominent are names such as Hurley, Collins, Hogan, Bohan, Walsh, Fitzgerald, Murphy, O'Hea, O'Mahony, O'Neill, Harrington and Lynch who have replaced much of the fleet with a number of larger vessels purchased abroad, capable of staying at sea for extended periods. In a hopeful sign, these fine boats, up to 80 feet and more in length, show that while undertaking large financial commitments the young men, confident in their own ability, are ensuring that fishing remains an activity in the harbour. A mooring pontoon was put in place to improve berthing at the World's End in the 1990s. In 2010 landing facilities at Adams Quay were improved and the Lobster Quay was repaired and extended. The finance injection into these facilities indicates a change of policy at official level and in time, with management and organisation, may realise the potential of the industry in Kinsale. The industry, operating from the pontoon and new landing facilities at the World's End, looks to the future with some optimism.

5

Threats and Harbour Defence

Because of its natural qualities as a harbour and recognition as one of Irelands leading ports, Kinsale developed a range of services, which made it a focus of maritime activity on the south coast and a generator of wealth through victualling and the provision of facilities for seafarers. Until the late eighteenth century, it was Ireland's primary naval base and in the nineteenth century the harbour became the centre of a thriving fishing industry.

Kinsale also attracted those who were enemies of and at war with England in the era of discovery and colonial expansion. It was seen as a suitable and proximate base from which an attack on England could be launched. The idea of getting at England 'through the back door' was particularly true in the seventeenth century when some of the most significant events in the history of these islands were played out and at least partially determined at Kinsale. The threats did not just have an impact on Kinsale itself but on the island of Ireland and on England. It was patently evident that enemy aggression had to be curbed. Defence of the harbour and its rich agricultural hinterland was imperative. Various strategies were employed, which included the construction of castles, towers, walls, blockhouses and forts, using the most up-to-date fortification design. Observation posts, early warning and signalling systems were located on prominent headlands. When the Royal Naval Dockyard was established at the World's End it was the most important naval installation on the Irish coast, emphasising the role of Kinsale in the defence of the realm.

An early defence structure was the stone wall built across the narrow neck on the Old Head of Kinsale, effectively making the headland a promontory fort. It was built to protect Dún Cearma, a pre Christian settlement.[1] The Newenham drawing of 1750 shows the full extent of the barrier and the two keeps formed part of the late medieval coastal defence. The wall incorporates Dún Mhic Pádraig constructed by the Norman de Courcy family who held extensive lands in the area. The classic defensive qualities of the site perched on the narrow isthmus of cliffs high above Hole Open Bay offered an additional foil against an advancing enemy.

In Kinsale Town, under a charter of Edward III in 1334, provision was made for the erection of a wall to control and monitor trade and the movement of goods and people. It was not until 1381, when raiding Spanish and French galleys entered the harbour seeking shelter, that the inhabitants were spurred into action. The burgesses, members of the Corporation, began building a defensive stone structure at their own expense. Later the project was financed through the taking of murage, a special wall tax that was collected from all ships in the harbour.[2]

The wall, as the interface between the town and harbour, regulated activity. With its turrets, gates and narrow alleys (or sallies, as they are still known in Kinsale) that allowed pedestrian passage, it marked out and defined the town. It determined who lived inside and who was entitled to trade and set up business. The wall established limits, power and marked the economic bailiwick of the burgesses and the Sovereign.

More formal protection, which included a number of castle-like structures, was built into the wall at various points. Close to the foot of the Green Hill, where the wall from the Ramparts ran to meet the water opposite Scilly Point, a blockhouse was built. In the plan of the Siege of Kinsale 1601, drawn by Baptista Boazio, the structure is shown outside the wall and actually in the water, which effectively narrowed the entrance to the Inner Harbour. In October 1669 the

Corporation sought payment for the repair of the building including the construction of new batteries. Its defence function was confirmed in 1684 when it was reported that the building, then called the Queen's Blockhouse, had guns which were fired through portholes.[3]

As part of the reclamation process which involved encroaching into the harbour there was a proposal by Thomas Burrows in 1692 to build a quay out to the Blockhouse so that it would be accessible at all stages of the tide. B.H. St J. O'Neil, an expert on ancient fortifications, said that this connection would have linked the Old Blockhouse with the King's Fort, a substantial structure built into the wall where Higher Fisher (O'Connell) and Main Streets merge. In the 1880s what remained of this causeway was capped off when the road to the Pier Head was built.[4]

Despite efforts to maintain the wall, its condition was constantly a source for concern. 'In 1550 Sir James Crofts was instructed by the King to make proposals for the repair of [the walls at] Cork and Kinsale, choose ground and houses fittest to be fortified for the safety of havens and towns and was asked to encourage towns to strengthen the fortifications.' In 1586 it was asserted that 'many harms have been done of late to the town of Kinsale by pirates and men of war by reason the haven is open without defence and that there is a town which is not able to make resistance'. In 1598, three years before the Siege of Kinsale, it was reported that the 'walls are so spacious and decayed and their homes, for the most part built with clay and stones and without a strong garrison, could not be defended'.[5]

In reality, the walls, while having a defensive function, were more significant for the purpose of regulating trade and collecting tolls. At the end of the seventeenth century, large sections had become so dilapidated that both defensively and economically they had become ineffective. As the town gradually encroached on the harbour and expanded outside the medieval limits, particularly in the direction of the World's End, the walls became irrelevant. Having become redundant and obsolete, significant sections including the gates and castles became derelict and ruined. No traces of the walls remain in the modern town.

On 22 September 1601, a fleet of 26 Spanish ships, carrying 3,500 soldiers, entered the harbour under a stormy autumn sky, having embarked originally at Lisbon, then part of Spain. Because of the poor condition of the walls they quickly took possession of the town and drove the inhabitants out.

The subsequent episode, which involved the siege of the Spaniards in the town and the Battle of Kinsale itself, was one of a series of engagements in the seventeenth century which had implications for the English monarchy, in relation to conquest, colonisation, dominion of the seas and the Reformation. The Spaniards were not just a threat to the security of Kinsale town and harbour but to Ireland and England and, in the wider European context, influenced relations between England, France and Spain.

By deciding to land at Kinsale it can be argued that the Spaniards planned to use the harbour as an intermediary launching base for an attack on England. The expedition to Kinsale was the last in a series of attempts to attack England, starting with the First or Great Armada of 1588. The reasons for these maritime expeditions are varied and complex but arose directly because of military assistance provided by Elizabeth I to the Calvinist burghers of the Netherlands against the Spanish domination they had endured for many years.

The Netherlands was important to Spain as it provided transit ports for the passage of ships carrying essential corn supplies from the Baltic. England's interference in Brittany leading to the defeat of the Catholic League, which was supported by Spain, in 1598 at Blavet exacerbated the antagonism that existed between England and Spain. It was here that Juan del Áquila, later to command the Spanish forces in Kinsale, had a significant role. The irascible Galician-born Spaniard lost the sixteenth-century citadel of Port Louis on the bank opposite the harbour of Lorient. By coincidence, Charles Blount, who fought on the English side in that engagement, later faced del Áquila at Kinsale as Lord Deputy of Ireland.[6] Both the Netherlands and Port Louis were essential to Spain and their loss reduced its maritime strength in the Atlantic.

Another source of the conflict was the religious question which divided Europe at the time. Elizabeth I, Queen of England, was a moderate reforming Protestant. On the other hand Philip II, King of Spain, who died in 1598, was the leading Catholic monarch in Europe and as an advocate of the Counter-Reformation would have been disposed to support his Irish co-religious.

War at sea in sailing ships was an evolving phenomenon in the sixteenth century. The discovery of the Americas by the Spaniards put new emphasis on the maritime. Large consignments of gold and silver were transported across the Atlantic from ports in the Caribbean to Seville and Cadiz in Spain. The English looked enviously at the wealth potential of these fleets and the opportunities they presented to replenish depleted finances. Letters of marque were issued to consortia of English shipowners who fitted out vessels for the purpose of intercepting and capturing the Spanish fleets and bringing their valuable cargos to England.

To curb these attacks and the growing influence of the English, Spain attempted a number of armadas, beginning with the Great Armada. Each of these, which attempted to land a Spanish army on English soil, ended in failure. In reprisal, an English fleet in June 1596 under the command of the Earl of Essex, Francis Drake, and Charles Blount sailed to Cadiz and succeeded in destroying a large section of the Spanish fleet there.[7]

Spain by the end of the 1590s was on the back foot and anxious to reassert its traditional influence at sea. A possible means of curbing English aggression emerged in Ireland where there was growing antipathy, particularly among the Ulster chieftains, towards the aggressive Tudor policy of colonisation and conquest. A confederacy of the Irish clans, led by Hugh O'Neill, inflicted major defeats on the English at Enniskillen, Clontibret, Blackwater and most decisively at the Yellow Ford in 1598. After many requests for his assistance and inspired by the Irish success, the new King Philip III responded positively.

At this critical point Spain delayed, which gave the English time to recover. By September 1601 when the Spanish fleet, depleted and storm damaged, arrived at Kinsale, Blount (now the Lord Deputy) had succeeded in restoring much of England's military superiority in Ireland.

The suitability of Kinsale as the landing point for the Spanish has been a constant source of debate. From the Irish perspective a landing in the north, on the Donegal coast, where the Irish success against the English had been concentrated, was the preferred option and one to which del Áquila himself subscribed. The Admiral of the Spanish fleet, however, Diego Brochero, insisted on Kinsale, a decision frequently presented as a significant reason for the ultimate failure of the expedition.[8] The advantages of this option, from the Spanish perspective, are rarely if ever articulated. It must be remembered that the objective for Spain was ultimately to invade England and a port such as Kinsale offered the best possibility of providing the base or a bridgehead from which to launch an armada. Located on the south coast of Ireland, it was already familiar to the Spaniards and, in addition, the prevailing westerly winds facilitated swift passage to home ports in Spain and the ability to intercept English privateers more easily.[9]

A month after the Spanish arrival, the English Lord Deputy set up camp on the hills surrounding the town and began a process of 'investment' or laying siege to the Spaniards, bombarding the town. His first objective was to win back the harbour, which was facilitated by the fact that the Spanish fleet had left. After vigorous Spanish defence Barry Óg Castle at Rincurran and Castlepark overlooking the harbour were won back by the English. With the harbour open and also access to supplies and reinforcements possible through Oysterhaven Creek, Blount was in a stronger position.[10]

The Irish were tardy in making the winter march from Ulster to Kinsale. Eventually, after persistent pressure from del Áquila, an army of over 3,000 Irish arrived late in December 1601 and camped at Coolcorran on a hill to the north of the English, creating a siege within a siege. On the morning of 24 December the Irish moved in three sections to connect with the Spaniards in the town. Blount with the English army at Camphill became aware of the movement and advanced quickly to intercept. Hugh O'Neill, apparently surprised by the sudden English intervention, retreated towards Dunderrow and made a stand at Millwater, west of the town. Considerable confusion spread among the Irish and, unfamiliar with battle in the open field, they were outmanoeuvred and the soldiers fled. The battle quickly degenerated into a rout.[11]

The Spaniards in the town after ten days asked for parley, to which Blount promptly agreed, giving the Spaniards shipping and safe conduct. For the King of Spain, Kinsale marked a radical shift

in policy. It was the last armada attempt by the Spaniards and in negotiating the Treaty of London in 1604 Spain was forced to acknowledge England's growing maritime reputation and influence throughout the world. Soon afterwards, the first English settlements in the Caribbean were established and the East India Company was set up in the early 1600s. Spain had at least begun to share with the English the sun that was said never to set on their empire.

For the Irish, the defeat at Kinsale led to the Treaty of Mellifont in 1603 and eventual submission to the English. They were now subject to major change in relation to language, systems of governance, ownership of land, customs, religion and conquest which, apart from control and domination, led to widespread plantation where the older settlers were replaced by the 'New English' colonisers.

In the post-battle period the Kinsale Corporation pleaded with the Privy Council to restore its Charter rights. These were granted with the provisos that the Corporation improve the defences of the town by repairing the walls and contribute to the construction of Castlepark Fort (later renamed James Fort) on the site of the tower house destroyed during the siege, to forestall further threats and defend the harbour and town.[12] For the town the battle marked a period of profound change. The dominance of the old Anglo-Normans, who had sought accommodation with the native Irish, was eclipsed. They were replaced by new settlers who pursued a vigorous policy of colonisation through conquest, were advocates of the reformed religion and in Kinsale

James Fort, 1604 (left) and Charles Fort, 1680.
Courtesy John Collins

took every opportunity to establish their position and exploit the harbour's natural qualities as a port.

The location of James Fort is striking not alone for the beauty of the location but also for its defence capability. Almost totally surrounded by water apart from a narrow isthmus of land between the beach and the Dock Bar, the Fort is situated on a steep slope, 100 feet above sea level. It provides a viewing point for observing activity in the town and shipping movements in the harbour. The construction was directed by Paul Ivye, the noted fortifications expert, who had previously completed Elizabeth Fort on Jersey in the Channel Islands. Work at Castlepark began in 1602 and was considered to have overrun its planned construction time when opened in 1604. The imposing structure consists of a five-sided curtain defence outer wall with large bastions at each corner and a ditch outside. Incorporating the latest contemporary features in the art of fortifications, the main bastion overlooking the 'new' Blockhouse was the site of the main battery. There the strong artillery was mounted. The bastion had access to a tunnel through the curtain wall connecting the Fort to the Blockhouse by means of a high-sided covered way that would be a last resort for escape by boat if the Fort had to be abandoned. Inside the main wall was a second line of defence consisting of a four-sided structure with demi-bastions at each corner. The flagstaff stood on the southern corner. In the heart of the complex were substantial towers which housed the garrison.

Although designed to the highest standards, a weakness in regard to its specific defence purpose became evident in that it did not have a view of the open sea through the harbour mouth. The deficit was improved to some extent by constructing a 'watch' building on the pathway to the Blockhouse. It is placed on the highest point of the headland, giving an improved view of the open sea and a better opportunity to monitor shipping approaching the harbour.

More seriously, however, it proved vulnerable to cannon placed on elevated ground at Compass Hill across the river on the very first challenge to its defence qualities. In November 1649 Cromwellian soldiers took possession of the town and then attacked Castlepark, to which a number of Royalists holding out against the Parliamentarians had retreated. The fire was directed by a former gunner at the Fort,

Sam Pett, who aimed cannon at specific targets, creating maximum damage and leading to the surrender of those sheltering within the walls.[13]

Forty years later in 1690, during what is described as the Second Siege of Kinsale, Williamite forces, in the process of overcoming the residue of support for James II in towns such as Kinsale, attacked the Fort, where the garrison surrendered after a barrel of powder exploded. The story of this encounter will be elaborated later. Suffice to say at this point that, when surveyed subsequently by Sir William Petty, the Fort was declared inadequate for harbour protection and it was suggested that it would be more useful if converted for use as a military hospital.[14]

Reflecting the importance of the harbour a second Blockhouse, with a similar function to the older structure at the entrance to the Inner Harbour, was erected where the Castlepark promontory dips sharply into the water touching both the Middle and Outer Harbours (see plate 3). The 'Blockhouse at the end of the land' was fortified with a battery of guns which were trained on the channel at blank range. Viewed from various points in the harbour, the building is an iconic structure. Still in place is the corbel-roofed magazine where munitions were stored. A seventeenth-century French map of the harbour indicates a blocking chain from the building drawn across to the opposite bank on the Lower Road, using a mechanism described as a '*cabeston de la chaisne*'. On arrival in the harbour in March 1669 Cosimo de' Medici noted the barrier, reporting that 'the Port is closed at night with beams, bound together by strong chains'.[15]

O'Neil, the fortifications expert, in 1940 said that the Blockhouse was the earliest defence structure built on the headland in the sixteenth century.[16] However, a report on excavations undertaken in the period 1974 to 1998 disputes this assertion and estimates that the structure was not built until the 1620s. It is most probable that some building occupied this prominent headland which, apart from any defence function, would have been used for observation and the monitoring of shipping in the harbour. After falling into disuse in the eighteenth century, as Kinsale's status as a shipping port declined, it functioned at the height of the fishing industry for the storing of boxes, baskets and net mending.

Other forms of fortification are associated with quay walls on the Bandon River. Many, now dilapidated, mark landing places on which goods were handled. The more important were located on the bends of the river where the water runs fast and deep. Those at the top of creeks were accessed by boats on a flood tide, such as Ballinacurra, which was presided over by White Castle at Ardcloyne. Apart from identifying important transport hubs, stores and milling facilities situated close to the quays, they became the focus of activity for the landowners, who lived in the nearby tower or fortified house, and their tenants. (For the position of defence structures on the Bandon River see map on p. 163.)

The rectangular stone-built structures of the fifteenth and sixteenth centuries constructed close to the quays had design features similar to the Norman defence towers. They were three or four storeys high with an internal stairway and provided comfortable accommodation for the owner and his family, with facilities for the obligatory hospitality offered to visiting overlords and their retinues. The architectural style of the towers may still be appreciated at the Old Head of Kinsale and at Kilgobban.[17] Norman influence gave way, with the arrival of the new English settlers, to roomier, better-lit accommodation, as is evident at Shippool and in the features of the house at Mountlong on Oysterhaven Creek. These included modified defence features such as battlements, machicolation, gun loops and bartizans.[18]

A field survey of the tower houses in the Kinsale area reveals that they are strategically sited so that a line of sight from one to others was possible. The visual networking provided a means of signalling news of ship arrivals and movement. Kilgobban Castle near Ballinadee, described as 'very tall and slender', was ideally situated to receive and transfer messages.[19] The survey showed that from its battlements looking southeast there was visual contact with the ruined bartizan at Ringrone over the dip in the intervening land at Kilnacloona. From Ringrone, although diminished in height due to the weathering and the removal of stone, the remaining machicolation at Ardcloyne Castle can be seen at the top of the winding Ballinacurra creek (see plate 11). Ringrone, as befits the seat of Lord de Courcy, Baron of Kinsale, had visual contact with Dún Mhic Pádraig at the Old Head with sight, just possible, skirting the elevated sea cliffs at Killowny, Ballynaboola and

Passing under the
'tall and slender'
Kilgobban Castle.
Author's collection

Passing under the
'tall and slender'
Kilgobban Castle.
Author's collection

Ardkilly. In addition Castlepark and Barry Óg Castles, both destroyed during the Siege of Kinsale in 1601, could be seen from Ringrone. Tradition has it that a fort at Kilnacloona was located in the line between Kilgobban and Ringrone. This would have protected the ancient crossing point on the river which linked the foot of Cappagh Lane to the Courcies. Upriver, north of Kilgobban, other castles were visually linked. Knocknagappel could be seen from Carriganassig but no trace of either remains. Sharp bends on the river provide vantage points as at Castlepark, Ringrone, Carriganassig and Shippool where two stretches of water could be monitored simultaneously through narrow gaps in the high-sided creeks.[20]

Following the Desmond rebellion, the subsequent plantation of Munster in 1585 and the Battle of Kinsale in 1601, the new settlers were granted fertile lands on the banks of the Bandon River which gave them easy access to the sea.[21] Those who had received land felt vulnerable and threatened as the dispossessed previous occupiers became belligerent in seeking to win some redress.[22] The sense of wrong, exacerbated by the banning of the Irish language, Irish dress, access to public positions and business opportunity was deepened in 1605 during the reign of James I when Catholic priests were prohibited from ministering openly. Taken with the Act of Supremacy the laws were a severe blow to the Old Irish and Anglo-Normans. These restrictions persisted during the reign of Charles I and subsequent regimes.

At Kinsale the Southwell family had received substantial property through which they exerted control, influence and developed success-ful business interests. Richard Boyle acquired lands upriver where he settled people from Somerset who established the new walled town of Bandon; to provide protection from those who had lost their lands, the Bandon Militia was formed in 1622. 'It was able to muster 44 horses and 550 foot, well-armed with pikes muskets and swords, horsemen staves and pistols.'[23]

The seething bitterness which had been festering from the time of the Munster Plantations could not be contained. Enraged and embittered, the Catholics rose in rebellion, starting in Ulster in October 1641 and spreading throughout the whole Island, with horrific reports of notorious incidents.[24]

In Kinsale the Royalist Tristram Whetcombe, describing himself as Mayor in a letter to his brother in London, gives an account of how 'the rebels persisted in their cruel and tyrannical ways'. He describes how he focused on those who continued to occupy and claim ownership of tower houses in the area and admits to pillaging and burning all the houses he could and hanging any who were captured 'whether man, woman or child'. Continuing, he writes that 'assistance, in the form of Lord Baltinglass's men and powder, arrived by sea' to Kinsale and with these reinforcements he first turned his attention to the Longs of Oysterhaven and Barry of Kinalea (Rincurran) who had come together at Belgooly. After viciously putting down this opposition the loyal Kinsale Mayor turned his attention to the houses on the Bandon River.

The Roches at Ardcloyne (White Castle) were attacked first. Next the focus switched upriver to Dundaniel which was burned with 'the rebels and provisions within'. Carriganassig Castle on the western bank opposite and a little below Shippool was bombarded for thirty hours by ordnance brought by boat from Kinsale and at the same time attacked from the land by the Bandon Militia. When it was possible to approach the castle, Whetcombe burned the building and described how the garrison surrendered. 'The fire at Carriganassig continued all night and next day until at last were brought forth such a pack of roasted rogues as never in a man's life were seen and at last as many as were not burned enough were hanged.'[25] Soon afterwards, Shippool Castle, belonging to the Roches, surrendered and Kilgobban was abandoned, leaving all the defence structures on the river firmly in the hands of those loyal to the King.

It was a highly complex period politically, with divisions and alliances based on religion and on varying degrees of loyalty to the monarch. In the upheavals that followed the 1642 rebellion and the Cromwellian settlement of 1652, the descendants of the early Norman settlers became known as the 'English rebels' and the older Irish natives were classed as the 'Irish enemies'. Both these groups maintained adherence to Catholicism which defined them as the enemy of the new settlers who were distinguished by their Protestant beliefs. Some of the recent arrivals were also linked to the emergence of Republican politics in England, eventually leading to the beheading of King Charles I in 1649.

In the various settlements after the defeat of the rebels and the forfeiture of land, Richard Boyle, the Earl of Cork, received Dundaniel and his son assumed the title Lord Kinalmeaky and became Governor of Bandon. Innishannon passed to the Adderlys and Shippool and its surrounding lands came into the possession of the Herrick family. Part of Barry Óg's lands, east of Kinsale, were added to the property of the Southwells. John Long was arraigned at Cork and executed for his role in the rebellion. The family lost rights to Mountlong, control over Oysterhaven and shipping to Belgooly. Tristram Whetcombe was acknowledged for quelling the rising and securing the river and the route to the open sea. He was declared 'a loyal monarchist' by St Ledger, the Lord President of Munster.[26]

At the same time as the rising in Ireland, a Civil War in England generated further threats that would supersede events in Kinsale. Unpopular taxation measures, King Charles I's claim to absolute rule and divine rights of the monarchy gave rise to strong Parliamentary opposition. Republican ideas of commonwealth evolved which sought to replace the authority of the King by a representative Parliament. Puritanism and individual responsibility were the underlying principles. Civil war erupted in England and after a long campaign the Parliamentary forces under Oliver Cromwell emerged successful, ultimately leading to the arrest and execution of the King in 1649.

In Ireland Cromwell had particular antipathy towards Catholics, especially those who had participated in the 1641 rebellion and committed atrocities against Protestants. Conveniently he was also interested in Ireland because a successful campaign would make tracts of land available for plantation. He also recognised that Ireland's ports, including Kinsale, posed a threat because they offered suitable locations for the organisation of resistance, had the potential to launch a bid to restore the monarchy and had the means of controlling the collection of customs and taxes.

Towards the end of the English Civil War the King's fleet, which had gathered in Holland for refitting, was commanded by Charles I's German-born nephew, Prince Rupert. He had established Royalist bases at Jersey in the Channel Islands and St Mary's in the Isles of Scilly and looked to Kinsale in an overall strategy of restoring the fortunes of the monarchy. Kinsale Harbour, because of its natural qualities and the town's professed loyalty to the King, ensured that Rupert's fleet would be welcome and could avail of the Southwell victualling services.

Initially, all boded well when the fleet arrived in Kinsale on 23 January 1649 after a swift passage from Holland. Prince Rupert found a fleet of Irish privateers commanded by members of the Confederation of Kilkenny at anchor in the port. They were strongly anti-Cromwellian, and supported Rupert. In fact, on arrival in the harbour he found that the Irish privateers had captured 'a very rich prize brought to Kinsale ... her lading was said to be 18 tons in silver bars and 40 bags of coin'.[27] The capture by members of the

Confederation was appreciated by the Prince, as it demonstrated how sources of Parliamentary revenue could be limited.

Within a week of Rupert's arrival, news of Charles I's execution reached the town. The Prince immediately 'put himself and all his officers in mourning and even the ensigns, jacks and streamers of all the fleet were altered to a colour suitable'. Rupert called the population of the town together, presumably at St Multose Church, and had Charles II proclaimed King 'with all the solemnity that the place was capable of'.[28] This recognition of the new king came eleven years before the 'restoration' actually took place in London.

From Cromwell's perspective the royal fleet in Kinsale was a potent force and a threat to the safety of transporting an army to Ireland. It was also seen that Rupert was capable of becoming a focus for royal support. To deal with the threat, Cromwell attempted to keep Rupert and his fleet confined in Kinsale by establishing a blockade at the mouth of the harbour. In the age of sail this was an intricate task to effect as change in wind direction and the set of the tide made it difficult for vessels to maintain a windward position to enable the blockading ships to pounce on the royal fleet should it attempt to break out. The naval exercise was commanded by Robert Blake and Richard Deane, noted captains of the Parliamentary fleet, who displayed superb seamanship and handling skills.[29]

With the blockade in place from May to October 1649, Cromwell was able to land at Dublin with his army of 13,000 infantry and cavalry from Milford Haven. From there he undertook an aggressive military campaign in Ireland which involved transferring his army's baggage train by sea from Drogheda to Wexford. From there he continued the process of forcing the country into submission.[30]

When the authorities at Youghal, Cork and Kinsale submitted to Cromwell, recognising the possibility of the destruction that could be inflicted, the royal fleet was under great pressure as 'no longer could Prince Rupert lie at anchor safe under the guns of Castlepark'. On 16 October a storm hit the Kinsale area and blew the Parliamentary ships temporarily out of position, which gave Rupert the opportunity to leave the harbour. He was pursued by Blake to Lisbon and into the Mediterranean but evaded capture in a series of cat-and-mouse engagements. Blake was replaced by Captain William Penn, who continued the pursuit. After sailing to the Caribbean in a hopeless final effort to reverse Royalist fortunes, Rupert became more and more disconsolate. Eventually, aboard his last remaining ship *The Swallow*, he returned across the Atlantic to France where he laid up the vessel on the Loire in 1653. The ship's figurehead was the image of Saturn, the symbol of hibernation and hope, in which Rupert anticipated the restoration of the monarchy.

By the time of Cromwell's death in 1658 dissatisfaction with the Commonwealth was increasing in England and the tide of opinion was turning once again towards the monarchy. In 1660 Charles II, son of the executed King, who had taken asylum in the Netherlands, returned to the throne in London at the invitation of the people. Prince Rupert was restored to a prominent role in the Navy and was joined by the King's brother James, the Duke of York.[31] James was a noted seaman and an accomplished naval tactician and was, thirty years later, destined to make a major impact on Kinsale.

The King's restoration created its own turmoil. Following two decades involving civil war, regicide and commonwealth governance, a strong anti-Catholic puritan-inspired ethic persisted. But instead of bloodletting and revenge towards former opponents, a pragmatic approach was adopted by the restored regime. Retribution against those responsible for the execution of Charles I was selective. While some were severely punished, expediency dictated that others, recognised for their ability and experience, were not just spared but even preferred in appointments. The restored King, faced with threats from the Dutch until the truce in 1675 and from French aggression subsequently during the reign of Louis XIV, took an accommodating stance.[32]

Examples of realpolitik had particular relevance to Kinsale Harbour and illustrate how tensions were kept in check when danger threatened and defence was required. Prince Rupert overcame antagonism towards Samuel Pepys, who had cooperated in the Commonwealth project. He not alone managed to survive but, due to the good offices of Robert Southwell of Kinsale, prospered, rising to high office in the Navy Board, and would have directed shipping to Kinsale for victualling. Southwell also had the ear of Prince Rupert who had received support of the family while blockaded in the harbour in 1649.

A change at the heart of naval command could see an ordinary seaman with practical seafaring ability, such as William Penn, rise through the ranks to become admiral. He became a committed Royalist after the restoration, even receiving a knighthood, and cooperated with Rupert whom he had relentlessly pursued across the Atlantic while a supporter of Cromwell in 1651. For his services to the Commonwealth he had been granted estates in Cork. Part of his duties included the governance of James Fort in Kinsale where his son William junior visited him.[33] While in Ireland the younger Penn developed his Nonconformist beliefs through contact with Quakerism in Cork. He was eventually forced to leave England for America in 1681 where he founded a new colony, which came to be known as the state of Pennsylvania.[34]

In Ireland a similar pragmatic approach was evident. The Southwell family in Kinsale who had received lands during the reigns of Elizabeth I, James I and Charles I, supported Prince Rupert in the Harbour in 1649 and yet became victuallers to Cromwell's fleet. When Charles II was restored to the throne in 1660, the family continued to prosper through the extensive web of contacts nurtured by the younger Robert. The complex matrix of services, which they had established in Kinsale by the end of the seventeenth century, were indispensible to whoever ruled and were in constant demand.

A great exponent in the art of survival in this period of expediency, change and flux was Roger Boyle, another son of the Earl of Cork, who demonstrated remarkable skill in winning the favour of whoever was dominant. James I, in 1625, gave him the title Lord Broghill but during the Commonwealth period he supported Cromwell. After the Restoration of the monarchy in 1666 he was dubbed Earl of Orrery by Charles II, and given extensive powers with responsibility for the defence of the Province of Munster. He was particularly concerned about the Dutch and the French and how they could use the latent resentment of a dissenting population in Ireland. Orrery saw this as a threat which highlighted the need to focus on improving the defence of Kinsale Harbour.

The Dutch came to prominence at the beginning of the seventeenth century when they and the English East India Companies were rivals in exploiting the wealth of the Orient. Using similar methods of administration, military engagement and shipping operations, a successful period emerged for both countries in terms of their economies and opportunities for colonisation. The rivalry developed into more aggressive confrontation when Dutch ships were harassed by the English as they passed through the narrow Dover Straits on approach to their own ports. In the period 1650 to 1676 the two countries were at war on three separate occasions. Much of the war was conducted at sea by remarkable commanders on both sides. Prince Rupert and the Duke of York led the English Fleet with some success in the English Channel but in 1653 were defeated at the Battle of Ter Heijde by a fleet of lightly armed fishing boats under the command of Admiral Maarten Tromp. The great Dutch admiral, Michiel de Ruyter, in 1667 produced a shock for the English by sailing up the Thames to Chatham and capturing the *Royal Prince*, the pride of the Navy Board.[35] Aware of the Spanish strategy in undertaking the expedition of 1601 to Kinsale, Orrery was perturbed at the success of the Dutch and the threat posed by the possibility of attacking Kinsale to divert English attention away from the richly laden Dutch fleets in the Channel.

By the mid-1670s the ever-growing threat of the French under Catholic King Louis XIV became more significant, which forced the English and the Dutch to recognise the danger to both posed by the French King. The alliance was copper-fastened when the English Parliament deposed the openly practising Catholic King James II, who had succeeded Charles II, and invited the Dutch Prince William of Orange to become King of England in 1688.

Orrery's anxiety concerning the defence of Kinsale became even more focused with the very real possibility of a French invasion. In 1667, having surveyed the harbour, he recommended that batteries be placed on each side at the entrance. Captain Greenville Collins' chart of 1696 shows ruins on Shronecan Point at the entrance to Sandy Cove, which may have been the site selected on the western side. He requested that six guns be placed at Rincurran, where Charles Fort was later constructed. On the Castlepark side, Orrery recommended that the defence of the Fort, built in 1604, be improved by the

The Devil's (*left*) and Charles (*right*) bastions at Charles Fort.
Courtesy Irish Examiner

placement of thirty guns at water level. He also proposed the use of a strong chain across the harbour and other preventative measures. Requests for the stationing of fourth- and fifth-rate frigates at Kinsale 'to cruise and attend the Harbour' were included in the suggestions.[36]

Eventually it was decided that the defence of the harbour would centre on the building of a 'showpiece citadel'. The project had been sanctioned by Charles II in 1667 on the site at Rincurran, provided by Robert Southwell, where the ruins of the Barry Óg Castle were still visible. It was described, prematurely as it turned out, as the ideal location where 'all objects are visible seaward from their appearance on the horizon'. The Fort, designed by William Robinson, is recognised as a fine example of a pentagon-shaped bastioned structure. Many of the features were borrowed from de Vauben who, as fortifications expert to Louis XIV, influenced military building throughout Europe. Locations as far apart as the walls around the city of Lucca in Tuscany and the blockhouse at Camaret-sur-Mer in northwest Brittany, both having trade links to Kinsale, had defensive features similar to the new fort which was substantially complete in 1681 and named Charles Fort by Lord Deputy Ormond.

The major features of the Fort are its five bastions. The 'Kinsale', now known as the 'Devil's', and the 'Charles' are substantial, as attack was expected to come from the seaward side. Both are large bombproof casemated structures designed to accommodate a second level of cannon. The other three bastions – the 'Cockpit', the 'Flagstaff' and the 'North' – face towards the land. Between these are the curtain walls broken with externally splayed gun embrasures. Placed at these openings were eleven large cannon, capable of firing 24 lb balls, on sloping limestone mountings at a gradient designed to absorb the recoil. Various other ordnance and powder, stored in the explosion-proof magazine, provided the defence against ships entering the harbour that 'must sail within a pistol distance'.[37]

The Fort, towering over the mouth of the harbour, was a deterrent to any enemy approaching from the sea. However, the high ground to the north and east made the Fort vulnerable if attacked from the land. Defence was also weakened by the tower and the church of the ancient Teampall an Trionóide located at a point overlooking the new Fort. Because of its proximity it was demolished and relocated to Ardbrack, leaving only the well and the burial ground, which are still in use, at the Fort Hill.

Apart from its imposing defence features towards the sea, the choice of location at Rincurran was poor and difficult to justify when previous history is considered. The earlier Barry Óg Castle on the same site was taken by George Carew, the second in command on the English side during the Siege of Kinsale prior to the Battle in 1601. The account shows how exposed the site was to the surrounding high ground. Using the height and setting the angle of the cannon to the correct inclination, Carew overcame the stout resistance of the Spaniards inside: 'He did score out his ground markers and with his quadrant took the true level so as the want of light was no hindrance.'[38]

After completion, Thomas Phillips inspected Charles Fort in 1685 and commented that 'it being so ill situated under the hills that it is a very hard matter to cover the inhabitants thereof on any occasion that they have to stand by guns or the sea batteries'. Phillips' drawing of the Fort sketched from the high ground above Sally Port clearly illustrates how it was exposed to fire from that position.[39] Within ten years of completion, its vulnerability was exposed by the forces of William of Orange in what is sometimes referred to as the 'Second Siege of Kinsale'.

The prelude to this engagement was the deposing of James II as monarch in London. He had succeeded to the English throne following the death of Charles II in 1685. Unpopular with the people, he was removed after three years, primarily because Parliament was alarmed at his open espousal of Catholicism. In 1688, with the approval of the English people, William of Orange, who had married James' daughter, accepted the crown and James was deposed. He fled to France and was received at the court of Louis XIV from whom he received support.

Kinsale was the chosen landing place in Ireland from where James would launch his campaign in a bid to retain the kingship of Ireland and win back the throne in England. A fleet of 22 ships set sail from Brest in February 1689 with 1,200 French soldiers aboard. The army was augmented by French reinforcements and Irish supporters who rallied from all over Munster. The King came ashore at Castlepark, which subsequently was called James Fort in recognition of its illustrious visitor. Crossing the river to the town, James and his retinue were received 'enthusiastically by the Corporation and the people amid flowing banners and booming salvoes'. Having enjoyed hospitality in the town he went by carriage to Charles Fort where he and the French held court for a number of days.[40] In appreciation of the French, 'universal thanks [was] due to them from this Kingdom in general for transporting His Majesty thither, we having the first of his presence in this Country'.[41]

Leaving Kinsale, James travelled to Cork, Lismore, Kilkenny and finally Dublin, 'pushing aside cordons put in place by those who supported William of Orange'. In June 1690 William himself landed at Carrigfergus to support the resistance in the northern part of the country, particularly from the people of Derry who vehemently rejected James. After many months' suffering under siege, they were relieved when three ships sent by William broke the barriers across the River Foyle. James' forces, having been repulsed at Derry, then conducted a disastrous campaign in Ireland. His army was defeated at the Battle of the Boyne in what has become an iconic episode in Irish history. Further defeats followed at Aughrim and Limerick. By this time James, seeing that further campaigning in Ireland was doomed, had already left for France sailing out of Kinsale.

Nevertheless, Kinsale, Cork and other towns in the south maintained their support for the deposed King. John Churchill, the Duke of Marlborough in command of the Williamite forces in the south, was determined to stamp out the residual Jacobite opposition. He sailed for Cork in September 1690, besieged the city and after five days, it surrendered.[42]

Attention then turned to Kinsale whose townspeople retired to James and Charles Forts. Under the command of the Dutch Major Ernest von Tettau, an 800-man detachment of Marlborough's army crossed the Bandon River at Innishannon and advanced towards Kinsale on the western bank. They encountered no resistance at Ringrone as its garrison had retreated to James Fort, making a defence of 400 men. After initial resistance the Dutch forced the defenders to retire to the inner fort. Concentrated in the confined space, carnage followed when a barrel of powder exploded, killing eighty. The effect was devastating, and the survivors put down their arms and surrendered.

Attention now switched across the harbour to Charles Fort, where its vulnerability was fully exposed. The Dutch and English placed artillery on the elevated ground at Bawnavota, overlooking the fortification. A continuous thirteen-day battery began which pounded the rampart between the Flagstaff and Cockpit bastions. The wall was eventually breached, forcing the garrison and the Governor, Colonel Edward Scott, to seek a truce. Under the terms, the garrison received safe conduct and the Fort was handed over to William's men.[43]

Following the campaign a settlement, written into the Treaty of Limerick (1691), ensured the position of an ascendency class through the vigorous application of the blatantly discriminatory Penal Laws. The policy effectively excluded 80 per cent of the population, mostly Catholic, from ownership of land, business, access to the law and power or benefit from the shipping that was attracted to Kinsale.

Edmund Burke later wrote that the campaign was 'the ruin of the native Irish and in a great measure too the first races of the English'. When the laws were applied, many of the soldiers who had supported James opted to go abroad through Kinsale and join Irish regiments on the continent. Many of the Irish who remained on the island, the majority of whom were women and children, joined the ranks of 'indentured servants' who were transported from harbours like Kinsale to the West Indies.

At Kinsale the pragmatism of the authorities was once again evident, having no difficulty in changing allegiance and adapting to change. In 1689 James II, the Stuart Catholic King had been received with lavish hospitality. By 1695 the Corporation decided that the new regime would henceforth be remembered annually for the 'deliverance of Protestants of this Corporation out of the hands of their implacable enemies of the Roman Catholic persuasion'.[44]

Following William's campaign, James Fort was examined from the perspective of harbour defence. William Petty declared that the Fort had little to offer and would be more useful if adapted as a military hospital. Seventy years later in 1776–77, Charles Vallancey in comparing the relative defence merits of Charles and James Forts was more positive about the latter. He said that a 'sum of money expended on the Old Fort (James) would be more advantageous having a better command of the channel'. In the appendix to his Military Itinerary of 1796 he too was scathing of the Charles Fort site in terms not dissimilar to earlier criticism. 'A more injudicious situation than Charles Fort could not have been fixed on.'[45]

Charles Fort, however, together with the town barracks established early in the eighteenth century, continued as military installations until the withdrawal of the British forces in 1922 following the signing of the treaty establishing the Free State. The Fort served as a training base for soldiers of British regiments before transfer on tours of duty to other overseas colonies. On occasions it had garrison duties when called to deal with civil disturbances or quell insurgency trouble that occasionally arose in the surrounding districts.

After the signing of the treaty the Irish Civil War followed in 1922–23. Anti-Treaty or Republican forces undertook a campaign to disrupt the functioning of the new Free State government and occupied Kinsale. The Commandant, Tom Kelleher, then set about torching all the old establishment buildings which included Charles Fort. The Fort remained in a ruined state until the 1970s when efforts to conserve the magnificent structure as a tourist attraction were initiated by the Board of Works.

A second strategy adopted by Kelleher was to disrupt transport and access to the town by bombing the bridges and roads, cutting off land connections with Cork, Bandon and the surrounding area. The only means of getting supplies and relief to the people was by sea. The old steam drifter *Maryland*, owned by the Robertson family, was pressed into service, bringing badly needed food from Cork. The sight of black smoke belching from its tall funnel as the vessel came up the harbour was the first indication of relief for the community who gathered anxiously at the quayside. The boiler section, topped by the dome-shaped release valve of the vessel, can still be seen in the mud of the Scilly Dam after the hull of the *Maryland* became a wreck.

Eventually the State forces, similar to Marlborough's army in 1690, approached by way of the Castlepark side of the river to relieve the town. Crossing by boat, they were fired on briefly from Compass Hill by the retreating Republican forces. There were no casualties and the town was subsequently occupied by the Free State authorities.[46]

The conflict between France and England that continued during the eighteenth century was often complicated by changing alliances in Europe and by the War of Independence in America, where both nations had extensive colonial interests. In 1757 England achieved a significant victory over a large French fleet gathering at Quiberon Bay in preparation for an all-out invasion of England.[47]

This defeat along with the earlier 1690 debacle in Ireland did not deter the French. Inspired by the Republicanism of the United Irishmen and forceful arguments put forward by Wolfe Tone, a fleet of forty-three ships set sail from Brest bound for Bantry in west Cork in December 1796. Unfavourable weather and a lack of preparedness by the Irish ashore resulted in the failure of the attempt. The commitment of the French was such that two further expeditions were undertaken which, however, were competently put down by the

English. Nevertheless, the expeditions posed serious questions about the effectiveness of coastal defences in Ireland. To deal with the threat one of the strategies employed was to establish an early warning system of coast-watch capable of signalling messages if an enemy fleet was spotted. On the most elevated site of the Old Head of Kinsale, above the narrow connection to the headland, a slender square tower was constructed in 1804. Originally weather-slated with an entrance door at second-floor level, access was by ladder and on top defensive features such as bartizans and parapets were put in place.[48] The tower has magnificent sweeping views over the sea to the horizon with visibility of over 50 miles on a clear day. Similar towers were placed on the Seven Heads to the west and on Barry's Head and Robert's Head to the east. From these structures the first sight of the enemy could be signalled by means of flags to other towers around the coast, and to the coastguard authorities at Summer Cove, Oysterhaven or Howe's Strand and from these the Navy and the Military could be alerted.

While Charles Fort and the local military barracks continued to maintain a complement of 800 soldiers in the town up to 1922, the need for elaborate defence installations was reduced after the defeat of the French at the naval battle of Trafalgar in 1805 and Napoleon's army at Waterloo in 1815. The possibility of further foreign naval armadas or expeditions became remote. In any case, naval warfare from the early nineteenth century tended to be conducted, in set-piece engagements, involving ships far out at sea.

During the wars of the twentieth century the ability to gain intelligence by observation from the land nevertheless remained significant. Kinsale, like other areas on the coast, built a series of small bunker-like pillboxes on the headlands for coastal defence personnel whose function was to report on shipping movements and suspect activity that might pose a threat.[49]

In modern warfare the need for specific structures to provide defence against possible threats has become redundant. The ruins of these buildings at Kinsale, though, are a reminder of major incidents in the maritime history of these islands where the harbour played a significant role.

6

Piracy, Smuggling and Wreck

Apart from threats by enemy armadas, rebellion and civil unrest, further instability was generated by the activity of pirates, smugglers and wreckers, which had the capacity to play havoc with the economy. Piracy was the scourge of the authorities in seaboard communities. It was particularly rampant on the west Cork coast where many hidden anchorages provided the bases from which pirates could swoop on ships bearing valuable cargos. They then returned to the security of the secret shelters where the rule of law was lax among people who, surviving on their wits and native cunning, actively connived in the operation. The maritime historian John de Courcy Ireland said that rapacious piracy thrived among an impoverished dispossessed people who used the rocky, indented coastline as 'a nursery and storehouse of pirates'. As well as availing of the cover provided in secluded coves, the pirates took on supplies of food and water and enjoyed 'a good store of Irish wenches which resort onto them'. At official level the pirates were viewed 'as a great hindrance to overseas trade', particularly that coming from the West Indies which found its landfall on the Cork coast.[1]

Piracy is associated with a merciless bloodcurdling disregard for life. Gratuitous torture and cruelty were inflicted on captives to

144

provide amusement before they were dispatched to watery graves. Yet pirates were highly organised. Essential for survival, a strict code of practice evolved among the crews. Disciplined ships and self-regulation were the norm for shipboard life. Captains emerged from among their peers, with specific responsibilities and duties allocated to each crewmember: navigation, gunnery, sail repairs, carpentry, bo'sun's duties, etc. A code determined how and when booty was distributed, based on the share principle similar to the arrangement for bounty payments in other aspects of maritime activity.

In 1610 measures were introduced to counter piracy on the Cork coast. Laws were enacted to prevent tavern, innkeepers and alehouse owners catering for 'lewd and wicked pirates' and if the proprietors did not cooperate with the authorities they would be apprehended and punished. The authorities went so far as to propose that certain remote islands in west Cork be 'laid waste and unpeopled'.

Kinsale Harbour, because of the naval presence, was not frequented by pirates. Yet their impact was significant as was evident in the pardon granted to Patrick and Richard Meade of Kinsale for trading with pirates in 1583.[2] And on entering the harbour, east of Bulman Buoy, is Hangman Point, a prominent 200-foot cliff rising sharply above the sea. A gibbet erected high on the rock was a macabre reminder of the punishment meted out to those who fell foul of the law at sea. Similar chill warnings were familiar at the entrances to other harbours. In the Isles of Scilly approaching New Grimsby Sound from the north, between the islands of Tresco and Bryer, is Hangman Island which gives the leading line in navigating the tricky entrance. Other places of public execution were at Volewijk on the northern entrance to Amsterdam and most notably at Tilbury on the estuary of the River Thames, where the gruesome spectacle of executed pirates hanging in chains acted 'as a great terror to all persons from committing like crimes'. The *London Gazette* reports how six Irish in April 1675, posing as passengers aboard 'a very rich ship the *St Peter of Hamburg* bound for France', murdered the master and three of his crew and sailed the vessel to the west coast of Ireland. The vigilance of Robert Southwell, who was Vice Admiral of Munster, is credited with having the pirates captured and executed. Their heads were set up at different points along the coast, including Kinsale, a grisly sight at Hangman Point.[3] Other punishments, including periods in jail, time in the stocks or transportation, were handed down. But more frequently these were reserved for offences relating to smuggling and wrecking.[4] (For positions of places associated with piracy in the Kinsale area, see plate 3). References to piracy in Kinsale go back to 1380 when Thomas of Walsingham reported that a number of French and Spanish galleys took shelter in Kinsale Harbour after a fleet from the southwest of England forced them to suspend their plundering activities. The anxiety generated by the arrival of these foreign pirates confirmed the need for a town wall and gates to control access through which the movement of goods and travellers could be monitored.[5]

In 1398 a Kinsale ship, *The Mary* was reported at Sluys, the port to the city of Bruges, then the commercial centre of the Netherlands. She was chartered by a Catalan merchant for a voyage to Valencia on the east coast of Spain. The crew, however, mutinied, murdered the merchant and then, as a pirate ship, sailed to Brittany, the Isles of Scilly, Waterford and Dublin, selling off the cargo as they went.[6]

In another reference to piracy Thomas Hanyagh, described as a Kinsale man, was accused in 1449 of freebooting and with other Kinsale mariners was charged with taking a Bristol ship and a Spanish prize.[7]

Richard Colle brought piracy directly to Kinsale with the connivance of the local noble Barry Óg of Rincurran. In July 1548 the Sovereign wrote to Lord Deputy Bellingham saying that 'Pirates prevent victuals and succour operating in the harbour itself. Of late cometh Richard Colle with a pinnace and 18 or 20 men and married Barry Óg's aunt and dwelleth in his castle within our haven and our liberty. There he remained and would not suffer none to come to the town but taketh them and spoileth them which is a great hindrance to us'. The report concludes with the enquiry, 'If it lieth in our power to deal with him we know not, what is your will therein?' In the complaint the Sovereign hints clearly at the complicity of the Barry Ógs, Lords of Kinalea. They had been granted the fisheries, custom and the harbour of Oysterhaven and were widely connected in the area; they were related to the de Courcys of Ringrone and the McCarthy Reaghs of Kilbrittain, both of whom had knowledge of and involvement in piracy. The account is an example of the endemic nature of piracy at the time and the difficulties that existed in dealing with the problem in Kinsale and on the west Cork coast in the sixteenth century.

Although the career of the individual pirate was relatively short, on average not more than five years, the scourge continued relentlessly until the beginning of the eighteenth century. The official response to curb the activity was to have naval ships patrol the coast. Sir Thomas Button, a Welsh seaman who had played a role in winning back the harbour for the English during the Siege of Kinsale in 1601, was based at Kinsale. He was commander of the *Phoenix*, becoming Admiral of the King's ships on the coast of Ireland from 1614 until his death in 1634.

His successes included the capture of a Captain Flemminge, who was hanged in chains at Youghal, and his company executed at Cork in July 1616. Off Oysterhaven, Button took the pirate vessel of a Captain Austin following an eleven-hour encounter, leading to more hangings.[8]

Piracy on the Irish coast was not confined to the Irish or the English. During Button's period, North African corsairs were active on the western approaches. They raided Baltimore in July 1631 and took 109 captives to the Barbary Coast where they were sold as slaves and servants. The original intention was to enter Kinsale but the plan was changed when the corsairs learned that one of Button's ships was in the harbour awaiting supplies. The particular episode has become known as the 'Sack of Baltimore' and is part of Ireland's maritime lore.[9]

The effectiveness of patrolling the coast was limited and as a strategy it was costly. To improve the situation, a radical change of policy was introduced by King James I in 1607. It was the offer of a pardon if a pirate voluntarily withdrew from the activity. One of those who received the amnesty was Captain William Baugh, which had direct implications for Kinsale. Baugh had been pirating ships off the west of Ireland, from the Orkneys to the North African coast, and as a condition of pardon he agreed to come ashore and negotiate the details directly with the Admiralty. En route, aboard his ship *The Lion*, like a reforming gambler, the pirate captain could not resist one last play when three French vessels laden with tempting cargos were encountered at sea. He captured the ships and an estimate of Baugh's personal share was close to £4,000. The inappropriate lapse of trust exacerbated an already delicate international situation and elicited a strong protest from French diplomats to the London authorities. After his arrival at Leamcon near Long Island Sound, Baugh, whose pardon was now in jeopardy, agreed to sail for Kinsale. There he placed himself in the custody of Captain Henry Skipwith, Governor of the Fort at Castlepark, while the naval authorities pursued his case.

The image of romantic adventure is often associated with the activities of pirates. Despite a callous reputation, the handsome Captain Baugh ingratiated himself with the people with his recently acquired wealth, including a gift of 900 pieces of eight which he presented to Skipwith. In accepting the plundered goods the Governor was compromised, giving the pirate the security he required before he delivered his sails to the authorities ashore and thus rendering himself unable to leave harbour. His largesse not alone bought hospitality for Baugh at the Fort but also the affection of Skipwith's daughter where romance blossomed at Castlepark.

There was a limit to what charm and gifts could buy, however. Delicate diplomacy with the French and the Lord Deputy's reluctance 'to have any meddling in the affairs of pirates' required that Baugh appear before the Admiralty Court in London. Much of the original booty was by then pilfered and dissipated. The Court had the function of resolving the various and conflicting interests and at the same time upholding the King's policy of granting pardon to pirates. The judgement was a classic fudge where Baugh was criticised severely but still retained a portion of the plunder which in an obscure legal interpretation was compensation for amounts that had been hived off by various officials after being landed in Kinsale.

Baugh died soon afterwards. The affair, much of which transpired in Kinsale, exposed the weaknesses inherent in dealing with pirates, the vacillation of the authorities, and the complicity of officials at all levels, despite protestations to the contrary. The pirates themselves viewed Baugh's surrender in Kinsale as undertaken in bad faith which cast doubt on the credibility of the authorities and damaged the promise held out by the pardon. Many, in fact, returned to pirating with 'more appetite and malice'. Needless to say, little of the plunder was returned to the original owners from whom it was looted. By 1614 the policy of appeasement and pardon was seen as a failure and under the Irish Piracy Act of that year it was laid down specifically that pirates were to be hanged by the shore, which no doubt, provided further spectacles at Hangman Point.[10]

Pirates cruised the craggy coast off Kinsale seeking vulnerable prey. While rarely entering the harbour, they had a temporary haven on which to land stolen goods and restore supplies of water and provisions close by at Bullen's Bay. The submerged reefs in the area are a dangerous lee shore in a southeasterly and ships, drawn on to these rocks in poor visibility, presented easy pickings and wrecking opportunities for the people of the area.

Anne Cormac, a vivacious girl in her teens, came to live in this isolated community in 1695. She lived with her father, William, in a fine house on the edge of Bullen's Bay. The spirited young woman shared in encounters with the sea and witnessed at first hand what accidental sea wreckage and nefarious maritime activity could produce. Her father, a successful Cork lawyer, emigrated with his daughter to the Carolinas in America where he had acquired a plantation. After a short time, despite her father's best efforts, Anne, now sixteen years old, was drawn to the sea and soon met and married a small-time pirate by the name of Bonny. Ambitious and not satisfied with her husband's low-level involvement, the young bride while ashore at Nassau in the Caribbean fell for the charms of 'Calico' Jack Rackham, a notorious and ruthless buccaneer who from 1718 to 1720 terrorised the seas and coasts of Bermuda and Hispaniola aboard *The William*, a stolen sloop.

Pirates consorted with women not just as partners but as associates who ashore aided and abetted the clandestine activity. Females rarely went to sea as the cramped conditions, the violence, heavy drinking and masculine milieu made shipboard life an unlikely option for women, and in any case a woman's presence would have been highly disruptive. Anne was the exception. Dressed as a man, she relished the sea-going life, actively participating in the piracy. She is on occasions depicted bare-breasted, vaulting over gunwales of vessels grappled together, with a cutlass in hand and had the reputation of being a merciless accomplice of Rackham. A number of pregnancies interrupted her sea-going but after short periods of confinement and having the babies fostered, Anne returned to sea and piracy.

Woodes Rogers, who called frequently to Kinsale, was an English privateer. For a short period he was appointed Governor of the Bahamas with a specific brief, directly from King George I, to hunt down the pirates who were creating havoc in the area. One of his captures was Rackham and crew, which included Anne. They were charged and found guilty and the mandatory punishment of hanging in chains at Gallow's Point in Port Royal was handed down. On appeal Anne's sentence was reprieved as she was pregnant. But her callous unrelenting toughness could not be illustrated better than in her final words to Rackham as he was about to face the hangman, when she is reputed to have said, 'I am sorry to see you here, Jack, but if you had fought like a man, you would not now be hanged like a dog.'

It is reasonable to speculate on how Anne's formative years at the Old Head of Kinsale may have given her a taste for piracy. No precise information is available about her after Rackham's death. There are reports that she abandoned piracy, was reconciled with her father, remarried and had eight more children.[11]

By 1730 the incidence of piracy had greatly reduced due to more aggressive strategies adopted by the Navy Board which had constructed a number of fast frigates, including the HMS *Kinsale*, capable of overhauling pirate ships at sea. Also punishment and scenes such as those visible at Hangman Point were a strong deterrent.

Piracy was not the only illicit activity conducted on the high seas. Smuggling and activities connected with shipwreck were rampant off Kinsale. Hitting at the heart of the town's economy, smuggling was the evasion of toll payments on the import and export of designated goods and dealing in products that were prohibited by the authorities. The activity thrived at times when tariffs were high and scarce goods were in demand.

In the eighteenth century more than half of all tea, tobacco, brandy, wine and pepper landed in Ireland was smuggled. Eighty per cent of fleeces were illegally exported because trade in Irish woollens was restricted in 1699 as these products were oversupplying the market, reducing the price available to English sheep farmers. Sheep nevertheless remained an integral part of Irish agriculture and running the gauntlet to the French coast was profitable for the Irish smuggler. Apart from traded goods, smugglers also transported fugitives from the Williamite Wars to join the Irish Brigades fighting in various conflicts on the continent.[12] Sources of the illicit goods shipped into Ireland were ports such as Nantes, Roscoff and the islands of Guernsey and the Isle of Man, which were noted smuggler haunts.

In the early years of Charles II's reign more determined efforts to curb smuggling were introduced, by strengthening customs and preventative procedures and recruiting additional searchers, gaugers and informers. To avoid detection the smugglers devised ingenious methods of secretly transporting the goods. Watertight timber casks, which could be hidden in rocky inaccessible inlets, were used for carriage. Aboard vessels tobacco, spices and brandy were concealed in hollow masts, and in false and disguised bulkheads. The law was manipulated by altering the alcohol concentration of the liquor which involved sophisticated distilling processes.[13]

Because of the risk of being observed, smugglers tended to operate on more dangerous, less frequented parts of the coast. Landings took place at night, often in poor misty weather when visibility was down. Six-oared seine boats were manoeuvred alongside remote rocky ledges where some shelter might be expected in the lee of a high cliff. But in these conditions there was the constant risk from the 'scend' of the surging sea which could leave a boat holed or capsized.

One of the locations used in the Kinsale area was in the bay south of Money Point known locally as Bog Hole. 'Bog' in the name may be derived from *boc*, *bac* or *tobac*, variations of the French for tobacco. With Farmer Rock a danger in the bay, Bog Hole was a classic location for the clandestine handling of banned goods. The products, small in volume but financially valuable, were spirited away by the community who lived on this exposed, remote and difficult-to-access part of the harbour.[14]

On the opposite eastern shore at Middle Cove, the French Consul Coquebert de Monbret visited the area in 1790 and described a conversation he had with the daughter of a household in the area. He clearly indicates that the peasant girl, with whom he conversed in French, had visited Lorient on the west coast of Brittany and hints that the purpose of these trips was related to smuggling.[15]

Entering Oysterhaven, east of Kinsale and close to Ballymacus Point, is Pointe Éalú or Ealaidore, which was associated with smuggling. Also known as Watcher's Point, it had wide views of the open sea, giving early warning for those engaged in the nefarious activity. Jack Connor, a well-known smuggler in the seventeenth century, was one of those responsible for giving the area its dubious reputation.[16]

Another method of trading in contraband was to link up with French and Dutch smugglers at sea who, like travelling salesmen, sailed along the coast and supplied fishermen with tobacco and liquor. They were called 'floating grog ships'. Conchúr Ó Síocháin from Cape Clear describes how tobacco and brandy were purchased from Lord John, a Dutch trader in 1895. Subsequently, while weatherbound in Baltimore, his vessel was searched by customs officers who discovered the illicit goods under nets in the hold. In this case, having been arraigned before the local magistrate, the fishermen were treated leniently and received a small fine. Ó Síocháin suggests that the fishermen had been informed on.[17]

The role of the informer was important to the authorities and the system on which the detection process greatly depended. As an incentive the informer received between one third and a half of the seized goods if the evidence was strong enough to support a conviction. Generally the community did not cooperate with the customs authorities and tacitly tolerated the activity of smugglers. Even the clergy admitted that smuggling held no moral opprobrium for the people, saying that 'they cannot be convinced it is a sin'. Particular community contempt was reserved for the informers who, when discovered, were viciously attacked. In 1735 *The Dublin Evening Post* reported the murder of an informer at Kinsale by a group of unemployed Cork weavers. He had revealed the identity of the captain of a ship with a cargo of woollen cloth destined for Portugal.[18] Other punishments known to have been meted out to informants in the Cork area included having their tongues cut out.[19] Following the hazardous task of landing, the goods were sequestered away to secret storage locations. From here they were distributed through the countryside on packhorses, usually at night. Passing through a network of contacts the illicit trade was eventually sold at outlets after being hawked by pedlars from fair to fair which broadened the consumer base and trading opportunities.[20]

In walled towns the objective for the smuggler was to get the goods through the gates and trade openly in the market. It was a form of 'laundering' in that the prohibition would then be lifted and the goods would have gained in value by being available on the open market. In Kinsale the smuggled goods were transported from isolated landing places such as Bog Hole or Sandy Cove, carried over the 'Saddle' at Ringrone and ferried across the river to the sand quays in the marsh at the foot of Commoge, Cappagh or Ballinacubby. The marsh was open to the river before the causeway, bearing the road, was constructed in the nineteenth century.[21] On calm, dark nights at high tide, with rowlocks muffled to reduce the creak of oars and blades gently dipped in the water to avoid the sound of the splash, the contraband was secretly brought ashore. For the curious observer, who might come on the furtive activity, the surrounding area was reputed to be haunted. Older members of the community still refer to Cappagh Lane, which overlooks the marsh, as 'Botharín na Spride' in Irish meaning 'the haunted lane of the spirits', which might frighten off the curious or those who would inform the authorities.

The final stage in transporting these goods to market was the short journey that involved passing through Nicholas Gate in the town wall where access was monitored and tolls collected. At this particular gate, however, corrupt officials were reputed to be in collusion with the fraud. Because of the incidence of smuggling, the gate in Irish was known as 'Geata na nGabhar' – gabhar being an Irish word for contraband. By the end of the seventeenth century the loss of revenue was such that the Corporation ordered the permanent closure or 'blinding' of the gate. While the opening has long since been removed, the surrounding area is still known as Blind Gate and a reminder of covert activity in the town's past.[22]

At sea complex ploys were used to divert attention and frustrate pursuers. An account in the *Annals of Kinsale* for 30 May 1739 describes how an Irish smuggler got on the far side of a net shot by French fishermen, which blocked a customs cutter in pursuit as it then fouled the nets. By the time the excise men had cut themselves free 'the sun was rising on a new day' and the smugglers had disappeared over the horizon. The authorities claimed that 'the accident prevented a sizable seizure of wool'.

The case was doubly embarrassing for His Majesty's officers in that when the French men followed the cutter to Kinsale in an effort to retrieve their nets, the fishing boat was also seized. The action created a diplomatic incident with the English representative in Paris being summoned to the French court to explain. The Secretary to Ireland, Burchett, was asked to investigate. He reported that the reason for taking the boat and gear to Kinsale was not as a result of interference in the pursuit of the smuggler, but to teach the French a lesson not to fish so near the coast, as Kinsale 'fishermen were reduced to beggary'.[23] The outcome was that the property was returned to the French and the smuggler was not apprehended.

Apart from preventative measures initiated by the Navy Board, legislation was introduced to prevent smuggling and improve surveillance. Swift customs cutters were placed on the coast from 1730 and much later, in 1809, water-guards were established. In 1822 the different agencies amalgamated and reorganised to form a coastguard service.[24] Its function was to act as a maritime guard having observation, detection and defence roles in the post-Napoleonic era. The officers served at sea in revenue cutters and ashore lived in stations built around the coast. In the Kinsale area, the remains of solid military-style buildings still stand at Howe Strand, the Old Head, Oysterhaven and at Summer Cove, which was designated as the lead station for the area in 1858.

The determination of the authorities to deal with smuggling produced results. By 1850 the incidence was greatly reduced in communities where it had hitherto been rampant. Apart from coast-watching duties, the coastguard worked closely with custom officers monitoring the movement of vessels and in Kinsale they provided information to the harbour authorities to assist in the collection of dues.

Coastguards were trained in sea rescue and saved many from drowning. The pole, now in poor condition at Sallyport near Charles Fort, is a reminder of the training methods practised by the officers in the use of rescue equipment. The procedure involved firing a rocket, with a breeches buoy attached, from the shore over a stricken vessel which when attached to the ship enabled the crew to be safely drawn ashore. One of many rescues undertaken was of the *Glaramara* which dragged her anchors between the Sovereign Islands on a night in February 1883. All hands were saved despite the severe weather.[25] The grounding of the *City of Chicago* on the rocks of the Old Head of Kinsale on the evening of 22 June 1892 with 360 passengers

Coastguard station at Summercove, Kinsale on hill to the right, *c*.1896.
Courtesy Lawrence Collection

could have been a disastrous tragedy but for the intervention of the coastguard. They assisted 200 in climbing to safety up the steep cliff at Ringurteen Point. The remainder were taken off by boat without a single casualty.[26]

Despite the positive work undertaken by the coastguard there was suspicion among the community towards them because of their association with the garrisons at the barracks in the town and Charles Fort. Secondly, to avoid the temptation of becoming complicit in smuggling or being compromised by the community, the officers lived in isolated compounds and avoided familiarity with local people. Many were English and this contributed to their non-acceptance. A total complement of seventy men operated in the Kinsale area.[27]

The memory of a child of one of the officers gives an account of life at the new Lispatrick station on the Old Head in the period 1917 to 1922.[28] Together with the three families of lighthouse

155

keepers, twelve coastguard families made up this isolated community. They had plentiful supplies of fish which were caught from the rocks accessed by steps to Gunhole or Cuas Gorm on either side of the headland. For the more adventurous a jack yard was rigged on which a young person was lowered to gather seagull's eggs from the cliffs. Each family had its own plot in which vegetables were grown and hardy goats, which could survive the harsh conditions, were kept to supply milk, cheese and butter. When there was a surplus of kid goats they were fattened and slaughtered for meat. As fresh water was a problem on the headland, rainfall from roofs was stored in tanks or drawn from a small well at Gunhole. The group were mainly self-sufficient and socially quite viable as a community.

However, difficulties arose in dealings with the locals whose lives were comparatively poor. This was particularly true for the children who attended the local school where they encountered hostility. Antipathy towards the coastguard was heightened during the War of Independence when the authorities felt it necessary to deploy a party of the Essex Regiment on the Old Head to 'defend the colony against possible attack'. The families were, in fact, under siege and, as supplies and services could not be supplied by road, HMS *Tring* was used to land goods by sea at the Cuas or Gunhole.

When the Treaty was signed in 1921 and adopted by the Free State government, the British-sponsored coastguard operation was disbanded and the families on the Old Head returned to Britain. The end of the old regime coincided with a change of emphasis away from preventative duties toward a focus on search-and-rescue services. Under the Irish government, the coastguard continues on a semi-voluntary basis at the Old Head and at Summer Cove in Kinsale Harbour, where it provides an invaluable service and support particularly at times when tragic loss or a coastal emergency arise.

Among the various methods put in place to collect revenue in Kinsale was a system of customs control which was established under the provisions of the first charter in the fourteenth century. The officials, appointed by the Corporation, reported directly to the Sovereign. The original Custom House was Desmond Castle located inside Cork Gate at the top of Chairman's Lane which gave direct access to the Inner Harbour. As the town developed, encroaching further into the harbour, the customs office was moved to the Market House, now the Museum. In the eighteenth century, at the busiest period of harbour activity, the Custom House was relocated to Lower Fisher (O'Connell) Street where it functioned until its closure in 1992. Since then the work of the customs has been undertaken by mobile units on land and at sea and is coordinated from Cork. At Fisher (O'Connell) Street the office was on the edge of the waterfront, close to the Town Rock, with its own landing place which was incorporated into the new Pier in the 1880s. The customs and excise operation required bond houses in which goods were stored until required and dues were paid. Extensive warehousing at the Glen and at the Custom House itself was built for this purpose.

Customs revenue collection systems changed over the centuries. Major developments were introduced in 1643 to finance the English Civil War. Excise or 'riding' men monitored the movement of goods on land and in 1809 a preventative water-guard using fast cutters was established on the coast. The customs office at Kinsale carried a large staff. Records for 1815 show that the harbour authorities employed a collector at £100 per annum and other officials such as port and tide surveyors, tide and land waiters and ten boatmen. Also included was a surveyor of excise and a gauger.[29] The surveillance area extended from Robert's Head at the entrance to Cork Harbour to the Galley Head, a total of 26 miles, which included hundreds of inlets, bays and harbours. Latterly, reflecting the low level of activity, the staff complement was reduced to just one officer, for whom it was an impossible task to maintain even a minimum level of surveillance.[30]

Apart from the customs and excise function, officials had responsibility for immigration in the port, mostly concerning foreign sailors who landed and were paid off at Kinsale. The office also was the intermediary between shipping companies and the families of crewmen at sea on long voyages. Wives or mothers went to the Custom House to receive the 'half pay', which was sent through the office to provide support for the family at home.

Among other functions conducted by customs was to board a ship on its arrival in harbour from a foreign port. On the starboard side of the mast the yellow 'Q' signal flag was flown which signalled a healthy ship and that it was requesting 'free pratique' or clearance for the crew to go ashore and conduct business. The officers would also check that crew members were healthy and not suffering from contagious illness. If there was sickness aboard, the individual would be quarantined and prevented from leaving the vessel until cleared by the medical officer.

Another health-related aspect of the customs officer's duties was the disposal of dead animals found in the harbour or river. When a carcass was discovered it was taken from the water and properly buried. A bounty was awarded to the individual who undertook this work upon presentation to the customs officer of a severed ear or tail of the animal as evidence.

Of great significance were duties involved in taking depositions from survivors after a ship foundered or ran aground. The task was undertaken by the customs authorities in their capacity as Receiver of Wrecks. They had the legal statutory role of apportioning blame which could be used in evidence to decide on insurance claims and salvage rights and to act as the intermediary between the different stakeholders who claimed ownership of the cargo or the stricken vessel itself. The goods included what were jettisoned and left scattered on the sea after a ship grounded or cargo shifted, causing the vessel to list. Flotsam, which was cargo that broke loose and went overboard, was also included in the fraught process of making judgement calls between competing claimants who were often in conflict.

Many attempts were made to regulate issues around ships that were wrecked. As evidence was invariably confused, decisions were difficult to determine. Under the Merchant Shipping Act of 1894 the role of the Receiver of Wrecks was set down. The objective was to prevent looting, to arbitrate between various claimants and return goods to the owner. The receiver also acted as broker in the event of a dispute and determined the payment due to the salver who may have incurred expense or been exposed to risk in saving the goods. If the owner of a wreck could not be found then the goods were divided in three ways: to the local authority, the state coffers and a portion to the finder.

Shipwreck often occurs on dark nights in stormy conditions, producing danger and panic among passengers and crew. Wrecking, the active procuring of a wreck, was associated with the use of false lights, misleading signals or corrupt pilots who drove vessels onto rocks so that accomplices could ravage and pillage. Incidents were extremely rare but when caught the perpetrators were punished 'by death as in cases of felony without the benefit of clergy'. Novels such as du Maurier's *Jamaica Inn* and the film *Whisky Galore,* based on fiction, have contributed to promoting a false and a rather romanticised image of wrecking.

More common were situations that arose when a ship, in danger of going aground on a perilous shore, led people to focus on the possible benefits that the stricken vessel might produce for themselves in terms of wreckage or salvage. In those circumstances the possibility of saving the ship or the unfortunate crew and passengers became a matter of secondary importance. It was not unknown for survivors who managed to scramble ashore to be robbed and even murdered to prevent them giving evidence that could bring a conviction. Attempts to put a sea code in place go back to 1266 when the French drafted the Rules of Oléron to prevent malpractice. Even though the code became the basis of maritime law throughout Europe, the 'plundering and destroying of vessels in distress … and wilful obstructing the escape of any person endeavouring to save his or her life' continued into the eighteenth century.

From these examples of criminality at one extreme, there is still the quite legitimate practice of beachcombing and the collection of flotsam lost from a ship, which was common on the coasts near Kinsale. Seen as the sea's bounty, material such as timber was used for roofing, floorboards, lintels, fencing and even for boatbuilding. A bolt of torn canvas from a wreck would provide a suit of sails. The justification for taking possession of material in these circumstances was that it had been abandoned and if not salvaged would be destroyed by the sea. It was a form of scavenging and was perceived to be 'as legal as breathing' in a culture around wreck where the people are the passive recipients of the sea's largesse washed up on beaches or fouled on rocks. The attitude to possession and sense of ownership were further reinforced if the finder had risked injury in descending a cliff face, giving a further claim to at least a share of the value. After a storm in Kinsale Harbour in 1990 when a small sailing boat went ashore on the rocks at Scilly a local man openly proclaimed to the owner that he was taking possession of gear he had salvaged from the boat. What was taken was small but the incident illustrates very well the ambiguity attached to practices around wrecking which are endemic among people who live close to the shore.[31]

Particular examples of the sea's bounty show that Kinsale was no different from other coastal areas. In a report to Sir Robert Southwell from the Governor of Castlepark Fort in 1687 there is an account of retrieving several casks of brandy, floating off the Old Head of Kinsale after a French trader went down. This was only a portion of the liquor as the authorities, who went to investigate, were the butt of 'the rudeness of the country people who drank so plentifully of the brandy that some died on the place and others so ill thereof that it is thought many will follow them'.[32]

In the following year by contrast, Southwell in a letter to Samuel Pepys reported that 'butter (apparently lost overboard from a ship) beaten into the rocks not far from Kinsale, was raked out with poles and sold later for 9 livre', an example of how enterprising wreckers benefited from what the sea threw up.

When the *City of Chicago* became wedged on the rock of Ringurteen Point at the Old Head in 1892 some of her cargo spilled into the sea. After four days she broke her back and as the vessel's iron hull ground on the rocks her hold split open, tipping sides of cured bacon into the sea. These were quickly garnered by local boats and provided food for many families in the area for a considerable period afterwards.[33]

Salvage was also attempted on the *Falls of Garry* which foundered off Ballymacus Point in April 1911. The cargo of wheat aboard the hapless ship was acquired by the owners of Jagoe's Mills, near Kinsale before she sank completely. The cargo, however, was contaminated by salt water and declared a total loss. A female figurehead from under the bowsprit was saved and for many years was mounted on a block on the lawn of Acton's Hotel in Kinsale.[34]

Many other vessels were wrecked on the rough craggy coast off Kinsale Harbour, in the rock-strewn Bullen's Bay and on the submerged reefs off Courtmacsherry which were traps for numerous sailing vessels in foul weather and poor visibility. These locations provided easy prey for looters and wreckers.

Pirating, smuggling and wrecking were all part of the nefarious underbelly of a busy and successful port. Seafaring at best was a hard and tough experience. It was inevitable that taking advantage, legitimately or otherwise, would arise from the unfortunate circumstances that occur at sea.

7

Bandon River

The Bandon River was the transport link to much of the Kinsale hinterland and was used extensively prior to steam power and the internal combustion engine. While slow and dependent on weather and tides, the river bore enormous quantities of cargo to and from landing places in the baronies of Kinalea, east of the Harbour, Kinealmeaky on the northern bank of the river, Carbery to the west, and the Courcies on the southside.

Apart from its significance as a means of transport, the river provided water for industry in the Bandon, Innishannon, Kilmacsimon and Ballinadee areas. Each settlement was the commercial hub of an extensive countryside and rich agricultural hinterland. In a 12-mile navigable stretch, the river was the connection to Kinsale and through the harbour to the wider world.

Bandon, at the other end of the navigable link, was one of the new towns established at the beginning of the seventeenth century to advance the colonial process and to secure the settlement. It quickly became the second largest town in the county (next to Cork) with a population in 1821 of just over 10,000, twice that of Kinsale.[1]

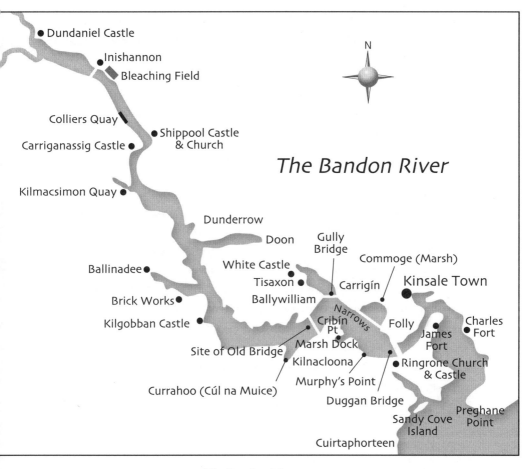

The Bandon River.

Apart from the settled towns and the valuable land close to the river, the territory was occupied by 'Irish enemies and English rebels'. They were barely tolerated by the urban authorities as demonstrated in presentments to the Corporation at Kinsale which describe the native population as 'strangers and foreigners'. However, when it came to economic interest, expediency prevailed. If the market required extra produce it brought in goods from the outlying areas with access to the river. The trading burgesses of Kinsale acquired or built castles and tower houses located in the most favourable positions. They established landing places on the riverbank where the tide ran fast and deep and at the top of creeks such as at White Castle. The ruins of Rincurran, Ringrone and Kilgobban remain. Shippool Castle (or *Poll na Long*) was built by Philip Roche in 1544 under licence from Henry VIII. The de Barrys constructed a fine structure at Dundaniel, which stands on an important site where the rivers Brinny and Bandon come together. It was close to a ford, one of the earliest crossing points on the river.

Describing the river, Samuel Lewis in 1839 said that it was navigable to Colliers Quay for ships up to 200 tons.[2] Skilled pilots, appointed by the authorities for their seamanship, experience and knowledge, guided vessels to this point. Each section of the passage presented different problems and so important was the task that at its second meeting in December 1870 the Kinsale Harbour Board designated Pat Kelly and Dan Kiely as river pilots. They also fixed the dues at 1d per ton for cargo inward and ½d outward, rates which would encourage exports. Having arrived in Kinsale and depending on wind direction, vessels often carried sails as far as Murphy's Point where they were furled. Then the long, slow progress upriver began with the help of local knowledge and the assistance of incoming tides. Kedging was used, which involved the laying ahead of the ship's anchor by its tender and then having the vessel haul on its own cable. The river presented a number of hazards for the ships as they had poor steerage with little 'way' and the high freeboards were subject to the effect of the wind in the narrow channel. Skill and knowledge were required of the pilot and skipper, with special care needed in approaching the opening swivel section of the Western Bridge. The pilot had also to contend with extensive mudbanks, deceptively covered by water on both sides of the river at the Folly, Commoge and across the river at Ringfinnan. As the fairway narrowed, stretches of mud at Currahoo and Ballinadee had to be avoided. On occasions, vessels were blown on to the wide banks off Killany, the Doon and Dunderrow in strong westerly winds. Overcompensation in avoiding the eastern side had vessels aground south of Kilmacsimon. Further on, the pilot headed for the deep water off Rock House and the bend at Carriganassig. The helm was then instructed to cross to the bend under Shippool. The approach to Colliers Quay was gained by gently 'crabbing' across the stream. In 1900 to assist navigation the Harbour

Board purchased and placed 120 stakes to mark the channel, which for a period provided guidance.

While the river is tidal to the bridge at Innishannon, Kilmacsimon and Colliers Quays were the navigable limits for commercial traffic. Kilmacsimon provided the port facilities for Bandon and, as it was essential for the manufacturing interests of the inland town, the Act of Parliament, which established Kinsale Harbour Board, made provision for representation from Bandon's distilling, brewing and agriculture interests. Four meetings a year were held at Kilmacsimon.

The importance of Kilmacsimon Quay was constantly highlighted by Lord Bandon, a member of the Board, who was concerned at the condition of the quay walls and slipways. Coal, maize, fertiliser and cement were landed and stored in extensive warehousing. Exports consisted of large quantities of eggs, butter, oats, corn, wool and manufactured products such as whiskey and beer. Timber was felled from the surrounding woods on the riverbanks and taken for use as pit props in the coal mines of South Wales.[3] Older members of the community remember up to twelve vessels in the 1940s waiting to discharge cargo. The handling of goods gave employment to local men as casual dockers, supplementing meagre incomes from fishing and small land holdings.

Prior to the tsunami that followed the Great Lisbon Earthquake on 1 November 1755, which later hit the Irish coast, it was possible to travel on the river to Bandon in shallow-draught lighters. There was enough water for the East India Company to have waterborne access to the iron smelter which it established at Dundaniel in 1612. The earthquake that struck Lisbon, killing 35,000 of its inhabitants, had its epicentre 200 kilometres west of the city in the Atlantic.[4] The underwater fissures created an enormous wave which sent a sudden 10-foot-high surge of water sweeping into Kinsale Harbour, flooding the town and Market Square. It roared up the valley of the Bandon River becoming even more vigorous as it narrowed in the upper reaches. People, boats, buildings and the bridge at Innishannon were swept away.[5] The impact on the river bottom was similar to a wave crashing on a beach with a force that shifted large stones, carried away banks and radically changed water levels. The effect, in practical terms, was that the river above Innishannon could no longer be used; vessels could now get only as far as Kilmacsimon and Colliers Quays.

Because of the economic importance of the river as a means of transport, its extension west of Bandon, by the construction of a canal, had been actively considered. In 1631, plans were drawn to build a navigable waterway from Colliers Quay to Bandon.[6] Further reports and surveys undertaken included a proposal by P. Aher of Cork in 1800 which showed the location of locks, weirs, and sluice gates to build an aqueduct to the west of Ballineen which would carry ships a further 18 miles to Dunmanway, the final destination.[7] Debate among property owners and vested interests followed, each putting forward arguments about the precise route which would produce the best advantage for themselves. Ultimately the project was considered overambitious and in fact was superseded in the nineteenth century by the emergence of the rail system and the construction of the road network, which for the first time offered alternatives to waterborne traffic.

Apart from the landing places and quays associated with the tower houses, there were many locations on the waterfront which acted as the interface between the river and the land. Small, rocky ledges and sheltered coves can still be identified at the end of overgrown pathways zigzagging their way from high ground to the riverbanks. The remains of more formally constructed sand quays are still visible, some totally dilapidated, which can be identified by the corner stones still standing. While they functioned, straining horses drew cartloads up the wheel-rutted inclines from the vessels lying at the quays.

As the name suggests, the quays were used to land sand, sometimes referred to as sea manure, which was dredged from the Swallow in Kinsale Harbour off the Dock beach. Vast quantities were spread on the land as fertiliser. The sand consisted of lime, which is the breakdown of shell and marine organisms, and compensated for the acid content of the peat soil prevalent in the Bandon and Innishannon areas. In fact George Bennett, writing in 1862, tells us that these boats unloaded the lime-rich sand and returned to Kinsale filled with turf and other agricultural products from upriver.[8]

The distribution of the sand throughout the area was a large and complex operation which in itself generated economic activity.

An acre of land required a typical boatload, which made up twenty cartloads, each weighing 5 or 6 hundredweight. Smaller consignments were carried in bags straddled on horses' backs. At Kinsale alone 250 carts transported the sand to the hinterland.[9]

The availability of this material in the Kinsale area was particularly suitable for the growing of potatoes which 'are mentioned specifically in 1665' and 'by 1700 were in sufficient quantities in the Bandon valley for a specific tithe to be levied upon them'.[10] While Kinsale Workhouse, drawing its destitute from the wider Poor Law catchment area, recorded a very high incidence of mortality during the Great Famine (1845–50), some of the worst impacts were mitigated in the limited Kinsale/Bandon area because of the more productive potato farming.[11]

In addition the fecundity of the crop created opportunities for other enterprises. A starch mill was established at Belgooly which took the surplus in the potato crop from 1832. In 1835 a near riot took place when the owner attempted to cut the price of the raw material. The growers planned a mass protest, which was stood down at the last moment, because a proclamation on public posters, issued by the Kinsale magistrates warned that anyone attending would be transported to Australia for seven years.

The taking of sand was encouraged by the authorities 'for the benefit and importance of Kinsale' as it cleared the silt and maintained the fairway which was essential for naval operations and the expansion of harbour services. The issue was discussed at Whitehall, London, in the presence of King Charles II in February 1669. There it was decided that sand could only be taken from the 'said banks below Rincorran and near the Blockhouse and take away all that they shall need for their lands', in other words, from the harbour itself, emphasised even more by a ban on the taking of sand from Sandy Cove.[12]

The process of collecting the soil-enriching material was labour-intensive work. One method involved dredging, using a self-closing mechanism which was lowered to the bottom, where it sank into the sand and was then retrieved by hauling on the connecting line to the surface. A more basic method was to shovel the sand into a boat in shallow water on a rising tide. Evenly supported by the water the floating craft remained sound, avoiding structural damage which would occur if allowed to ground. The temptation on occasions was to overload and, with little freeboard, the boats foundered, sometimes with tragic consequences.[13]

Despite the difficult, dangerous and hard work it is reported that the sand boats presented a wonderful scene in a favourable breeze as they sailed to the quays on the river. After the Famine there was a decline in the use of sand but the practice continued up to the 1950s.[14]

The remnants of six sand quays are still visible in the Kinsale marsh. Prior to the construction of the road causeway, the area flooded on each tide, with water flowing unhindered from the river. The quays close to Ballinacubby gave direct access through Nicholas Gate to the town market for agricultural produce, fish and smuggled goods. In addition it was to these landing places in 1830 that stone, quarried across the river at Kilnacloona, was carried for use in the construction of St John the Baptist parish church. Surrounded by the high ground of Cappagh, Knocknacurra and Commoge, and long before the World's End road was built, the marsh was of significance in the seventeenth and eighteenth centuries.

After the road-bearing causeway was built the link with the river was cut off and the quays fell into disuse. In the middle of what was essentially a barrier, sluice gates were inserted to control the flow of water in and out of the area. Close by are the remains of walled banks, which suggest that a canal was considered to maintain the water link with the river. This connection to the town became unnecessary after the construction of the road system and the emergence of steam rail.

On each tide quantities of salt water enter the marsh through the sluices and trapdoors in the wall. By mixing with fresh water, which flows from the surrounding hills, the area has evolved a brackish habitat that produces a diverse and interesting ecology. The alder and the reed growing in the wet marshy conditions provide sheltered feeding for wading birds and a variety of flora and fauna. Commonly seen in the marsh are shelduck, mallard, greenshank and redshank and the odd flash of brilliant colour from a darting kingfisher.[15]

The availability of extensive forests on both sides of the river attracted a range of industrial activity to the area. (The Bandon River was frequently referred to as *An Glas Linn* or 'the Green River'

Loading pit props at Shippool Castle, 1900. The church was removed in 1968.
Courtesy Tony Bocking

because of the sylvan reflection in the water and was described in these terms by the Spaniards when they arrived in Kinsale in 1601.) The ironworks established by the East India Company at Dundaniel, shipbuilding at Kilmacsimon and Kinsale, limekilns at Shippool, the brickworks at Ballinadee and tanning at Bandon used large quantities of timber for fuelling the manufacturing involved.[16]

Three hundred English settlers, familiar with the process of smelting ore, established an ironworks at Dundaniel in 1612. The ore was mined in Ireland or brought in by boat using the river for transport. A hundred tons of timber was cleared from the forests to produce the 25 tons of charcoal that was required to yield 10 tons of pig iron. The charcoal, fired in furnaces, was reddened by water-powered bellows to generate the intense heat needed for smelting. Anchors, chainplates, bolts, nails, rudder pintles and gudgeons, mast hounds and the myriad other fittings required for ship building were produced from the material.[17]

Two ships, of 500 and 600 tons, were completed for the East India Company at Kilmacsimon in 1613 and in 1700 the 120-foot-long HMS *Kinsale* was built at the Dockyard. Each of these vessels, which were approximately equal in size, would have required 40 acres of wood for construction. At that rate of felling, with no plan for replanting or coppicing, the area was quickly denuded of trees, which also had the effect of depriving lawless groups, known as rapparees and tories, of cover. Forest stripping would expose 'ye wild Irish and uncover the wood kern from their hiding places who created a constant threat to the new settlers'.[18]

The brickworks at the entrance to Ballinadee Creek drew on large quantities of timber to fire the ovens in the process of manufacturing brick. The slob and sand, the basic materials, were available from the river and were dried in moulds. The riverside operation, noted for the billowing, smutty smoke it produced, was run for generations by the Crowley family. The bricks were used extensively in Kinsale. A Famine project, started in the area for the purpose of linking Ballinadee to Kilmacsimon by a roadway to transport the brick, like many similar projects at the time was never completed.

An industry, which was also dependent on water from the river, was the manufacture of linen at Innishannon. For bleaching purposes flax, the raw material, was spread on the flat low-lying surface close to the water of the river which today is the location of the local GAA grounds. The industry was introduced to the area by the Adderly family who had received lands in the aftermath of the 1642 uprising.[19]

The river is the natural boundary of baronies, parishes and townlands. While it provided the transport medium between Kinsale and Bandon, it was also crossed from one side to the other. Initially locations were chosen based on their suitability for the construction of a ford where the river was wide and shallow. Deeper sections were crossed in ferries. Bridges offered many advantages but restricted the free movement of boats. Irrespective of ownership, control of these crossings was a powerful and valuable asset which on occasions gave rise to conflict. Regulation was required and a licensing system was put in place. The earliest reference to a ferry crossing on the river was

Ferry crossing (1937). *Courtesy Irish Examiner*

in 1240 when Philip de Barry of Innishannon was granted permission by Henry III.

Fording of rivers was associated with the building of weirs. Stones now scattered across the river on the bend at Curranure, just above Dundaniel, are the remnants of an early ford. Below the bridge at Innishannon close to the island of Innis Abhinn, from which the village takes its name, was Boithrín an Átha which loosely translates as 'the little road to the ford'.[20]

From earliest times crossings on several parts of the river were undertaken in boats. A significant ferry point was that from Carrigín at the foot of Cappagh lane to a landing on the opposite side in the townland of Kilnacloona. Before the causeway across the marsh was constructed in the early nineteenth century, Cappagh was the most direct connection from Kinsale through Friar's Gate to the river and 'over the water' to the Courcies. The river crossing at this point is still referred to as 'The Narrows'. Closer to Kinsale another boat ran from the World's End to the Dock at Castlepark which in the early part of the twentieth century was operated by the O'Donovan family. Crossing in all weathers, from the most pleasant summer days to winter sleet and near gale, the task of rowing the open boat was shared by the passengers. Memories remain of children travelling to school at Kinsale in the boat crabbing her way across, direction dictated by the tide. For attendance at church in Kinsale, the boat was often crowded with women protecting themselves and the children from spray and rain in their black, hooded cloaks. Christmas Mass was celebrated in the Kinsale Carmelite Friary at 6.00 a.m., which many from Castlepark attended, crossing in the darkness of the early morning. The landing places on the Kinsale side could vary from the Ferry Slip to either the Pier Head or the Lobster Quay depending on the wind and tide, of which the people were acutely aware.

Men, women and children had respect for the river and the inherent danger of travelling in an open boat. At a time when buoyancy aids and lifejackets were rare, people had an in-built sense of good seamanship practice and consciousness of safety. A well-remembered incident involving an argument that came to blows between two 'Courcy' men, which started on the Kinsale side of the river, was suspended for the duration of the ferry trip but resumed immediately on getting ashore at Castlepark.

While bridges facilitate the transport of goods and people, they can be an intrusion and frequently gave rise to conflicts of interest. Innishannon Bridge, 9 miles upriver, was the closest crossing to Kinsale until the nineteenth century. On 5 May 1665 Kinsale Corporation 'resolved to oppose the payment of money towards Innishannon Bridge' as it gave access to territory south of the Bandon, having a detrimental effect on traffic and commerce through Kinsale. Shipping interests in Kinsale and Bandon argued that bridges interfered with movement on the river. Added to this, it was argued that the necessary infrastructure, roads and access would be a levy on the rates. The emergence of liberal politics in Kinsale in the early part of the nineteenth century and the construction of a road system before the Famine persuaded the Grand Jury that a bridge was necessary and could no longer be postponed. A meeting took place at Kinsale Courthouse in October 1834 where it was resolved that the erection of a bridge would proceed. It was announced that a list would be opened inviting shareholders to contribute at an interest rate of not less than 7 per cent. This was a good return on investment and shows the confidence that attached to the project. Heard's Bridge, called

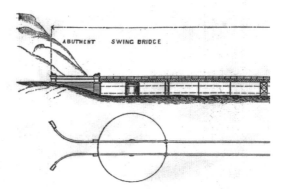

CONTRACTS OPEN.

BRIDGE OVER THE RIVER BANDON, NEAR KINSALE.

TENDERS are invited for re-building a long bridge situated three miles to the west of Kinsale, in the county of Cork, Ireland. It is to be contracted for towards the middle of March, at the ensuing assizes of the county of Cork. The new bridge will be 1500ft. in length, and consists of four parts, viz.: causeway, main bridge, swing bridge, and abutment. There are to be two separate contracts —the main bridge and swing bridge to form one contract, and the abutment and causeway the other.

Main Bridge.—The main bridge is to be composed of four parallel rows of lattice girders, 3ft. deep, eight in each row, and supported on cast iron screw piles, 12in. in diameter. Each girder is to be continuous over three spans, of 45ft. each span. The ends of the girders will rest throughout on double rows of piles, braced horizontally, vertically, and diagonally, except at the termination next the swing bridge, where they will be supported by two cast iron cylinders, 6ft. in diameter, and filled with concrete, and at the termination next the causeway, where they will rest on a single row of piles. The intermediate supports of the girders are to be two single rows of piles, four in each row. On these lattice girders will rest the cross girders, of I iron. On the lower flanges of the cross girders will rest curved plates, which are to support the concrete. Over this concrete is to be a layer of asphaltic concrete, which will form the immediate roadway. On each side of the roadway there are to be cast iron gutters, with pipes to carry off the water, and facia plates to hold the concrete and cover the ends of the cross girders. The hand-railing will consist of four horizontal rows of gas tubing, passing through cast iron standards.

Swing Bridge.—The swing bridge is to consist of four parallel lattice and plate girders, having cross girders of equal depth over the cylinder which supports it. This cylinder is to be 20ft. in diameter, leaving a clear span of 40ft. on each side. The parallel girders are to be 4ft. apart, and will support the cross girders, which are to project 3ft. The cylinder is to be filled with concrete, and carry the rolling gear. The hand-railing is to be the same as in the main bridge.

The Abutment is to consist of block-in-course masonry, set on a concrete foundation—the coping, parapet, and string courses to be limestone. The parapet to be ashlar masonry.

The Causeway is to consist of earth and stone filling, with a facing of stones set on edge. The parapet, coping and string courses are to be similar to those of the abutment. The base is to be protected with short timber piles well bound.

The filling for the abutment and causeway can be procured near the bridge. The stones, except limestone, can be precured in the neighbour-

Invitation to tender
for Western Bridge.
Courtesy The Engineer,
February 1878

after a Member of Parliament for the area, was eventually opened in March 1860 spanning the river from Kilnacloona to Tisaxon giving vital access from the Courcies to Kinsale.[21]

Timber was the material used in the construction and unfortunately was susceptible to attack from the marine beetle; after a relatively short period, this led to weakening and the eventual collapse of the bridge in 1878.[22] As people had grown accustomed to the convenience, there was no objection to a replacement in the quickest possible time which by then had the support and active participation of the Kinsale Harbour Board.

A design for the new bridge was prepared by S.A. Kirby, engineer for the Grand Jury and, after a tendering process, Brittle and Company were selected to undertake the construction. They had access to stone and the structure of the redundant bridge was used to provide a 'stage' or scaffolding. Materials were transported by ship and rail from England and the availability of 'cheap labour in the neighbourhood' provided local employment.[23] Constructed for the most part of iron, it was designed with a stone abutment at the southern side and a causeway at the other end, making a total span of 1,500 feet. With some reluctance the Board included an opening swing section at a cost of £600 to provide for the movement of ships upriver. Manually operated using a system of geared cogwheels it allowed vessels of up to 35-foot beam to pass through. The bridge opened business opportunities to local Kinsale and Bandon merchants and also was of benefit to the landowners on the riverside who had acquired property in the late nineteenth century through the Land League. The Keohane family, for generations associated with the river, had the task of maintaining and operating the swing section of the bridge and, under the direction of the Harbour Board, controlled access to the upper reaches.

The bridge was a success, apart from two problems that quickly became apparent. The first was a simple enough matter: cattle were reluctant to cross the timber end in the opening section when driven by stockmen to the fair each month in Kinsale. The second difficulty was more serious as it involved damage to the structure of the bridge and to ships. Vessels, as they lined up for the opening with little 'way on' and particularly in a northerly breeze, unavoidably made contact. In January 1883 the Harbour Board in consultation with the designer adopted a number of bye-laws. Vessels were required to furl sails and anchor at least 150 yards from the bridge. Warps were made fast to bollards and buoys laid, by which ships would be guided through, hauling on their own capstans. The ship was required to submit its 'intentions' to the men ashore, with strict rules not to attach ropes directly to the bridge. The regulations improved the situation and a hefty fine of £10 proved a deterrent. Nevertheless, in May 1909, thirteen stanchions and a 100-foot section of rail were carried away when the ketch *Atlas* fouled the structure.

The periodic closure of the bridge was not always attributable to damage caused by ships. In 1922, during the Civil War, it was bombed by Anti-Treaty forces in attempting to slow the advance of the Free State army. Similar damage was caused to the 'Stony Bridge' close by, which crossed the entrance to Ballinacurra and Blasby's Creek. This was an attractive humpbacked structure built in the nineteenth century. Merricks of Cork, well-known engineers, were contracted to repair the mechanical damage on the Western Bridge. The 'Stony Bridge' was replaced by the 'Gully' in 1925, using iron girders and faced with stone. It has a main eye and nine smaller openings through which tidal flow gushes four times a day.

To take Kinsale from the Republicans, the Pro-Treaty forces, similar to the approach of the Williamite army 200 years earlier, had no option but to advance on the western side of the river as all the bridges and approaches by road had been bombed. Reaching the Dock, the Free State soldiers crossed by boat from the Castlepark side and were subjected to gunfire from Compass Hill by the retreating enemy. Suffering no casualties, the State army took control of the town, now reeking of smoke from the burned-out establishment buildings and set about restoring all the access routes.

In the 1950s, defects emerged in the iron structure of the Western Bridge after the relatively short period of seventy years. Following considerable delay, a decision was made to construct another bridge closer to the town, crossing the river between the Folly and Ringrone. It was dedicated to the memory of Archdeacon Tom Duggan, Parish Priest of Kinsale, who in the 1950s had inspired many initiatives to revive the town's fortunes.[24] Designed by Cyril Roche, it was opened in 1977. There is no access for the passage of commercial vessels upriver. As a result, the river above the bridge is restricted to use by small pleasure craft as an amenity and some fishing activity continues in small open yawls.

Fishing on the Bandon River was a significant activity and an important source of food. In 1581 Robert Payne's description of south Cork records that, 'through this country runneth a goodly river called Bandon where is a great store of fishes ... salmon, trouts, eels and sometimes seals'.[25] Protection and conservation of the fishery, particularly salmon and shellfish stocks, were subject to high levels of regulation. In October 1721 Kinsale Corporation announced that the mussel stocks 'if preserved for one year longer will be of great advantage and that no fishermen rake or dredge in any part of the river above Ringrone Castle'. Similarly for oysters, the Corporation expressed its concern: 'whereas the bed of oysters in the Harbour of this town above Common point and Ringrone Castle hath been preserved by the Corporation for some years'. They went on to ban joulters from Cork 'taking away parcels before the town is first served'.[26]

These preservation measures reflect the importance of shell-fishing in the eighteenth and nineteenth centuries. Yet by the early 1910s, the native Kinsale oyster was extinct due, most probably, to overfishing and disease. An effort to revive the industry was made by the Government Fishery Department in 1938. This was not a success, nor was the effort of Castlepark-based Tony Hill who imported Pacific oyster spat and attempted to develop them on floating rafts in the river in the 1970s. A smaller family-based enterprise developing imported spat continues in the intertidal zone on the riverbank at Carrigeen and at Murphy's Point. The bivalve mussel, however, continues to flourish naturally. In the 1930s and 1940s banks of wild shellfish were harvested at the Gully Bridge and sent by train to Jamets in Dublin, a well-known gourmet restaurant. The picking of cockles and periwinkles, when extensive foreshore is exposed at low-water spring tides, continues to help supplement family incomes during the winter months.

Kinsale Harbour and the Bandon River were known for fine salmon but, like the shellfish, there were preservation concerns. In

Duggan Bridge with Ringrone Castle in the right background, 1977.
Courtesy Irish Examiner

1724 complaints were made that 'small fry and spawn are much destroyed by the seines of late, used in the harbour to the detriment of the fishery. We present that an admiralty court be called by the sovereign to enquire and redress the grievances.'[27]

Salmon fishing was conducted from the banks of the river using draught nets. One end of the net was fixed ashore and the remainder paid out from a boat rowed in a semicircle by two men. On reaching the shore the crew hauled the outer end of the net in short heaves, trapping the fish. When the salmon were plentiful there was competition among the boats as to which would be the first to get the nets in the water and get the extra 'shot' before the day was out. The sight of the silver fish flashing in the net towards the end of a haul generated great excitement. A four-lined verse penned by one of the salmon yawl owners reflects the enthusiasm of the fondly remembered Raikey Santry:

In Scilly Well the boats you see
Haul in their net with greatest glee.
Old Raikey who was always first
To shoot his haul or he will burst.

Salmon were fished at several upriver locations associated with particular families. Just above the Dock in Castlepark, fish were taken at the 'Five Stones' and close to the Gully Bridge is the spot known as 'Poll Diarmuid'. Fishing skills and knowledge of the habits of the salmon were passed seamlessly from one generation to the next among communities living at Ballinadee and Kilmacsimon Quay.

Fishermen had fraught relationships with the authorities over the centuries. A particular problem for the Kinsale Harbour Board was the difficulty of collecting dues from boat owners. This applied particularly to fishermen upriver who considered themselves to be outside the Board's bailiwick. Offenders in 1900 were summoned to appear before Magistrate Daunt at the Ballinspittle Sessions. No witnesses appeared, however, and the charges were adjourned. They were dropped completely in March 1901 for the reason that fishing was poor and to pursue the dues would be a waste of effort.

Income from fishing by its nature was uncertain and dependent on the size of catch. Payment was made on a share basis with approximately half to the owner of the boat and the remainder divided in pre-set proportions among the crew. Owners required men to crew their boats and at Christmas time, as was the custom prior to the start of the season, fishermen were paid 'bounty' money. The purpose was to acquire protective weather-proof oilskins, and in accepting the bounty the fisherman gave a commitment to a particular owner.

The draught salmon fishery declined and since the 1980s the number of boats has greatly reduced. In 1900 seventeen boats fished the river. By 2000 there were only one or two for a greatly shortened season. The reason for the decline was attributed to the practice of driftnetting in the open sea and across the entrance to spawning estuaries. The practice was banned in the 1990s and since then there is evidence of salmon returning to the rivers.

Weirs were an ancient and effective way of catching fish in the river. Knocknacurra (which translates from Irish as 'the hill of the

Draught net shot and haul at Scilly. *Courtesy Tony Bocking*

weir'), at the southern side of the marsh, and Ballinacurra ('the town of the weir') were the location of two. In the nineteenth century there were thirteen from Ballywilliam, on the bend just above the Western Bridge, to Laharn close to Shippool. A strand close to Ballywilliam House is known as 'The Weirs' and was until recently the postal address for the area. The structures made of timber and wattle frame trapped the fish behind on the falling tide. Records show that permission was granted in 1634 to 'cut six horse loads of wattle and stakes towards the reparation of a weir near Carriganassig Castle' on the riverbank opposite Shippool.[28]

Weirs, like other man-made structures, were seen positively by those using them but by others as obstructions. Richard Boyle sought to have 'weirs prostrated … whereby boats and fish may have free passage by water between these two towns', i.e., Kinsale and Bandon. The regulation of weirs and other fish-catching methods, described as 'fixed machines', can be traced back to Magna Carta in 1215 which interestingly makes provision 'pre-eminently to protect the poor from the aggression of the rich and the powerful'. The Fishery Laws of Ireland make specific reference to the Bandon River in relation to the removal of a weir seen as a danger to navigation which infringed individual free rights.[29]

Apart from its function as a means of transport and its importance to the economy of the area, the river provided recreational opportunities. The pleasures that can be derived from river activities are recounted by Jerome K. Jerome in *Three Men in a Boat* (1889). There the crew had 'air, exercise and quiet; the constant change of scene to occupy their minds and hard work to give them a good appetite'. Various accounts suggest that similar experiences were had on the Bandon River. Describing Kinsale in 1750 Charles Smith said, 'from Innishannon to Kinsale the Bandon River is extremely pleasant having several houses, castles and wood upon its banks which are high and beautiful. As one progresses down River it winds in an agreeable manner and at the end of each turn the sight is pleasingly entertained with the prospect of some neat seat or romantic building which open on the eye one after the other.' (See plate 12).

In the 1980s Gerald Gimblett went by boat in the opposite direction on a flood tide to avoid the possibility of going aground and being left stranded for many hours.

> It was beautiful with the high tide, to see the arbutus with its red berries hanging into the water as well as the other shrubbery in full bloom. Also to see some cattle standing in the river along the beach up to their knees, pictures that would be an artist's delight. On that cruise we went as far as Innishannon where we tied up to the root of a tree and went ashore for a browse around the village and enjoyed a cup of tea at a little shop. All the time keeping the tide in mind as we could misjudge it and be stranded.

Tea would not have satisfied the alcoholic thirst on some of the people from Kinsale who during the summer months regularly took the 'The Trip to Ballinadee' on a day's outing, as recounted in the poem by Phil O'Neill:

> They left one afternoon, this crew of jolly tars
> And each one carried his overcoat and a couple of cheap cigars.

With many sighs and fond goodbyes the girls around did flock.
Gone were their hopes when the crew cast ropes and cleared
the Short Quay dock.

Surviving a 'grounding', making water (a leaking boat) and many
escapades that would rival epic voyages, they reached Ballinadee and
after a convivial time ashore the day concludes:

So this, my friends, is the story of the jolly crew of tars
Who sailed one summer's day and came home in outside cars.
My bosom swells when history tells of this gallant company
Who ventured all in an open yawl on a trip to Ballinadee.

The close commercial ties between Kinsale and Bandon were made
possible by the river. The Harbour Authority, having jurisdiction over
the river, held a number of meetings at Kilmacsimon Quay where the
members travelling from Kinsale, having completed their business,
enjoyed the food and drink that were supplied. In the eighteenth
century there is a report that 'The officers and fishery inspectors gaily
spent a fair proportion of Harbour revenue in periodical junketing
to Kilmacsimon Quay … where on the sylvan sward they regaled
themselves with enormous lunches of roast and boiled washed
down in healths five fathom deep by copious libations of Billy Wise
returning to Kinsale at dewy eve'.

Similar indulgence continued after the Harbour Board was
established in 1870. Invoices for July 1879 show that 1½ gallons of
whiskey, 6 dozen ginger ale, 3 dozen stouts, 6 bottles of claret, 4 bottles
of brandy, 5 dozen bass ale and 2 bottles of sherry were purchased.
For food there was a leg of mutton, salad eggs, fresh butter, 4 bottles
of relish, pickles, bread, cheese and ham delivered for the meal. The
supplier was Richard Cogan, Army Baker and Contractor of Main
St, Kinsale, to whom £10-6-10 was paid. Harbour Board minutes
show that expenditure was under review. In April 1886 a proposal by
Commissioner O'Callaghan that each member would supply his own
lunch did not receive a seconder. It is clear that political junketing is
not just a phenomenon of modern times.

Other recreational pursuits that continue to take place on the river are rowing and swimming. Kilmacsimon annually hosts a regatta for which these activities are practised throughout the summer months. At present the river's economic importance is greatly reduced. But just as the Earl of Cork in 1634 recognised the value of some beautiful mussel pearls taken from the river, which he presented to his daughter, the Bandon River remains a precious resource of enormous potential, linking Kinsale Harbour to its extensive hinterland.[30]

8

Tragedy at Sea

Loss of life at sea is a constant reality for coastal communities. Every time a vessel sets sail there is the possibility of tragedy lurking in a darkening sky to windward or a freshening breeze angrily rising on a spume-laden sea. Deteriorating conditions can overwhelm a vessel and drive ships on to the iron clasp of a wave-pounded lee shore. Weather often described as 'thick', due to fog, mist or rain, restricts visibility, blanking out transits and clearing lines when close to the shore.

During the days of sail, before modern technology and the development of radio, radar, sat-nav, GPS and sophisticated weather-forecasting methods, seafarers were dependent on experience and dead reckoning. In Kinsale a tall mahogany box housing a mercury barometer at the Custom House Quay was consulted before leaving the harbour. At sea the leadsman, forward on the vessel with line in hand, would call out, or sound, the depth of water and with the assistance of a chart could estimate the distance off a particular danger or the presence of shoaling ground.

The expression 'wrung out of the sea' was used to describe how knowledge, the development of boat-handling skills and the ability to predict weather prospects were nurtured among seafarers. While natural caution was deeply engrained, accidents and tragedy did occur and on occasions involved loss of life, creating devastating grief and communal mourning. Fathers, sons, uncles and cousins serving on the same ship disappeared, sometimes without trace, leaving utter despondency for those at home. Children before they were born had lost their fathers. A young woman, Ellen Power (née Carroll) of Fisher (O'Connell) Street was a bride, a widow and a mother in a twelve-month period when her husband's ship, the *Ardmore,* with a cargo of livestock bound for Fishguard, struck a mine south of the Saltee Islands in November 1940. All hands were lost. Apart from the incidence of vessels foundering in the open sea, sometimes due to attack by enemy ships, the coast off Kinsale took its toll of hundreds of vessels making their approach to Cork, Kinsale and British ports. The Register of Depositions, the record of enquiries established to investigate shipping loss, was held at the Custom House and an examination of the details indicates certain patterns that tend to reoccur.

Fog, mist and reduced visibility were the most common cause of ships going aground and were factors in not being able to distinguish the light at the Old Head of Kinsale from Roche's Point at the entrance to Cork Harbour. In a howling southwesterly and driving rain, bearing away at Roche's Point takes a vessel safely into Cork Harbour. A similar change of heading mistaking the Old Head for Roche's Point leads to disaster in Courtmacsherry Bay.

Another common feature associated with the loss of ships off Kinsale was wind direction. A strong breeze backing in direction to the southeast is often the prelude to falling atmospheric pressure and foretells the onset of stormy conditions. Wind blowing from this direction is particularly disliked by Kinsale people as it tends to drive vessels in trouble onto lee shores at Hole Open, Bullen's Bay, 'the Burial Ground' at Cuirtaphorteen or the rocks of Sandy Cove Island.

Even within the shelter of the harbour, southeasterly gales create a sense of foreboding. In February 1691 the HMS *Swallow,* a fourth-rate frigate, broke up on the bank opposite Charles Fort and two crew members were drowned in a ferocious storm. In more recent

PLATE 13. *St Albans under sail, by A. Vernon, 2009. Courtesy Kinsale Museum*

PLATE 14. *City of Chicago* on the rocks of Ringurteen Point, Old Head of Kinsale, 1892.
Courtesy Tony Bocking

PLATE 15. *The Falls of Garry* aground at Ballymacus Point, April 1911.
Courtesy Christy Fitzgerald

PLATE 16. Sinking of the *Lusitania* with *Wanderer*, a Manx fishing vessel,
rescuing survivors, 1915. *Courtesy Post Service of the Isle of Man*

PLATE 17. Model of HMS *Kinsale* in Kinsale Museum. *Courtesy John Collins*

times – 1957 – a number of fine boats moored off the Pier, prior to the construction of the Yacht Club marina, were washed ashore with such force that they were left stranded in the garden of Acton's Hotel.

Approaching the Old Head from the west in the teeth of a southeasterly, vessels having difficulty in weathering the headland tend to make leeway into Courtmacsherry Bay, resulting in not having the sea room to wear around. In these circumstances a ship would lie abeam of the wind and drift onto the sea-breaking reefs around the Barrels and Curlaun Rocks off Garrettstown or the shore inside the Seven Heads, which was the fate of numerous vessels.

On a Friday afternoon, 8 December 1693, three vessels, the frigate *St Albans* (see plate 13), the galley *Shearness* and the *Virgins*, possibly a prize, were laying up for Kinsale after completing a tour of cruising west of Cape Clear. They comfortably weathered the Old Head. The *Shearness* entered Kinsale Harbour and the other two anchored outside, approximately 1 mile southwest of Preghane Point.

The subsequent events on that night were subject to an enquiry conducted at Charles Fort on 10 December. The investigation records show that two of the captains, Gillam of the *St Albans* and Hayles of the *Virgins*, went ashore in Kinsale and engaged in a bout of drinking. During the night as a southeasterly storm began to brew, the mate of the *St Albans,* in the absence of the captain, decided that he would seek the shelter of the harbour. In the winter rain and howling gale the vessel failed to clear Sandy Cove Island and went hard fast on the rock where she lost her masts and foundered. Fortunately, all hands survived by scrambling ashore on to the island. Early the following morning, oblivious of the night's happenings as the captains were returning to their ships, with the crews rowing the tenders, they capsized and drowned in the stormy conditions. The *Virgins,* which had held her position outside the harbour, survived. In the comprehensive report that emerged from the investigation, the ships' masters were severely criticised for their negligence. The investigation concluded with the recommendation that attempts should be made to retrieve the *St Albans'* fifty guns. At the time this was not undertaken but in 1976 the local Museum Sub Aqua Club did, in fact, locate these heavy cannon and brought them ashore for preservation at Charles Fort.[1]

While the loss of the *St Albans* was attributed to an error of human judgement and poor seamanship, the wrecking of two ships, *Lord Melville* and *Boadicea,* on 30 January 1816 was caused directly by the severity of a southeasterly gale. Troops who had fought at the Battle of Waterloo were being deployed to Cork. On arrival on the coast, the ships sailed too far west and anchored in Courtmacsherry Bay to weather out the storm before attempting to round the Old Head promontory. The anchors of the *Boadicea* did not hold and the troop ship dragged on to the jagged Curlaun and Drohid na Fina Rocks which lie between Garrettstown and White Strands. Charles Dickens in *David Copperfield* well describes the kind of terror witnessed that night off Garrettstown. People, gathered on the shore, 'all slant and with streaming hair' watched helplessly as the tragedy of the *Boadicea* unfolded in the raging sea. Amid 'the breakers that rose and bore one another down and rolled in interminable hosts', the vessel quickly broke up. Fifty, of the total complement of 300, survived by scrambling onto the sea-washed Curlaun, clinging to the rock until dawn.

Closer to the Old Head side of the strand, the *Lord Melville* survived the night. Earlier though, at the height of the storm, twelve soldiers attempted to abandon ship in a small tender, which capsized immediately, casting the occupants into the raging sea and to their deaths. The remainder, fortunately, were taken off safely the following morning before the ship itself was destroyed on the Muskraun Rock, a name coming from the Irish, appropriately associated with foul-smelling rat infestation.[2]

For weeks after the wreck, bodies were washed ashore and buried quickly in the sand. The eroding action of the sea and the shifting littoral was not a suitable resting place. Ninety years later the Cork philanthropist and historian Robert Day had the remains exhumed and reburied in the churchyard at Old Court. A memorial plaque to the victims of this terrible tragedy is set in the north aisle of St Multose Church in Kinsale.[3]

On 22 April 1822 the packet ship *Albion*, reaching the end of her regular voyage from New York to Liverpool, was knocked down in a vicious squall off Cape Clear. Captain Jack Williams, the skipper, was washed overboard. Losing her mainmast, broken feet above the deck, she carried away much of her sails and rigging. The pumps were not capable of handling the flow of water that she was taking through her damaged decks. With impaired steering she managed to get east of the Seven Heads. Severely disabled amid tangled rigging and torn sails, she was at the mercy of the gale and was driven on to the cliffs west of Garrettstown beach under what is now the Horizon Hotel. The agent at the nearby estate described the scene and the inevitable tragedy unfolding before him, looking from the top of the 60-foot rock. In the tempest the people could only look on haplessly at the despairing efforts of the passengers and crew who were unable to cling to the broken spars and torn lines. They were washed into the foaming seas and dashed on the shore as the *Albion,* now on her beam ends, broke up. Of the 25 passengers, one survived. Seven of the crew managed to get ashore.[4]

Off the entrance to Oysterhaven just east of Kinsale are the Sovereign Islands. On 11 November 1818 *The Sylvan* became 'hard fast' between the two rocks that form the Big Sovereign. The only survivor was a young boy who managed to scramble on to the rock and could be seen running frantically on the summit. Many attempts were made to rescue the lad, including one by the officers at Charles Fort. Each was abandoned because of the continuing and persistent gales. After three days of raging storm and high seas, a boat from Oysterhaven reached the lee of the Island. Jack Carthy, with a rope about his body, dived into the sea. Buffeted by the water which rose like hills he was lost from view in the breaking foam but succeeded in gaining the Rock. Then, fastening the rope to the shocked boy, both were drawn to safety amid great rejoicing, which even at this remove is still remembered in the folk memory of area.[5]

The most recent casualty on the Sovereigns was the 213-ton Dutch trawler *The Nelly,* which struck in November 1966. She was abandoned and became a total wreck after generating some controversy when a number of Kinsale men boarded her with a view to claiming salvage.

At the end of the nineteenth century, as dependence on sail declined, ocean-going vessels were powered by a combination of steam engine and wind power. One such was the *City of Chicago* owned by the Inman Company which set sail from New York on 22 June 1892. Cobh was her first port of call after the Atlantic crossing. The voyage was uneventful until she reached Brow Head on 1 July, when thick fog enveloped the ship. Anxious to maintain speed to reach Cobh by 9 p.m., the expected time of arrival, Master Captain Redford took the precaution of taking soundings to ensure that the vessel was not heading for shoal water. Despite this precaution Redford was on a course too far north and at 8 p.m. she ran up on Ringurteen Point on the western side of the Old Head of Kinsale. The depositions submitted by Captain Redford and the Chief Engineer to the Receiver of Wrecks on the following day give a clear account of what transpired. Fortunately, the wind was light and the sea calm. Visibility was so limited, though, that by the time land was spotted there was no possibility of stopping by going astern or of altering course to avoid the headland. The 360 passengers and 151 crew all survived by climbing the steep cliffs using rope ladders provided by the coastguard and local people. Others got ashore in the ship's lifeboats or were picked up by the tender *Ireland*, which was on standby awaiting the arrival of the liner at Cork. The ship's passengers included a delegation of three members of the Irish National League who were coming to Ireland to assist in moving the Home Rule debate forward.

'Hard fast' on the rock for three days the vessel broke her back, with the after section separating at right angles (see plate 14). The wreck provided a bonanza for the local people who transported the survivors to Kinsale and gathered the valuable flotsam that was discharged from the disintegrating vessel. At a later tribunal Captain Redford was reprimanded and suspended for nine months, being judged to have made way too fast in the fog and for the improper use of the lead line. The wreck continues to hold a fascination for amateur divers as it is constantly yielding up items of maritime interest.[6]

The wreck of *The Falls of Garry* (see plate 15), which went on the rocks at Ballymacus Point close to the entrance of Oysterhaven on the night of 22 April 1911, also attracts many divers to the site. She was a magnificent iron barque with square sails on each of four masts and was in the final stages of a voyage from Australia via the Cape of Good Hope with a cargo of wheat for England. While long and tedious, it had been an uneventful trip until the ship reached the English Channel heading to Falmouth for orders as to where the cargo was destined. At the entrance to the Channel the spirits of the crew were lifted by the supply of fresh victuals which were transferred from the HMS *Adventurer*. A fair breeze would have had the ship around the Lizard and into Falmouth in a matter of hours. The wind, however, freshened and to the utter frustration of the crew backed southeasterly, forcing Captain William Roberts to bear away and look for shelter in the lee of the low-lying Isles of Scilly. As it was not possible to remain 'hove to' there in the strengthening gale, Roberts decided to head downwind and make the 130 nautical-mile run for Cork Harbour. In the poor conditions he was too far west when the vessel arrived on the Irish coast and instead of Roche's Point his landfall was the Old Head of Kinsale.

'Hardening on the wind' in changing course for Cork Harbour, the captain was anxious about the ability of the ship to weather the notorious Daunt Rock at the western side of the entrance to Cork. So he ordered the ship to put about and heave to on a port tack. This would have the vessel heading off shore and towards the open sea, in other words 'to head out and head down', providing the opportunity to get a few hours of much-needed sleep. Again in the driving rain and poor visibility the wind this time veered, taking the ship in a more westerly direction than intended. Being hove to, such a vessel would tend to make leeway and take *The Falls of Garry* towards the land. This is exactly what transpired, when suddenly there was a call that the sea breaking on rocks to starboard could be heard. The situation was critical. The order to 'box haul' was given in a frantic attempt to change direction and avoid going aground. This involved getting the jibs 'aback', i.e. on the wrong side, and putting the helm down as the vessel by then helplessly gathered sternway. In such a large ship this was not effective and as a last resort the anchors were let go. The position was too far gone and the vessel grounded on a ledge. Immediately, magnesium-burning flares were ignited, hissing as they dispersed light in the mist-laden gloom. With the vessel on the rocks, emitting deep groaning echoes through her iron hull, the mate Henry Dixon gave orders that the tender on the starboard side be lowered and that a number of the crew take the ship's papers to Queenstown (Cobh) to make contact with Scotts, the shipping agents.

The remainder were taken off by the coastguard using the breeches buoy apparatus from the cliff top close to the dolmen known as the Prince's Bed. The captain and four others were the last to leave the vessel and immediately reported to the Receiver of Wrecks at Kinsale. As recorded in the depositions taken at the Custom House on 25 April 1911, the captain declared that the ship was a total loss and, while reserving his opinion, he attributed the reason 'to the strength of the tide and the scend of the sea'. The full complement of the 26-man crew was saved.

Attempts to salvage the 3,100 tons of wheat in bags were made by the owners of Jagoe's Mills whose business was close to a small boat-landing quay at the top of Oysterhaven Creek. This was abandoned as the cargo was contaminated, having come in contact with salt water and was deemed worthless.

In time the magnificent ship succumbed to the ravages of the pounding waves, disappearing under the tall cliff in 6 fathoms (36 feet) of water inside the iconic Sovereign Islands that rise out of the sea close by. She too has been a source of fascination for divers for more than 100 years.[7]

Tragedy within the harbour was a frequent occurrence. On a cold late-November afternoon in 1934, two Crean brothers from the World's End, while racing out to meet the incoming *Kathleen and May*, a small coaster, damaged their boat as they grappled alongside and were drowned in full view of their father who helplessly watched the incident from ashore. A terrible sadness descended on the town as a long period elapsed before the bodies were recovered. The remains of the older lad were dredged from the bottom by the steamer *Unique* and after twenty-one days the second boy was surrendered by the sea. Seventy years later the pathos and sadness of the tragedy are still recalled. The sense of loss followed by a fatalistic resignation is captured in the words of the play *Riders to the Sea* by J.M. Synge, when the mother, thinking of her lost sons, says, 'They are all gone now and there is nothing more the sea can do to me. I'll have no call now to be crying when the wind breaks from the south and you hear the surf in the east making a great stir. I won't care what the sea is when other women will be keening.'

In the days of sail and oars, men fished in lug-rigged drievers or in earlier times the distinctively shaped Kinsale hookers. Based on hard-wrought experience a skipper had difficult decisions to make in relation to safety. The economic reality was that no fish meant no income, which forced fishermen to sea when the weather prospects indicated that they should remain in harbour. Early on Saturday 15 October 1898 the loss of a boat and all hands was reported off the harbour. After a week being weather bound, David Cramer, a forty-year-old married man from the town who had a family of eight children, and skipper David Owen, fifty, his son Daniel, twenty-seven, and James Bowen, all of Castlepark, went to sea as the gales and storm abated on the Friday afternoon. They left the harbour in an open driever, in a moderate southwesterly. As the night drew in, they shot the nets under an increasingly threatening sky. Then, after a few hours, a cry for help was heard north of Black Head over the freshening breeze. The smaller boats had already returned to harbour but the crew of the *St Mary* went to investigate. In the quickly deteriorating conditions and poor visibility they abandoned the rescue attempt, running for safety themselves. At dawn the following morning some wreckage was discovered, washed up on Hake Head and Cuirtaphorteen under 'the Burial Ground'. It was quickly assumed that all hands on the driever had drowned. Michael Cotter, also at sea that night, reported that it was the worst weather he had experienced in forty years. The vicious storm on the same night grounded the liner *Mohegan*, which broke up on the Manacles off Falmouth with the loss of 100 lives.

The families of the men had to cope with the tragedy and the loss of breadwinners. Six of the Cramer children were under nine years of age. Within days of the wreck a public meeting was held and a subscription list opened, which for a period provided some relief.[8] In the subsequent investigation reasons were put forward for the loss including the possibility of the boat being run down by a larger vessel, but the precise cause remains unknown and can only be speculated on.

Collision at sea was a rare but traumatic experience for the crew when it did occur. Depositions recorded in the case of the Kinsale boat *Royal Princess* (Registration Number C 261), give a vivid account of an incident which occurred in the cold grimness of a November morning in 1892. Skipper Denis Gimblett described how at 7.30 a.m. after a night's fishing 6 miles south of the Daunt Rock lightship he observed a barque bearing down on him in a southerly breeze. The Kinsale vessel was struck amidships and sank in ten minutes. Fortunately, all hands abandoned ship safely and Gimblett hailed the master of the barque to 'back his main yard' in order that the crew of the stricken vessel, now vulnerable in a small tender, could board. The culprit, however, continued on his way, disregarding the fishermen's pleas. Despite their plight the crew managed to pick out the name *The Kilfauns* of Dundee on the stern of the barque. The depositions go on to say that 'having a defective paddle in a small boat we could only keep her before the sea and would not have made land only for the Kinsale boat *Water Nymph* (C 212) (see plate 18) who landed us safely ashore'. The loss of the vessel was put at £600 and compensation was pursued by the majority owners H. Williams, of the Kinsale Fish Company at Scilly. The crew of nine were all rescued on that occasion. A son of the skipper, who was aboard the *Royal Princess* that morning, was later lost at sea during the First World War, by then himself the father of a large family.[9]

Loss at sea is not confined to the inexperienced or to seamen unfamiliar with hidden dangers on stretches of shore that they fish. In a 'well found' open yawl, a crew of eight men pulling on four oars and coxed by sixty-year-old John Nagle of Lispatrick on the Old Head, headed out at 7.00 a.m. on a bright August morning in 1877. There was no wind but an ominous sea was running. On the way they safely passed inside Minane Rock, just off Black Head, which breaks in rough weather. Returning in the evening, however, the boat was swept on to the submerged rock and capsized. Some of the crew attempted to swim for shore, while others clung to the bottom of the upturned boat or scrambled for oars and other floating wreckage. They quickly drifted apart with five succumbing to the sea and the remainder rescued after some delay. During the following nine days the bodies of the drowned were recovered. An inquest was held, at which a detailed record was taken of the boat foundering and poignant accounts of identifying remains by the examination of scraps of clothing, button holes or a distinctive knitting pattern on a jumper.

The pain of these tragedies for the families and close-knit communities was relieved by the recovery of the bodies which were waked at doleful keening rituals undertaken by local women in the neighbourhood. It was a traditional expression of communal sadness, for which the women of the World's End in Kinsale were particularly noted.

Across Bullen's Bay, at Duneen close to Cuas Buí, there is a small triangular section in a field that is never ploughed. Here the crew of the foundered *Stonewall Jackson* were buried when the bodies were washed ashore. It is suggested that the ship was involved in smuggling, which would account for the fact that the loss did not receive great publicity. A story told in the area for many years after the sinking was that the unfortunate souls could be heard wailing for help on the eve of subsequent storms.

Tragedy also struck the fishermen who, full of expectation in the spring each year, came to Kinsale from the Isle of Man, Scotland and Cornwall. A number failed to return at the end of the season. In 1899 Manxman William Ball of Jurby was struck by falling rigging as his vessel, *Vivid*, lost her mast. Comforted in his last moments by his son, he was buried in St Multose after a service in the Methodist church. Throngs of people lined the streets of the town as the cortège passed.

Sixteen years later, at a spot close to where William was killed, other members of the Ball family, aboard the nobby *Wanderer*, were involved in the rescue of survivors following the sinking of the RMS *Lusitania*. The Old Head of Kinsale has become closely associated with the loss of the great Cunard liner on 7 May 1915, 8 miles south-southwest of the clearly visible lighthouse. This was at the height of the First World War, before America joined in the conflict. Captain William Turner, the ship's master, decided to use the prominent headland to get an accurate running position fix in preparation for the final stage of the voyage to Liverpool. The navigation exercise involved the ship maintaining a constant direction and speed over a fixed period of time which set up an easy target for an enemy on a predatory mission.[10] In the calm bright conditions a German submarine, under the command of Captain Walther Schwieger, fired one torpedo which sent the ship of 700 feet to her watery grave, only half as deep as her overall length, in under twenty minutes. Going down by the head, the bow section ploughed into the sandy bottom as the stern and four propellers rose in the air. Steam and smoke from the burning boilers belched explosively, hissing from the four disintegrating funnels in their Cunard livery of red and black. Of the full complement of 2,000 passengers and crew, 1,200, including 93 children, were lost (see plate 16).

In a number of inquests and enquiries that followed, the first-hand personal accounts of the survivors give vivid accounts from the moment of seeing the torpedo track towards the starboard side of the ship, the two explosions, even though only one torpedo was fired, and then the sinking itself. In terms of reporting, the log of the submarine skipper is impressive for its dispassionate coldness and the clinical account of the tragedy which created such human suffering and implications for the future course of the war. 'Torpedo out of stem tube on 700m (G-torpedo, 3m depth setting) track angle 90 degrees, estimated speed 22 sm [sea miles or knots]. The torpedo hits the starboard side, closely behind the bridge. The result is an exceptionally strong detonation with a very great explosive cloud ... We submerged to 24m and heaved to sea ... At 3.15 pm [65 minutes after firing torpedo] emerged to 11m and took a view around by periscope. Far away astern, a number of lifeboats are drifting; nothing can be seen any more of the Lusitania. The land and the lighthouse could be seen clearly.'[11]

In the passing years the shock of the sinking has receded but has been replaced by numerous questions concerning the vessel. For instance, instead of being an innocent victim, it has been suggested that the Lusitania was a legitimate target under the conventions of war that existed at the time. It has been shown that she could have been modified and quickly turned into a fighting vessel. The bridge equipment was far more sophisticated than that in standard use and was supplied by companies normally associated with the Admiralty.[12] It is also suggested that under the guise of being a passenger liner she was, in fact, carrying armaments from New York to the Allies in Europe, which may account for the second explosion that took place and caused the vessel to sink so quickly. A conspiracy theory even suggests that Winston Churchill, at the time First Lord of the Admiralty, cynically planned the circumstances that resulted in sinking the pride of the Cunard fleet to make America's involvement in the war inevitable. There is no evidence to support this speculation.

Reports of heroism among the survivors and harrowing descriptions of suffering and drowning are recorded. The cox of the Courtmacsherry lifeboat, which rowed to the disaster area, described the surface of the water as being 'as thick as grass' with floating corpses by the time he reached the scene.[13] Queenstown (Cobh) was the port at which the vast majority of the survivors were landed, including those aboard the Manx driever *Wanderer*, which was the first rescue boat at the scene. Many died of exposure, shock and hypothermia and the argument was made subsequently that more would have been saved if the order had been given by the naval authorities to land casualties at Kinsale, a considerably shorter distance from the site of the sinking.

The inquest, however, took place at Kinsale, in the courthouse on 19 May 1915. The normal reserve and stoic demeanour, a mark of master mariners, broke down in front of the jury and the coroner J.J. Horgan. Captain Turner, who had been saved from the water, having completed his evidence, gave way to uncontrolled sobbing during the course of the proceedings. The conclusion of the inquest was the verdict of 'wilful and wholesale murder against the Kaiser'.

The sinking of the *Lusitania* continues to hold great fascination. John Light, a retired US naval diver, in 1960 attempted to salvage the wreck. He succeeded in reaching the vessel and retrieved a number of items. In 1993, using remotely controlled diving equipment, Robert Ballard's photographic exploration techniques show the ship lying on her side, fouled by numerous fishing nets snagged in the hull. As she hit the bottom in 1915 sections of her superstructure broke off and are scattered about the sea bottom.[14] The wreck is now owned by American businessman Gregg Bremis who has undertaken a number of expeditions to retrieve sections of the ship and answer some of the questions.[15] In 2011 a major filming project was undertaken, showing most of the decks collapsed and the wreck covered in slimy marine growth. The sad remains of what was once a glorious ship is now a monument to the tragedy of war.

During both the First and Second World Wars a number of small local fishing vessels were sunk by mines or fired on by submarines that came to the surface to charge batteries. It was an opportunity to give the submariners some relief from the cramped and cluttered accommodation and replenish the foul-smelling air full of condensation and fumes. If fishing boats were in the area, crews were ordered to abandon their vessels, which were then sunk. German justification for these actions was that the boats were supplying food and therefore assisting in the British war effort.[16]

Kinsale men were casualties of the Second World War, 1939–1945, serving in the Royal Navy and on merchant shipping. Ted Tisdell was aboard HMS *Exeter*, which fought the German pocket battleship, the *Graf Spee* at the Battle of the River Plate in 1939. The *Exeter* was severely damaged in this well-known naval encounter, with many casualties, including serious burns to the Kinsale rating. After treatment on the Falkland Islands, Ted survived the ordeal and eventually returned home. Two Calnan brothers also saw action in the Royal Navy. Tom aboard HMS *Renown* was involved in the sinking of the *Bismarck*, which had created havoc to the North Sea convoys, and Timothy was drowned when the aircraft carrier HMS *Glorious* was sunk by the *Scharnhorst* in the Norwegian Sea in 1940.

Kinsale men served on Irish- and British-registered merchant ships. Ireland's neutral status was proclaimed with the letters EIRE and the Irish tricolour emblazoned boldly on the black sides of the ships. This was not enough to protect the vessels operated by Irish Shipping Ltd and those of the Limerick, Cork, Arklow and Waterford companies, which suffered many torpedo and gun attacks. The terrible circumstances of these crewmen's deaths were tragic, leaving many families bereft. Captain Frank Forde in his book writes that the *Irish Pine* was the saddest loss suffered by Irish Shipping. Of her 26-man crew, three were from Kinsale: Paddy Sheehan, John McCarthy and William Connolly. Towards the end of November 1942, at the height of German submarine activity in the Atlantic, the first worrying news of the *Irish Pine* filtered back to Kinsale when it was reported that she was overdue at Boston where she was bound for repairs. On 14 December the Harbour Board noted that the ship was missing, which had a numbing effect on the people of the town. The reason, however, for the ship's disappearance only emerged after the war when the log of the German submarine *U-608* was made available. It describes how the Irish vessel had been tracked for eight hours in thick snow showers and heavy rain on 15 November; two torpedoes were then fired, which sank the ship in a few minutes with all hands. The log admits to seeing red lights on her foremast, which signalled that she was 'not fully under command', indicating that she was at least partially disabled. This did not deter the Germans from consigning her to the bottom.[17]

Another incident at sea which had a happier outcome involved local Kinsale seamen Donie Buckley and Timmy Sheehan. They were left adrift in an open lifeboat after their ship *Ethel Knight* was attacked on the evening of 26 May 1942. She was part of a convoy making the voyage from Barry Dock to Trinidad. The crew abandoned ship and took to the four lifeboats. Soon one of the boats disappeared from view and was never seen again. For the remaining boats an incredible story of survival followed. They drifted in the South Atlantic for twenty-six days, living on a ration of two spoons of condensed milk and two ounces of water per man per day. Protected from the sun during daylight by a piece of canvas which at night was stretched to collect drops of moisture and condensation, the crew suffered severe weight loss, and complained of swollen tongues and boils on irritated skin. Fortunately, after four weeks they were picked up alive but in poor physical condition and were nursed back to health on the passage to Cape Town, where they were landed. Both Kinsale men returned to Britain where Tim joined another ship at Scapa Flow and Donie signed on *Pacific* at Sunderland. Later that year, at the tender age of twenty-two, young Buckley was among those lost when *Pacific* was sunk.

Records show other Kinsale families to suffer during the Second World War were the Farleys, Hayes, Hurleys, O'Connells, O'Learys and Alcocks. A wartime incident which was not the result of hostile enemy action was the grounding of the *Dunedin Star* on the coast of Namibia. Seven crew members of the ninety aboard were from Kinsale – three O'Driscolls, two O'Connells, Sonny Fives and Jack

Collins. All, including passengers, managed to get ashore and from safety watched their stranded ship pummelled on the beach before they were picked up and eventually arrived home, once again via Cape Town.

While Ireland was nominally neutral during the Second World War, Kinsale was constantly used by British trawlers busy fishing on the south coast to supplement the severely rationed food stock. Apart from seeking shelter, boats came in for repairs after bombing attacks from German aircraft or gun strafing. The Harbour Board minutes report on the survivors and casualties being daily landed at the Pier. Repairs were undertaken on the hulls of damaged ships by local shipwrights and the engineering services of Murphys, the Kinsale blacksmiths, and Merricks of Cork were much in demand. In 1941 alone the Board reported that 600 vessels paid dues.

By way of balance, out of the gloom of a winter's morning in January 1946 a converted fishing vessel, *FN 10*, arrived in the harbour. It had been commandeered by fourteen German prisoners of war and one civilian who escaped from internment at St Nazaire in France. The skipper, Commander Martin Clemen, explained that they had been forced to clear mines in the French port in the post-war period. Security, however, was lax around the Germans and the opportunity to take a boat and escape presented itself.

Initially, the arrival of the dishevelled German Navy men created excitement and a welcome break from the depressed atmosphere in the town. At Kinsale the ship was intensively searched and held by the Harbour Master while the crew received care and hospitality arranged by the local Red Cross. Hundreds of curious visitors came to the town to see the exotic-looking sailors who bore a whiff of daring and adventure. Within a week, however, incidents of anti-German feeling became evident among the townspeople whose families mourned the loss of close relatives. Fishermen aboard the British trawler *Iser,* at the time in the harbour, were openly aggressive towards the escapees and the growing antipathy was reflected in a motion of the Urban Council who proposed that electrical power to the vessel be cut off.

The Germans also created diplomatic problems for the 'neutral' Irish government. Eventually, a decision was made to hand the prisoners back to the French who sent a corvette to Cobh to which the escapees were transferred. On 11 February another French crew arrived in Kinsale, took command of the vessel and left the harbour.[18]

Commander Clemen at the end of internment returned to Germany from where he maintained contact with people in Ireland. He is quoted as saying: 'The friendship and understanding which we received there gave me new faith in mankind at a time when I needed it badly.' Afterwards, he retired from the navy and was ordained a religious minister.[19]

Seagoing was both an economic necessity and an adventure for many young men, even during periods of war. This was certainly true of the McCarthy brothers from Lower Cove who as boys had their seamanship skills honed in small boats, contending with the weather and tides that funnel through the mouth of the harbour. Mortimer and Timothy went to sea at an early age and after a number of years volunteered for expeditions to the North and South Poles, two of the most inhospitable places on earth. The brothers were on Robert Scott's ill-fated Antarctic expedition in 1912 aboard the *Terra Nova*, but survived. The Norwegian Roald Amundsen had, in fact, succeeded in reaching the South Pole in December 1911 but this did not end the Kinsale men's involvement.[20] For another member of the Scott expedition, the Kildare-born Ernest Shackleton, the Antarctic remained a fascination. As the Pole had been conquered, he set about planning the more arduous challenge of crossing the continent from one side to the other. In selecting his crew, Shackleton included Tom Crean, a Kerryman, Patrick Keohane from Butlerstown on the Seven Heads and Timothy McCarthy from Kinsale, all men of proven ability, to undertake the expedition aboard *Endurance*. In November 1914 the ship set sail for the Southern Ocean.

The vessel became trapped in pack ice in the middle of January 1915, which unfortunately led to the abandonment of the trans-polar project. Yet what followed has come to be recognised as an epic of endurance and survival. Twelve months after leaving England, the ship broke up from the pressure of ice on her sides. Now the crew were isolated on the barren snow-covered ice without any means of communication with home. The supplies that were salvaged from the stricken *Endurance* would provide sustenance for a limited period. Marooned and isolated, the crew saved three of the ship's small boats, which proved to be the only possible contact with the outside world. After fifteen months – ice-bound, with rescue an extremely remote possibility and the prospect of starvation a stark reality – they chose the most seaworthy of the open craft, the 22-foot *James Caird*, in an attempt to seek relief. A crew of six, which included Shackleton, Crean and McCarthy, set off on an 800-mile expedition to reach the small island of South Georgia. The hope was to make contact with a group of Norwegians who had a whaling station there. Persistent gales blew hard and fog and snow showers reduced visibility to a minimum. Constant baling was required as torrents of cold water crashed over the boat. It was reported that McCarthy's stoic optimism in the atrocious conditions contributed to maintaining morale. Finding South Georgia would be a tremendous feat in itself. Sextant sights were all but impossible and in the yawing conditions amid the large seas, maintaining a course was difficult with a small compass as the only navigation instrument aboard. After seventeen days the dim landfall of South Georgia appeared out of the mist. Contact with the Norwegians was made and arrangements were put in place for the evacuation of the crew of the *Endurance* who, until they saw the rescue boat would have had no knowledge that the *James Caird* had indeed succeeded in its heroic mission. The full complement of the original expedition was rescued with no loss of life.

Timothy McCarthy returned to England and almost immediately signed on as an able seaman on a merchant ship. In a most unfortunate irony, however, after his many death-defying exploits at the South Pole, this extraordinary mariner from Lower Cove succumbed to the horror of war and was drowned after his ship was sunk. Sculptured figures of the McCarthy brothers erected on the Pier road are a worthy monument to their achievements.[21]

The spectres of wreck, injury, loss and drowning are factors in the consciousness of all who live close to the sea. In more recent times, during the Fastnet Yacht race of 1979, in which fifteen lives were lost, many boats were brought to Kinsale with the assistance of the Royal National Lifeboat Institution (RNLI) or managed to limp into the harbour under their own power.[22]

The fury of the sea is a constant threat to those who earn their livelihoods in boats or enjoy the considerable pleasure of being afloat. The reality when it occurs is tragic, impacting deeply on the families and the wider community. In January 2001 the *Honey Dew II* did not survive a fearful night at sea. The skipper Ger Bohan and Tomas Jagla, a Polish crew member, were lost without trace. Both men left young families and a reminder of the pain the sea has the capacity to inflict. Kinsale has had many examples of sadness of which only a small number are recounted here. In 1989 Gerald Gimblett, whose family had been touched by tragedy at sea, succeeded in having a suitable monument in the form of an anchor constructed at Roger's Slip and in 2008 an artistic representation of the Kinsale hooker was put in place close by, as a memorial to all Kinsale seafarers.[23]

Ever conscious of the need to provide rescue services, the RNLI established an inshore boat operation in 2004 and a permanent station at the World's End in 2008. Dedicated to the saving of life at sea, it is a wonderful resource and while present in Kinsale for only a relatively short time, the lifeboat is greatly appreciated.

9

Shipbuilding

The safe haven of Kinsale Harbour, which for centuries offered a welcome respite for sailors, delivered a range of craft and skills for the maintenance and repair of ships when in harbour. Sail lofts, blacksmiths' forges, nail- and block-making workshops, rope walks, shipbuilding and repair yards all provided employment for hundreds of men who worked on the commercial and fishing fleets, ensuring that the boats were well found and ready for sea.

Two building styles developed on the Irish coast: clinker, in which the timber planks are overlapping, is associated with the Scandinavians who had access to extensive forests; the smooth carvel construction techniques of southern Europe were also common in Kinsale. This involved building hulls with planks butting one to another attached to solid frames. In both methods the garboard, or lowest plank, is fitted to the keel and then each plank is attached, building up to the top strake below the gunwale. Binding the planks together in the clinker system involved severe bending of the ribs or timbers of oak, which were made pliable by the application of steam in a special 'box'. Copper nails were hammered in from the outside through the plank and rib and then capped off with roves that were tapped smooth using a 'dolly' for 'holding on'. A locally owned pleasure yacht, *The Spray*, was constructed in the carvel style below the waterline while the freeboard section, which included a fine counter stern, was clinker built.[1]

Of the specialised tools and instruments used in boatbuilding, the adze is the best known. The master builder standing over rough, unprepared timber became proficient with the adze in shaping planks, which were fitted at different stages in the building process. The heavy keel was the first part of the craft laid to which the stem and stern posts were connected, all in line with the hanging plumb bob. As ships got bigger and native-grown timber became less available, the carvel methods of southern Europe were employed. Planks of oak were fitted to solid sawn forms already attached to the keel. Depending on the design, a transom was fitted to the post astern. Then the caulking took place – the process whereby oakum, or old rope, was served into the seams between the planks using a chisel and a strengthened wooden mallet. Contact with the water had the effect of swelling the material, tightening the seams and thus prevent leaking.

The availability of oak trees easily felled on the banks of the Bandon River provided the raw material for use in the dockyards and building facilities at Kinsale in the seventeenth and eighteenth centuries. Verdant banks of wood skirting the water produced the light-seeking spruce and fir trees stretching straight and upright for use as spars and slender masts. Natural tree bends of boughs twisting towards the sun overhanging the water's edge were saved to make strong-grained knees, breast hooks and futtocks. Large trunks of trees were cut into slender planks by two manned pit saws first stripping off the bark edge to expose the white timber. For builders of smaller boats, the material was provided by the local timber yard. This involved selecting the cleanest knot-free planks by turning them over, one by one, searching for flaws. A winter countryside walk, before the sap began to rise in the trees, in the company of a boatbuilder was frequently interrupted by spotting a bend in an ash tree which would be noted for future use.

The construction of boats was the end process that involved design and sail plans. The high structured castles fore and aft on vessels, originally platforms from which weapons could be fired, reduced in size and height. They became more pleasing, at least to the modern eye, reaching the height of elegance in the nineteenth-century tea clippers, which were noted for their speed. Whether the boats were large ocean-going vessels or small harbour tenders, the form and function were related and mutually dependent. Graceful lines generally ensured faster and more efficient sailing vessels whereas 'beamier', or broader, boats tended to have greater cargo-handling capacity. The development in design also applied to fishing craft and was driven by the need for efficiency and the commercial demand of getting the fresh fish to market. By the end of the seventeenth century, ships themselves had evolved into more cost-effective cargo transporters. Typically the overall length-to-beam ratio was increased from 3:1 to the more aesthetically pleasing 6:1, with size increasing from 100 to 1,000 tonnes. Multiple masts were stepped to take courses of sail. For handling, particularly when going to windward, fore-and-aft sails were run out on the bowsprit forward and hoisted on the mizzenmast astern. Vessels were a beautiful sight when under way in a fresh breeze, particularly on long, reaching passages.

The forward end of the modern ship is still associated with the term forecastle, or fo'c'sle. It was here that the ordinary seaman was accommodated, often in cold and damp conditions, where many a Kinsale man found a berth. Astern, the steering board mounted on the side of the vessel in ancient times was replaced by the rudder gudgeoned and pintled to the sternpost. The stern section was the more pleasant quarter where the ship's master and officers had their accommodation. The young trainee officers and cadets slept amidships.

The single square-sailed rig, which was associated in particular with the Viking longboat, was attached to a long yard and hoisted from its midpoint. It was effective with the wind from any point abaft the beam. Because of the need to sail in a windward direction, the fore-and-aft rig evolved with the yard becoming the lug or gaff and later the more upright gunter, attached almost as an extension to the mast by the halyard and held in place by timber jaws. In the latter half of the twentieth century the emergence of modern materials allowed for the development of steel rigging and metal spars, resulting in the introduction of the single-mast Bermudan rig, which is used by the majority of yachts today.

Various textiles and cloths were used in sailmaking. Up to the nineteenth century, calico was common. Then Egyptian cotton became available which was a stronger material. Sailors and fishermen made and repaired their own sails for the most part. In the nineteenth and twentieth centuries a sail loft, owned by Casey and Company, located opposite the Fish Shed, produced sails for the larger vessels (see plate 8). Dampness and the harsh conditions that these materials were exposed to caused mildew, resulting in the sailcloth weakening and rotting. Methods to reduce deterioration included the use of the bark from trees boiled in large cauldrons. The preservative qualities and the liquid when painted on the white canvas gave sails a tan colour and reduced the rotting process. In modern times sailmakers use nylon and other synthetic fabrics which are longer lasting.

The unspoken design criterion for boats built in Kinsale as elsewhere was that they were 'fit for purpose'.[2] The principle produced a shape and design which accommodated the functional requirements, the type of cargos they carried and the conditions in which they were to operate. Other influences that may have impacted on boat design were contact with the Netherlands and the efficiency of boats from France, Cornwall and the Isle of Man, which frequently called to Kinsale. From the late seventeenth century, draughtsmen were conversant with ship design as was evident in the HMS *Kinsale*, which was built at the Royal Naval Dockyard at the World's End in 1700. Nevertheless 'rule of thumb' methods continue to the present day. George Bushe, the noted Crosshaven and Baltimore based boatbuilder who died in 2011, used three essential measurements: length overall, the beam and the height from the hog, or top of the keel, to the mid taut (middle seat). He produced some of the most aesthetically pleasing and efficient boats sailing on the Cork coast. A beautiful line was the hallmark of the craftsmen, while having their own distinctive style. Boats might have features such as a gently curving shareline at the gunwale, a slight rake in the wine-glass-shaped transom, the hint of tumblehome in the upper strakes or the curve of a stem piece giving the subtle look that identified one boatbuilder from the next.

Owners and skippers took great pride in their boats. The East India Company, drawn to the Bandon River because of the plentiful supply of timber, built two ships at Kilmacsimon Quay. They were noted for the gilded sculptures on their sterns and the colourful figure-head forward under the bowsprit. One hundred years later, similar ornamentation decorated the HMS *Kinsale*, which is clearly visible on the model of the vessel in the local museum (see plate 6). On smaller boats, unlike the modern mass-produced craft, the traditional boatbuilder finished off with tasteful filigree work on the upper strake, without which it was considered incomplete.

From 1600 the history of ship building in Kinsale can be divided into two periods. The date 1800 marked a move away from large commercial and naval construction to a focus on smaller fishing craft and leisure boats, which continues to the present.

Apart from the East India Company at Kilmacsimon, there was a yard at Castlepark still known as the Dock. It is said that the facility was in place at the time of the Battle of Kinsale in 1601. A large deep cut into the land at Castlepark can be seen on the Greenville Collins chart of the harbour in 1693. The Bellin plan of 1764 names the area as '*Calle pour la Construction*'. In the early 1900s all that remained of this dockyard was flooded hole in the ground located close to the site of the present Dock Bar. From observations recorded at the time it would appear that the facility originally consisted of a grid on which ships were grounded to be worked on. It was also used for graving, where a compound of tallow, sulphur and resin was smeared on the ship's bottom to prevent the growth of weed and barnacles. Later copper plates tacked to the bottom had a similar effect. Evidence of the iroko-constructed grid was unearthed in the 1960s when the foundations for Castlepark village were being laid.[3]

Castlepark went into decline when the Royal or King's Dockyard was established at the World's End, across the river, in the area where the Trident Hotel is located today. There is not a precise date for the new location but it was operating from the middle of the seventeenth century at the foot of Dromderrig (appropriately meaning 'the hill of the oak'). Close to a ready supply of material, the new site was adjacent to some of the deepest water in the harbour. The outer knuckles of the berthing cambers are still visible even though the docks themselves have been filled in to provide car parking for the hotel. Excavations, undertaken in connection with sewerage works at O'Connell Street in

February 2010, showed the full extent of the Dockyard where ships of well over 120 feet could be handled. Writing in 1750, Charles Smith recorded that 'there was a dock and yard for the building and replacing his majesty's ships ... and this is the only port in Ireland where his Majesty's ships can be fitted'.[4]

On a wooden panel, close to the west door of St Multose Church, there is a reference to a curious boat that was constructed at the Dockyard. In Latin it commemorates a design for a prefabricated craft by the Kinsale-based shipbuilder Thomas Chudleigh. The craft, perhaps some form of barge, was taken overland, assembled on the shores of Lough Leane near Killarney and from the water was used by Cromwell's forces to take Ross Castle in one of the last actions of the Parliamentary campaign in Ireland in June 1652.[5]

> Causavit terries velificasse ratem.
> Velificasse ratem terris bene Kerria novit
> Rossensis turris capta labore probat.

This translates as:

> He caused a ship to sail on land
> Kerry knows it well, the capture of Ross Castle
> With difficulty proves it.

The Chudleighs were a prominent seventeenth-century Kinsale family, not just known for shipbuilding but also for their involvement in the political life of the town where members of the family on a number of occasions were elected to the position of town Sovereign. In July 1667, they were directed to construct 'a boom of masts and chains with which to lock up the Harbour', as part of the Earl of Orrery's plan to protect Kinsale from the Dutch threat.[6] By 1696 they had acquired water frontage close to the Town Blockhouse and were granted permission to extend the quay facilities and engage in the profitable business of servicing the ships that called to Kinsale.[7]

The vessel with which the Dockyard is most associated is the HMS *Kinsale* (see plate 17), launched in 1700, and also referred to on the plaque at St Multose. Interestingly, it hints at the professional rivalry that existed among the shipbuilding fraternity at the time:

ille ratem Regi cui dat Kinsalia nomen
Condidit ast alii laus dat magna fuit.

This translates as the vessel which Thomas Chudleigh's son 'built for the King to which Kinsale gives its name but great credit to another'. The 'other' was a Richard Stacy who also claimed to be the builder, both men wishing to be associated with such a fine vessel. It is possible that both Stacy and the younger Chudleigh were involved, one as the builder and the other the foreman who 'put the work through'. There is a suggestion that there may have been two ships called *Kinsale,* one being the Stacy ship that broke up in 1741 and possibly a second vessel, as there is a reference to a HMS *Kinsale* leaving Kinsale in February 1759 as a convoy ship with fifty-four sail bound for the West Indies. The Rev. J.L. Darling in his book on St Multose Church mentions that this vessel was sold out of the service and ended up as a hulk. There is some speculation that the vessel may have given the name Kinsale to a town in Montserrat in the Leeward Islands.

In 1666 the Earl of Orrery, supported by Samuel Pepys, was concerned at the poor condition of the defences at Kinsale Harbour and its inability to withstand possible Dutch aggression and later, after 1675 when the Dutch and English made peace, the threat posed by the French. Part of the defence strategy devised was to build up the fleet which placed renewed emphasis on yards such as Kinsale and the building of ships like the fifth-rate HMS *Kinsale.* Coming in 'the line', after the first-rate battleship and the second-rate armoured cruiser and so on, her function was similar to that of the modern fishery protection craft. In all, fifty-eight of these vessels were built. From their graceful lines and large press of canvas it is obvious that they were designed to act as the eyes of the fleet. A detailed model of the Kinsale boat, constructed by John H. Thuillier in 1939, may be viewed in the Kinsale Museum. The fine ship was 117 feet in length, 32 feet beam and had a draught of 12 feet; she bore 32 guns on a single deck and was limited in size by the depth of water available in the harbour. She sailed with a crew complement of 140.[8]

It was the period when the Navy Board named the ships after particular towns such as Kinsale. Another fifth rater, the HMS *Looe*, similar in size and purpose to the *Kinsale*, was called after the Cornish coastal town. She has an unfortunate association with the Cork coast in that she foundered on a rock at the entrance to Baltimore Harbour in 1697 and since then the danger has been marked by the familiar 'Loo' buoy.[9]

No Chudleighs remain in Kinsale, but to the present it is a name still associated with boatbuilding in the Isles of Scilly, re-emphasising the Kinsale link with these remote islands off the southwest of Cornwall.

The Royal Naval Dockyard itself was extensive stretching from the area now occupied by the Trident Hotel to the Ferry Slip. A sketch of the Kinsale waterfront drawn from James Fort in Smith's history in 1750 gives a view of the yard at the World's End. An accompanying comment says that 'this is the only port in Ireland where his Majesty's ships can be refitted'.[10] The legend attached clearly identifies the graving quay at the yard, the Custom House, Southwell's house, later to become the classical school, and the artillery or gun wharf and slipway. The section of the World's End road as it is today, linking the hotel to the slipway, did not exist and access to different parts of the yard was by way of the 'Drang', which is still in use. It is a narrow slope with a sharp descent wide enough for a horse drawing a gun carriage. All that remains of the Gun Wharf is a small stone structure protruding into the water close to the Ferry Slip, which is covered at high tide. Originally constructed at different levels with a derrick and lifting gear, it was used to step masts, lift guns and ship stores aboard vessels.[11]

Another outline of the dockyard was drawn by Charles Vallancey (see p. 68) in 1796 when he was engaged to survey defence installations in the south of Ireland because of the ongoing threat from the French. Identified on the drawing are boathouses, slipways, stores, a sawpit, paint store, nail store, sailmaker's loft and a mast pond where spars were placed for the purpose of seasoning.

Even though relatively small in terms of other British yards, the facility employed large numbers of workmen. At the height of its importance the town records for 1725 show that it carried a master carpenter with sixty joiners and turners, a master boatswain, forty shipwrights, a master caulker and his men, together with smiths, maltsters, coopers and their proper labourers.[12]

In the latter half of the eighteenth century the status of the Naval Dockyard declined, mirroring the general reduction in port activity at Kinsale. A number of factors contributed to this. First of all, the harbour had not the depth for the size of ship that was then considered necessary for the defence of the coast. This was recognised as a problem as early as 1694 when Alderman Hoare, Southwell's deputy in Kinsale, indicated that the bar, across the entrance of the harbour, limited use to the smaller fifth- and sixth-rate cruisers.[13] A second factor identified by Charles Vallancey in the 1750s which ultimately led to the complete withdrawal of the dockyard from Kinsale was 'the notable eighteenth century progress in boat building and marine engineering together with the general expansion in shipping rendered the old docks and harbour inadequate'.[14]

The Dockyard function as the naval backup for the transatlantic fleets to the colonies and the centre for the coordination of convoy facilities was gradually removed from Kinsale. The facilities, including shipbuilding, were transferred to Haulbowline in Cork Harbour and 1805 is normally accepted as the date on which naval activity finished at Kinsale.

From a building and repair perspective the date also marks the point at which the emphasis changed from large ship to boatbuilding with a particular focus on the fishing industry, the coastal trade and on the emerging use of the sea for leisure and yachting in the later nineteenth century. This was the spur for the emergence of a number of family-run boatbuilding firms.

Small private yards, some operated by one or two people under lean-to sheds at the gable end of cottages, had been turning out boats for centuries in sheltered coves around the harbour. Two of the more prominent in the nineteenth century were located close to the quays that stretched into the harbour from Lower Fisher (O'Connell) Street. Set back from the location of the Galleon Mast at Roger's Slip, George Brown had a yard. When launching a vessel from the slipway, a hawser was secured in the Scilly Dam to slow the sternway movement. The operation which required precision, practised for centuries, caused the west–east movement of the vessel as she became waterborne, to swing safely into a north–south orientation.

Great rivalry existed between this yard and that of Cornelius Barrett which occupied what is now the site of the Shearwater apartments. Each yard had its own sleek four-oared gig, manned by apprentices, who rowed out to make contact with an approaching vessel when it was signalled from Castlepark. A keen race ensued and the first to reach the incoming ship usually got the orders for the repairs and maintenance while in harbour.

The tradition of boatbuilding was continued by the Thuilliers, who had family connections with a number of the older builders. They established the business at the World's End, which continued until 1958. Extensive records, work diaries, business correspondence and written recollections provide first-hand evidence of the industry in Kinsale from 1800. Joseph Thuillier (1842–1921), for thirty years chairman of the Kinsale Harbour Commissioners, including the period when Pier Road and Head were constructed, recalled his father-in-law Jerh Coveney's account of working on the garboards of the *Lord Sandown*, hove down at the old Royal Dockyard in 1820. The vessel, owned by the McDaniel family, traded between Kinsale and St John's, Newfoundland taking general cargo and returning with timber. In another incident, as a young boatbuilder Coveney with other apprentices saved the damaged brig *Peru* by grounding her on the bank off Castlepark. Later, after the pilot escaped, it was discovered that she was a smuggler. She was seized and later broken up at the Custom Quay in Kinsale.[15]

Joseph himself was apprenticed to master builder Cornelius Barrett. His indenture, dated 1857, set out a seven-year period before becoming a fully certified craftsman. During his training he was subject to strict Victorian mores: 'he must promise not to waste the goods of his master or commit fornication nor contract matrimony within the said term ... not play cards, dice tables or other unlawful games ... not use taverns ale or play houses.' For the first two and a half years he earned a weekly wage of 4 shillings. In later life he recalled his days as an apprentice and gives an insight into the recreational activities of Kinsale society. 'At that time Mr Robert Heard, a prominent Kinsale landowner, was laying down the lines of the schooner yacht *Echo* built by Cornelius Barrett of this town, to whom I served my apprenticeship as a shipwright, a first-rate man. I was then a boy holding the battens and chalk line and it was there that I got my first lessons in ship draughting.' The Heards must have been well pleased for in 1893 Captain Heard of Pallastown had a 27-foot yacht, *The Otter*, built by the Thuilliers. Cornelius Barrett was the boatbuilder who produced the drawing of the Kinsale hooker contained in the Washington Parliamentary Report of 1849 that was requested by the House of Commons.

In the early 1860s Joseph and his brothers, Michael and Henry, established a yard at the World's End. The business prospered during the period 1862 to 1900 when the harbour filled with up to 500 fishing boats annually. The family built a number of boats for themselves and engaged directly in fishing. According to the diaries, the order books were full and the firm was in constant demand for repairs, sending skilled men to the strands at Scilly and Castlepark where boats were drawn up. At the end of each season there were a number of instructions for the fitting of jury rigs capable of getting damaged luggers back to their home ports in Cornwall and the Isle of Man.

Among some of the notable boats built by the firm was the 48-foot *Marion* in 1882. She was described 'as a splendid looking boat built substantially'. In 1885 the *Water Nymph* (see plates 18 and 19) was designed and built for Kinsale Fishery Company. Reporting on the launch, the *Cork Examiner* (17 February 1885) noted that her lines were said to be 'like those of a yacht ... and fitted with a steam hauling machine'. A sister vessel was built for the Thuillier fleet and to encourage fishing off the Galway coast the Congested Districts Board placed an order for *Richard Hall*, a 45-foot-keel-length boat constructed of red pine on framed oak, with the firm. This was a prestigious contract for which the family were congratulated by the Harbour Board at its meeting in 1886. There is evidence that the boat in fact was registered in the name of Stephen J. Fuller and fished out of Union Hall in west Cork.

The Congested Districts Board was a highly regarded government authority established to relieve poverty and promote fisheries in areas of small population. Its input, including the construction of piers

212

and shore-based facilities, was coordinated by Sir Thomas Brady, Inspector of Fisheries, who had commissioned the building of the *Richard Hall*.[16] Satisfied at the standard of construction of that vessel, the Royal Lifeboat Institution (RLI) placed an order for a similar craft but incorporating three watertight compartments. On the day of the launch Joseph Thuillier's work diary says that 'she hung on the ways for half an hour – we got the screw to her and she went off beautifully. Got three ton of metal from Perrots and got it in her. Got card from the Institution.' In finishing the project the diary recalls that Sir Thomas and Lieutenant Tipping, the RLI representative, inspected the boat in March 1887, and it passed all the tests. While the diary entry appears matter of fact, the launch of the lifeboat was a significant event for the town. Even so, on the day of the launch the work routine of the thirty employees at the yard continued regardless. The absence of any celebration may have been due to a number of evictions that took place in the parish on the same day.[17]

There are references to sailing for pleasure in Kinsale Harbour in boats built by the Thuilliers. Well-known yachts which raced regularly included the *Glance, Heroine, Spray, Swallow, Truant* and the *Tertia*, which was listed in Lloyd's Register of Yachts for 1925 as the only Irish-built boat. She was 35 foot LOA (length overall), 28 foot LWL (waterline length), 8 foot 6 inches beam and 4 foot 9 inches draught. Her sails, of 1,005 square feet in area, were made by Ratsey and Lapthorn. She is still fondly recalled by the older people in Kinsale who remember her epic contests with the Cork-based *Gull* as the whole town turned out at the Fort or Compass Hill to watch the end of the annual ocean race from Cork. The *Tertia* was owned originally by the Rev. Penrose, rector of Rincurran Parish, and skippered in her early years by Tommy Newman who remembered her leather-trimmed cockpit. He recalled her falling from the stocks and twisting her keel, which he claimed was the reason that she never won a race subsequently; and thus the stories of a seafaring community originate and are passed down through the generations.[18]

Apart from the yachts, the craft of boatbuilding in the town was synonymous with the Kinsale hooker, already discussed briefly when outlining Robert Southwell's association with the Netherlands (see chapter 2) and the fishing industry (see chapter 4). Many coastal areas in Ireland had their own version of the hooker. What distinguished the Kinsale and Galway hookers from the others was the tumblehome in the shape of the hull which, when looking from dead ahead or astern, appeared as a bulge on the side. It is argued that this feature was influenced by connections with the Netherlands. The Dutch prototype when heeling would hang a leeboard perpendicularly to facilitate a boat of shallow draught sailing more efficiently to windward. At a later stage, unlike its Galway equivalent, the design of the Kinsale version was influenced by the Manx lug-rigged nickeys and nobbies and the Cornish drifters, which had the effect of reducing the tumblehome on the side.

The first written mention of the Kinsale hooker was in a letter from Robert Southwell to the Lord Deputy in 1671 where he complains about the incursion of French fishing boats which were affecting the catches of the mackerel, pilchard and herring taken in the local hookers.[19] Building a Kinsale hooker, of which unfortunately no example survives, began with the half model, i.e. a one-sided model from which measurements can be taken (see plate 19) approximately 30 inches in length and which provided the basis on which the finished craft would be constructed. Lines were 'struck out' (drawn) on the layered model and the width taken at different points. Measuring from the 30-inch working model, the position of the frames and shape of the plank required for the 30-foot finished craft were determined by a matter of simple calculation. Generally, the Kinsale hooker was between 30 and 40 feet in length and of 15 to 20 tons. Originally decked forward with a cutter rig (single mast), they were adapted in the 1860s to include a mizzen. Conditions aboard all fishing craft were primitive with a fire, for cooking purposes, lit on stones in the bilge prior to the fish-boom period. At a later stage a 'donkey' steam engine was fitted to help in hauling nets. The names of some local hookers were *Water Witch*, *Water Nymph*, *Scilly Bell*, *Eleanor*, *Agnes*, *Seagull* and *Ernest*.

These craft were not designed by sophisticated naval architects, but wrought out of centuries of encountering particular conditions associated with the port, the coastline, the availability of shelter, handling facilities and function.[20] Accounting for what could be described as the nature of boat design, Ernest B. Anderson succinctly

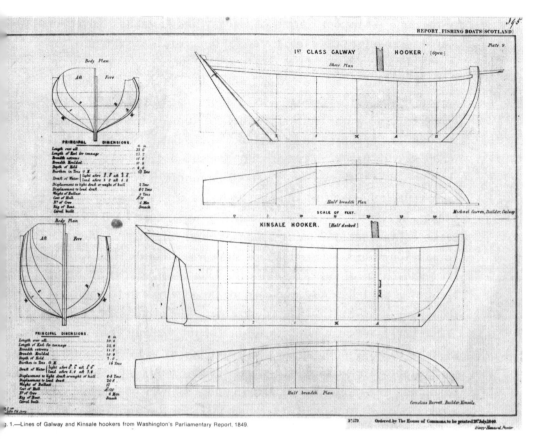

Fig. 1.—Lines of Galway and Kinsale hookers from Washington's Parliamentary Report, 1849.

Drawings of Kinsale and Galway hookers, Washington Parliamentary Report 1849. *Courtesy Michael Curran and Cornelius Barrett*

sums up the process: 'There are many local types of small craft built for fishing and in some cases carrying merchandise and each type was distinctive to its port or particular part of the coast. For instance the Donegal, Galway and Kinsale hookers, each bearing a resemblance to others in their rig but otherwise quite distinct and designed to suit varying local conditions.'[21] The physical conditions in which the craft operated were influential in the development of design and the sail plan.

Interesting drawings, produced for the House of Commons report on fisheries in 1849, provide the opportunity to compare the Galway and the Kinsale hookers. The plans are by the noted builders of the time – Michael Curran of Galway and Cornelius Barrett of Kinsale. The most noticeable feature of the boats is the extent of the tumblehome which runs from fore to aft, but more pronounced in the Galway version as shown in the body plan. The design implication was that the Galway boat was a more flat-bottomed, shallow-draught vessel with bluff apple-cheeked forequarters particularly suitable for the short, lumpy seas of Galway Bay. The whole bay is indented with small, rocky harbours that dry out at low water and the tumblehome allowed the boats to lie more comfortably against quay walls to unload turf and take on board general cargo when not fishing. In Kinsale there was a relatively wide, deep harbour with easier lying-alongside facilities. Outside and off the Old Head of Kinsale the deeper water creates a slow wave motion. The Kinsale boat evolved to cut rather than ride the rolling seas with its finer bow and the deeper bilge and cargo-carrying hold giving extra stability on the longer open-sea trips. The counter stern (the overhanging section at the back), which was not a feature of the Galway version, was included to avoid pooping (i.e., seas coming over the stern) and add to its impressive performance when heeled, giving extra waterline length and thus more speed. The stern on the Galway boat consists of a raked (sloped) transom (back) which takes the foot (bottom) of the rudder well forward, providing a turning moment close to the centre of the boat which facilitates manoeuvrability in the tighter confines of the Connemara harbours. The sail plan of both was the gaff cutter. The Kinsale hooker, however, also included a topsail which gave an extra press of sail and thus more speed in open water.

The proposition that the design of the hookers evolved in part out of local practice, responding to the physical environment, tends to be dismissed by a number of maritime historians. While acknowledging the Dutch influence on these craft, another view suggests that the emergence of the hooker shape came through the development of yachting and the staging of mock naval battles which were enthusiastically pursued in England during the reign of Charles II.[22]

Apart from a model of the Kinsale hooker in the National Museum, drawings for the House of Commons 1849 Report, work undertaken by Michael Tyrrell in 1998 and computer research by Pat Tanner of Meitheal Mara, nothing of the nineteenth-century Kinsale

PLATE 18. *Water Nymph* under full sail. Pen and ink drawing, 1903, by J.H. Thuillier. *Courtesy John Collins*

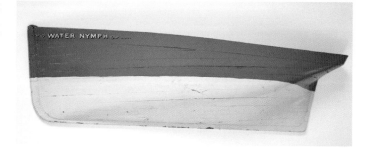

PLATE 19. Working half model from which the *Water Nymph* was built. *Courtesy John Collins*

PLATE 20. Patrick Murphy aboard the restored *Pinkeen*, 2009.
Courtesy Nick Rourke

PLATE 21.
Launch of
Kinsale and
Dock rowing
yawl, October
1994. (*L–r*):
J. O'Regan,
J. O'Brien,
N. Keohane,
W. Dillon and
C. Hurley.
*Courtesy
Southern Star*

PLATE 22. (*L–r*) Maurice and John Thuillier in fresh conditions racing 470 class dinghy, 1973. *Courtesy D. Tucker*

PLATE 23. (*L–r*) Jack Tyrrell and Joe Thuillier assessing a Department of Education boatbuilding competition, 1979. *Author's collection*

PLATE 24. Kinsale boat skippers, 1960: (*L–r*) Pat Collins, Michael Coakley, Jerh O'Donovan, Richard O'Connell, and Denis Collins. *Courtesy Pat Collins*

boat remains. On the Galway coast, however, the western boats are still active as demonstrated at the Cruinniú na mBád Traditional Boat Festival annually at Kinvara. The sailing capability of these ancient craft is excellent, even in the calmest conditions with little wind.

In Kinsale, builders modified design incrementally, influenced by the efficiency and performance of the boats from Cornwall and the Isle of Man which filled the harbour in the latter half of the nineteenth century. Change was also required to accommodate the new techniques introduced for driftnetting, which gave the term 'driever' to all boats engaged in that type of fishing. By the end of the nineteenth century the tumblehome was no longer a feature of the Kinsale hull, which was by then similar to that of the Penzance drifters. In the 1860s a mizzenmast and sail were fitted for the purpose of keeping the boat head to wind, modelled on the Manx nickeys and nobbies. Some boats were lengthened by adding sections to the hull and sail plans were adapted for the use of the dipping lugsail which improved speed when sailing to windward. Nevertheless, the term 'hooker' continued in use to describe these craft. Old men in the 1960s remembered the boats in their working days and observed how they vied with one another in striving to improve performance through the tweaking and altering of rigging, similar to the practice of tuning in modern racing yachts.

When fishing activity declined in the harbour with the emergence of the British-based steam drifters in the 1920s, all aspects of Kinsale's economy became depressed, including the boatbuilding industry. By 1940 all that remained of the Thuillier yard was the boiler and rusting steam engine that once powered the large flywheel for the belts that drove the saws. The business was reduced to a one-man operation and continued by John Henry Thuillier who, having worked in a civilian capacity for the Royal Navy, retired to Kinsale. Not deterred, however, by the decline, he built eight 10-foot gunter-rigged dinghies which raced regularly in the harbour and became the basis of the Kinsale Harbour Sailing Club, now Kinsale Yacht Club. While in his eighties, still able to wield an adze and use an auger, he built *Pinkeen*, a Colleen class Buchan-designed sailing boat, in 1952. With two other boats of the same class they formed a beautiful one-design fleet in the harbour and regularly cruised the west Cork coast. *Pinkeen* was the last timber-built yacht at Kinsale and can be seen regularly sailing in Cork Harbour, having been expertly restored by Patrick Murphy, a grandson of the builder (see plate 20).

The death of John Henry Thuillier in 1958 ended a long tradition of boatbuilding in the town. In the 1990s with the revival of coastal rowing in the harbour, a number of timber boats were produced by Ray O'Callaghan. These sleek racing craft, constructed of spruce, larch, oak and ash, were a legacy of the working timber yawls that raced to meet the incoming vessels in the past. They can be seen competing at different venues on the Cork coast during the summer months.

Petrochemical and fibreglass materials are now almost universally used to build the small vessels afloat used for fishing and recreation. Attractive boats satisfying function and safety requirements are turned out by Gearoid Fitzgerald in Kinsale and the Kingston brothers at their yards in Kilmacsimon and Middle Cove. They are continuing a craft that is an essential part of all seaboard communities and will continue for as long as water flows in the harbour.

10

Regattas and Water Sports

On entering Kinsale Harbour the embracing shelter of the surrounding shoreline is immediately appreciated, becoming even more secure as the town appears around the corner of the Blockhouse at Castlepark. The lower reaches of the Bandon River, in a meander of acute bends, give the harbour its reputation as a safe haven of exceptional charm (see plate 12). At Ringrone the river flows in a northeasterly direction for a mile and at Scilly it swings dramatically to the south as the stream heads for the open sea. Apart from shelter, the rocky shore provides natural landing places between the strands and beaches, which for centuries have been used for pleasure and recreation. For those fortunate enough to own a sailing craft, the delights of Bullen's Bay, Trá Buí and Oysterhaven are available. A trip to Sandy Cove offers a sense of discovery, adventure and the opportunity to land on the island with its sandy beach, where blowholes and shallow caves can be explored. On the rocky edges that provide nesting for swooping herring gulls, seals can be observed from above, moving gracefully in the still blue water. Not so long ago, rounding the Old Head of Kinsale for the small-boat sailor held a little of the foreboding of Cape Horn and only rarely were the pleasures of Courtmacsherry Bay or further west even contemplated.

Swallow, one of eight sailing dinghies built in the 1930/40s. *Author's collection*

Open rowing boats were common in the past. Each year in May and June, from the middle of the nineteenth century, clinker-built craft were drawn out of winter storage and had ceiling boards, stern and fore-sheets fitted. The boats were cleaned, scraped, painted and, depending on the condition of the timber, had gleaming varnish applied to the topsides. Paint was brushed into the bilges with particular attention to the laps between the timbers and planks. On the bottom, white was common. Care was given to the waterline which showed two or three inches of boot top appearing like a neat shirt cuff when the boat was properly trimmed in the water. Older boats usually had thick pitch applied to the bilge to stop leaks and, after winter storage, boats were sunk to the gunwales for a week or so to swell and tighten up the planks. Corks from sherry or porter bottles, garnered during the winter, were fitted to the bungholes. With a baling can under the stern sheet, oar leathers checked, painter made fast and rowlocks, known as spurs, tied with lanyards to the resins, all was shipshape for the season. When afloat, the pleasure derived from boating is elemental. The sound of water lapping gently on a timber hull at a calm mooring or spray flecking freshly varnished gunwales is the perfect encounter as sea and timber make contact. Men and boys did the rowing with the ladies sitting in the stern, perhaps steering with arm resting on the tiller. Crafted spoon-shaped blades at the end of tapered oars were a source of pride to the careful owner who learned to feather the stroke when rowing. When shipped, the oars were placed with the blades forward in naval style so that seawater would not drip on the passengers.

Bathing expeditions were a feature of the summer and included quite elaborate picnics of lunches and sometimes tea al fresco. A large basket was kept in readiness, filled with heavy china and cutlery, and appeared with the prospect of fine weather. Depending on wind and tide, Lower and Middle Coves, Money Point or the Platters and Dishes at Castlepark were the favourite locations. The Platters and Dishes is ideal as a landing place and sheltered in a northerly breeze, and the name is derived, according to Kinsale woman Maureen Murphy, 'from the curious rock formation which made a series of platforms'.[1] At Jarley Cove, now more commonly known as the Dock Beach, the Harbour Board gave permission to the Kinsale Amusement Committee in 1895 for the erection of bathing boxes to avoid the possibility of slipping towels offending modesty.

Lennox Robinson, the playwright, noted that the Dock was popular among 'local cads' and the soldiers from the military barracks and Charles Fort across the harbour. The young recruits created scandal and shock as they frequently swam in the nude.[2] This gave rise to complaints which were brought to the attention of the Harbour Board in 1911 and Commissioner Reardon, after whom the slipway at Scilly was called, objected to the soldiers swimming in full view of the public. A compromise was reached, following discussions with Captain Hewitt of the barracks, which allowed for 'bathing parades' at Castlepark every morning between 5.30 and 7.30 a.m. Also the military had permission to swim under the ruined hotel close to the concrete seat on the Lower Road and from secluded rocks at Summer Cove where permission was given to place a springboard. These arrangements appear to have worked as no further complaints are recorded.[3]

For those without boats, several well-remembered swimming areas were popular. Sally Port at Charles Fort, the steps at Carrig Oisín, and Carrigín, with its diving board accessed through Commoge or by Cappagh Lane, were frequented during the summer period. Important for centuries was the ferry that plied the river between the Ferry Slip on the Kinsale side directly to the Dock at Castlepark. On fine summer days large numbers from the town enjoyed swimming at Jarley Cove, Sandy Beach or the Platters and Dishes after walking through the gently rising fields, close to the ivy-covered ruins of James Fort.

The ferry service, which had been franchised to the O'Donovan family of Castlepark in the nineteenth century, suffered from the lack of adequate landing facilities. Highlighted was the need for a breakwater and slipway but repeated requests went unheeded. In 1957 the operation of the ferry passed to the Kinsale Development Association. The service was in terminal decline as the availability of road transport became more common and the opening of the Duggan Bridge twenty years later rendered the ferry unnecessary.

In the late nineteenth century the stunning beauty of Castlepark became a popular venue not just for swimming and picnicking, but also for the playing of football, cricket and dancing in the fields around the Old Fort. These activities were a social outlet for the prominent people of the town and the military stationed at Charles Fort and the barracks. An army band was ferried across to provide music on Sundays. But the use of the area as a recreational venue led to complaints because of the trampling of crops, the frightening of cattle and owners being abused when they confronted the offenders. At the Harbour Board in August 1887 the landowners said that they did not object to people enjoying themselves but requested that a line be drawn at the playing of games and romping through the fields.

The natural attraction of the harbour also appealed to visitors from outside. Wishing to portray a genteel image, Kinsale was

An Saorstat arriving at Kinsale Regatta, 1930, with ruined hotel on the left.
Courtesy Irish Examiner

described in 1806 as 'Bath in miniature', encouraging people to come and enjoy the bathing facilities in the chalybeate springs at Scilly and Summer Cove for the health-giving properties of the iron-impregnated mineral water.[4] The early tourism initiative proposed a hotel on a site overlooking the Lower Road at Scilly which was planned in conjunction with the extension of the railway to the town. The building reached roof level but was abandoned and remained in a ruined condition until 1970 when the site was developed as a domestic house.[5]

The major aquatic event of the season was the Regatta which was enjoyed by all sections of the community, joined by many travelling from Cork city and other parts of the county on a day excursion.

In August 1854, at which the Royal Navy was represented by HMS *Advice*, it was reported that 'the aquatic sports of this time-honoured regatta have been in existence longer than is included within the recollection of even the oldest lover of naval festivities'.[6] This implies that Kinsale hosted a regatta going back at least to the middle of the eighteenth century. After the train link to Kinsale was established, hundreds of people arrived from Cork, with others coming by sea on the paddle steamer *Prince Albert* to enjoy the spectacle. The annual sea passage continued into the twentieth century when the steamer *Morsecock* and later *An Saorstat* took over. The passengers coming for the 1911 Regatta had the excitement of going to the rescue of the three-man crew of the sailing yacht *Heroine* which foundered on Bulman Rock when racing. Ashore, the throngs enjoyed 'the splendid band of the Kings Royal Rifles', listening to the music from outside the enclosed promenade, which was reserved for the leading citizens who were admitted at 1 shilling per head. The majority of the travellers returned home in the evening. A small number, however, stayed overnight to enjoy the All-Night Regatta Dance which in 1947 started at 10 p.m. and continued until 4 a.m. the following morning.[7]

In modern times the refrain 'When it is August Bank Holiday it is Kinsale Regatta' fixes the date of the festival, chosen to coincide with the annual holiday period for Kinsale emigrants living in England. In earlier times the date varied; as Samuel Lewis in 1839 wrote, 'a regatta is held in July or August which is well attended'.[8] Kinsale was not the only venue at which these maritime festivals took place on the coast. The Feast of the Assumption, 15 August, became firmly associated with Cobh Regatta which followed after the Courtmacsherry and Glandore Regattas, to which Kinsale yachts would sail and participate. Stories recall crews being awoken to a report of a 'light cool' apparent off Money Point, which indicated the prospect of a breeze for the run to Cork Harbour. For a few days the crew would enjoy the racing afloat and the social activities ashore. At night they would bunk down aboard under a canvas cover drawn over the boom.

For the Kinsale Regatta, local boats were joined by yachts from the Royal Cork and Royal Munster clubs in Cork Harbour. A report of the 1898 event records that the Cork one-design fleet took part for the first time. Subsequently, these open gaff-rigged counter-stern

Tertia heading for Scilly in a moderate northeast breeze. *Courtesy Denis Gimblett*

boats graced the event for many years.[9] Mentioned in the report of the racing were *Minx* (A.H. Julian) and *Little Devil* (Miss Gubbins), who finished within four seconds of one another. Other boats in the class were *Querida* (A. Fowler) and *Maureen* (M.J. O'Sullivan).

The sportsmanship among the crews of this class and the gentlemanly conduct associated with sailing in general was well reflected at the regatta held on 11 July 1907. Sailed in a moderate southwesterly on a beautiful day, no more than four lengths at any stage in the race separated *Sybil* (A.H. Allen) and *Maureen* (then owned by G. Crosbie). The close competition forced the skippers to overstay the windward mark allowing *Little Devil*, sailed by Captain Ormansby, to slip ahead which, with nothing but the run ahead, assured the captain of almost certain victory. Confirming the old adage that a race is never won until the finishing line is crossed, a slippery hitch on the spinnaker gave way, causing the sail to drop in the water and slow the boat, allowing the others to pass. The report goes on to say that 'much sympathy was expressed to the Captain for his bad luck'. The disappointment was even more acute when only two minutes separated first and third after 20 miles of close racing. In the sporting manner of the day the disappointed captain would no doubt have acknowledged the winner in leading the customary three sharp cheers.

Racing took place in all weathers and damage was a regular occurrence. In the Ocean Race of 1900 *Tertia*, whose performance all Kinsale people followed with interest, carried away her mast off Barry's Head and was towed to Kinsale by the steam-powered *Vagrant*.

A feature of the time was the interest that the yachting press took in reporting the sailing excitement and competition that was part of the sport. The usual course set for the yachts started at the Pier Head taking the fleet around Big Sovereign and from there to a flag boat southeast of the Old Head. On the way home the Big Sovereign was left to port and Bulman Buoy to starboard. At the 1900 Regatta, fierce squalls from the northwest created flukey 'cat's paws' stretching across the harbour. On the run to the Sovereign there was anxiety about the anticipated gybe with the risk of carrying away the mast, which in those days was stepped through the deck down to the keel. Despite the foreboding, the boats rounded the island safely and then, close hauled, encountered huge seas that broke on their windward quarter, flowing in torrents from the sails and pouring out through the scuppers on the lee side. *Vanity* lost her bowsprit and *Cyane* carried away her forestay but managed to run safely to Cork Harbour. On the same day, *Jabberwalk* beat local boats *Spray* and *Glance* in the smaller class. In such weather, boats suffered broken spars and gear, torn sails and no doubt frantic baling was required to stay afloat. The reputation of sailors could be destroyed by poor seamanship or gain mythic status if they successfully came through the difficult conditions.

Boats in Kinsale raced in classes according to size or tonnage under handicap. Races were referred to as matches. In the 1907 programme the largest boats, between 15 and 23 tons, were followed by vessels of between 5 and 15 tons. Smaller than these, boats were sailed in two classes according to length, not exceeding 24 feet or 18 feet overall. The larger boats normally sailed set courses of 20 miles and a distance of 12 miles was laid for the smaller craft.[10]

Tough, uncompromising competition was a feature of the fishing boat matches which were crewed by the men who worked them. These races had the added edge of substantial money being the prize for success. Prizes of £8 for first and £3 for second were available for the first class fishing boats when five went to the line in 1898. In a strong northerly breeze the *Rover* (M. Driscoll), *Bonnie Maggie* (R.A. Williams), *Susan* (J. Coughlan), *Stella* (C. Farley) and *Water Nymph* (Thuillier brothers) started at the Pier and, taking all the harbour buoys to starboard, they raced to the Daunt Rock lightship. At the end there was little between the boats as they beat up the harbour having made great time in the fresh reaching conditions. In the tight racing, *Susan* and *Stella* collided with no quarter given and scant regard for the rules of yacht racing. *Stella* obviously came out of the incident well as she finished first, followed by *Rover*, then *Susan*, *Water Nymph* and *Bonnie Maggie* in fifth place. No doubt Skipper Farley and his crew celebrated well into the night.

The usual sportsmanship among the yachting fraternity was occasionally compromised when valuable prizes were on offer. The Regatta held on 29 July 1861 was a case in point. 'Corinthian' in a *History of Yachting in the South of Ireland* writes that 'to carry out the sports in a spirited and worthy manner Sir John Arnott MP presented the meeting with a splendid Challenge Cup value 50 guineas with twenty guineas added … to become the property of the gentleman winning it twice with the same vessel'. With such prizes, competition was intense and to ensure fair sailing a rule was adopted 'prohibiting the use of shifting ballast or bags of shot and that all ballast be under the floors or in lockers'. The aim of the rule was to prevent the practice of moving weight to the windward side of the boat to improve performance.

In Kinsale many of these trophies were presented by the British regiments serving in the town. A link with this sponsorship is the Thuillier Cup raced annually during the Kinsale Yacht Club April League. The silver trophy was originally presented by the Royal Enniskillen Fusiliers in 1871 and won by Michael Thuillier. The cup was presented to the Club to acknowledge the long tradition of yacht racing in the harbour.

In the nineteenth century the Regatta was the social event of the year in Kinsale. Organisation and management were in the hands of an elite group and military personnel stationed in the town. A perk was free access to the enclosed promenade and also, with their partners and acquaintances, entry to 'a ball which was numerously and fashionably attended'. Fifty years later in 1937 the Regatta Committee had become more representative of the population as a whole. The stewards and officials were identified by a cotton badge pinned to the coat lapel which set them apart, with authority to control the crowds and organise the events ashore and afloat. Proud to wear the badge, each steward was admonished in the programme with the warning that 'the strength of the chain is marred by even one weak link. Don't you be that weak link'.[11]

Position in the social order was not confined to participation in activities ashore. The report of the 1858 Regatta shows that the fishing boats were included only as an afterthought: 'the real racing took place in yachts after the start of the hooker races'. In retrospect, the lack of appreciation of these fine boats is difficult to understand as under way in a fresh breeze they were a magnificent spectacle.

Aboard the yachts a fine distinction existed in the relationship between the owner and the 'paid hands', based on principles of naval command and authority. Paid hands were employed aboard larger sailing craft to maintain the boat and rig. Usually men of seafaring experience and expertise, they were often the most competent sailors aboard. On occasions this gave rise to tension when conditions got tough and the 'hand' had to take charge. At the end of the nineteenth century it is said that owners complained about paid skippers and crews having everything their own way on race days and that they, the owners, were no more than passengers. They agreed that while paid hands were essential, they must understand that their duty was to obey rather than command and under no circumstances was a 'hand' even to touch the helm. To mark their status in the pecking order, the paid hands were required to stand on the counter astern before the start and at the end of racing.

The Regatta Committee, 1958. *Courtesy Cork Examiner*

From the social and community perspective the most successful years of the Regatta were from the 1930s to the 1960s when the festival in early August coincided with the two-week British holiday period. Those who had emigrated during the depression returned home to family and friends to enjoy the annual festival. To provide added entertainment for the wider public, swimming and water carnival events, tug-o'-war, fancy dress and firework displays were introduced. Under the guidance of dedicated people, preparations were undertaken for weeks in advance, including the decoration of the Pier Road and Head in colourful bunting.

Rowing was a significant feature of the programme on Regatta day. Competition was arranged for two- and four-oared 'pleasure' boats, six-man fishing yawls and seine boats complete with their nets. Four-oared gigs were rowed by members of the coastguard, military and naval reserve forces. In 1886 sculling races were organised for boys less than fifteen years of age in fishing punts, using a single oar held in a cutaway hold on the transom at the stern. The skill was used to get a short distance on the water in sheltered conditions.

Crews of the armed services were disciplined and obeyed the rules when overtaking and rounding marks. For other participants oars often became entangled in the heat of competition as boats converging on a turning mark frequently fouled one another. With the prospect of a financial reward, the races gave rise to displays of bad temper and the use of coarse language. The offended could make an objection to the stewards, which usually produced an indeterminate result leading to an unsatisfactory conclusion.[12]

Rowing became more formalised in the twentieth century when rowing clubs were established at the Dock and other locations on the Bandon River. The crews of the four-oared coxed 'pleasure' boats trained not just for Kinsale Regatta but for other events at venues in the Cork Harbour area. The annual arrival of the boats, which came bottom-up on lorries and underneath were packed full of supporters from clubs such as St Finbarr's, Blackrock, the Coal Quay in Cork and White Point in Cobh among others, was eagerly anticipated in Kinsale. In preparation for the rowing season the Dock Club began training in May with the majority of the crew from the Castlepark side of the river and a small number from the World's End. On calm evenings as dusk closed in, the strike of blades turned up the phosphorescence in the darkening water. The crew beat out the stroke like a Roman galley on the placid water to the echoing count of the cox as the boat cut out a fine bow wave. Groups of local supporters gathered at the river wall casting a critical eye, inevitably comparing the current crew with those of the past.

Before the Duggan Bridge was built, on race day the rowing started at Murphy's Point in the townland of Ringfinnan which to the finish was a course of approximately a mile and a half. A bend at Common Point and a slight turn to the right approaching the end line, complicated by the influence of the tide, required astute coxing. The crews stretched and strained to the encouraging roars of the supporters on the riverside. The cry 'Come on, the Dock' evokes scenes described by Virgil 2,000 years ago:[13]

And now the shouts from the shore
Grew twice as loud as all the watching crowd
Cheered, filling the air with a din.

Racing to the finish line at the Pier Head, the boats:

Abreast they cleft their furrows all the sea
Torn up by oar strokes and biting prows.

With success local heroes were created. Many a quick wager was laid between rival supporters as the jostling, cheering crowds on the World's End road followed progress to the finishing line.

Interest in these boats died out in the 1960s and competitive rowing was dropped from the Regatta programme. In March 1992 a small group formed the nucleus of a committee which met in the Outdoor Education Centre to re-establish a club in the Kinsale area and in recognition of the tradition across the river it was called the Kinsale and Dock Rowing Club. It was decided to affiliate with the Coastal Rowing Association which consisted of fifteen clubs from different parts of the Cork coast. The boats were constructed of timber and were 21 feet in length. The sport of coastal rowing comes from the tradition of working boats with the competitive element arising originally out of commercial necessity. As already mentioned, when the approach of a vessel at the harbour mouth was announced, apprentices of the rival boatyards raced to the incoming vessel for the prize of getting the contract for the repairs to the ship. During the height of the fishing, buyers in boats raced to the incoming fleet to strike a price for the catch before it was landed. The practice continued into the twentieth century when trawlers or small coasters arrived in the harbour: the first rowing yawl to arrive alongside would be used exclusively to ferry crew, carry provisions and assist in providing a range of services while in port. The new rowing club tapped into this tradition. A black-painted yawl designed by Rob Jacob and built by Ray O'Callaghan was launched in September 1992. Since then many hundreds of people, varying in age from under twelve years to veterans in their fifties, have competed at regattas in Kinsale and other venues throughout the island (see plate 21).

In August 1998 the Kinsale and Dock Club hosted the All-Ireland Coastal Rowing Championships. Forty clubs participated in twenty-one different race events. Eight lanes were laid between the Duggan Bridge with turning buoys moored off the Marsh Dock, giving the required distances for the various categories. Logistically, it was a mammoth task to cater for so many crews afloat and thousands of visitors ashore. The event firmly established the club as a popular harbour-related activity offering rowing and experience on the water to many and includes participation by whole families.

Reflecting the different communities in the harbour, regattas also took place at Summer Cove. The report for the second Thursday in August 1904 said that 'the delightful weather brought crowds from the surrounding districts' and 'the pretty little village appeared to great advantage'. Five yachts started, with *Heroine* beating scratch boat *Spray* by two minutes. The course, starting off the 'promenade' at Summer Cove, took the boats around Scilly (Crohogue) Buoy and out to Bulman twice. The course enabled the viewing public ashore to see the full race. Three drievers or working boats, with lug rigs, sailed the same course. There was also an extensive programme of rowing events involving the coastguard and the garrisons of both Charles Fort and the Barracks. Competition was organised for ladies and gentlemen rowing in two- and four-oared craft. The band of the Loyal North Lancashire Regiment provided the entertainment and novelty events such as a walking race to the Post Office in Kinsale, a barrel race and pig-and-pole contests provided much enjoyment.

While there is some truth, particular for those who suffer *mal de mer*, in Doctor Johnson's assertion that 'the pleasure of going to sea is getting ashore again', nevertheless the urge to get afloat in a well-found boat and sailing on the glistening sea in fresh conditions is a constant attraction. In the pre-engine days, crews rigged boats at moorings, bent on sails and, sweating on the fall of halyards, hoisted heavy gaffs, yards and topsails aloft 'to two blocks'. The expression describes the hauling limit of the rope before tying off on the mast cleats. When racing, boats jostled for the most advantageous position on the starting line, as the seconds were counted down for the signal to start and, more often than not, bore away at the start from the Pier Head in the prevailing breeze. Having rounded Scilly Buoy, sheets

An early photo of yacht racing in Kinsale shows *Heroine*, *Glance* and *Spray*
sailing for the O'Connor Cup, 1893. *Courtesy R. Jago*

were hardened in as the boats came on the wind. In the close racing
any attempt to overtake when going to windward was difficult as it
involved sailing through the opponent's lee. Alternative possibilities
might arise by breaking tacks in the wider stretches of the Outer
Harbour or working the wind shifts that produce the lifts. After the
windward mark the boats bore away with sheets checked and sails
trimmed for the brisk reach to the next mark. The craft creamed
along, as water dripped from the bobstay before the stem buried itself
again in its own bow wave and, with the curved bilge exposed, the
wake tantalisingly clung to the counter astern.

Apart from the regattas there is mention of racing under sail in
Kinsale taking place on a regular basis in the early nineteenth century.
It described competition between the best fishing hookers, pilot cutters
and yachts sailing as one class under the title 'Hake Club of Kinsale'.[14]
Specific instructions laid down that only three sails could be used –
main, jib and stay sails, avoiding topsails. Regular challenge cups were
presented and a photograph taken in 1893 (above) shows the *Spray*,
Glance and *Heroine* running towards Scilly, with the old hotel ruins
prominent in the background, sailing for the O'Connor Cup.

In the 1930s enthusiasts established the Kinsale Sailing Club which during the season arranged racing twice weekly and was organised formally with its flag officers, rules for competition, officers of the day, presentation of prizes, and social events such as the laying-up supper each year at Acton's Hotel. Initially eight gunter-rigged dinghies formed the basis of a small one-design fleet with sailing confined to the limits of the harbour. Throughout the 1940s regular reports on the racing appeared in the local press. For the mixed classes the handicapping system used was excellent with little separating the competitors on corrected time each week. Formality was the order of the day with results recorded using titles such as Mister, Miss, military rank Brigadier or Commander, of which there were a number retired in the Kinsale area, and for younger members, Master.

In the 1950s Knolly Stokes had three Colleen class boats built, *Pinkeen, Colleen* and *Spalpeen*. Even though one design, they sailed with a fleet of mixed cruisers and provided a wonderful spectacle on racing days. The fleet began to expand with the arrival of the first Dragon class boat – *Sleuth* – brought to the harbour by a retired British naval officer in the 1950s. The second boat in the development of this fleet was *Beduin*, owned by local man Dick Hegarty who enjoyed great success. Subsequently these elegant craft with their counter sterns became well established and formed a separate class. A later generation of Dragon owners had many achievements internationally, including Conor Doyle and Tony O'Gorman who between them won the Edinburgh Cup on a number of occasions in the 1970s. By this time the club had changed its name to Kinsale Yacht Club. The old burgee of the white anchor on a red back was changed to a gold portcullis, the harbour arms, on blue.

In the early 1960s the Albacore class was introduced to the harbour by John Jacob and John Petch. Designed by Uffa Fox, the heat-moulded, diagonally planked 15-foot dinghy with its straight stem was an attractive boat and a delight to sail. It was a stable craft and in a breeze capable of planing at great speed.

At about the same time the blue-sailed Enterprise class, 13 feet 9 inches in length, was introduced. The fleet grew quickly and, when combined with boats from Cork, had more than twenty racing regularly. While a little tender they were great performers and helped

Dick Hegarty and one of
his many sailing protégés,
Justin Coleman, 1945.
Courtesy Mary Hegarty

to hone the skills of many members. Designed by Jack Holt they were sailed in Kinsale until the middle of the 1970s. By this time the original sailors in the class, looking for more stability and size, established the Fox-designed Flying Fifteen fleet. It was a fin-keeled, spinnaker-flying craft which again brought success nationally to such helms as Eddie Sheehy and David Tucker.

For various reasons these classes went out of fashion and are no longer sailed in Kinsale. Currently, the predominant one-design class is the Squib, which is a stable craft, with fleets of fifteen in a full muster. Wednesday evenings for many years have been reserved for cruiser racing. The boats range in size from some of the largest yachts sailing on the Irish coast to the 24-foot Westerly GKs. Based on various handicapping systems they provide very competitive racing.

For short periods, high-performance boats such as the two-man trapeze-rigged 470 class were sailed but after a season or two tended to fade (see plate 22). Its junior counterpart, the 420, and versions of the Laser established themselves in the 1980s and continue in the harbour, raced by younger club members. In the 1960s in seeking to popularise the sport, Kinsale Yacht Club introduced the Irish Yachting Association, now the Irish Sailing Association, training scheme for young people. The three-stage course with a strong emphasis on racing has produced some fine sailors, many of whom have become instructors themselves. At the beginning an assortment of small boats was used, which had survived from the older days when racing was based on mixed classes. In the 1970s the gunter-rigged Mirror dinghy was adopted as the boat recommended for the juniors. These red-sailed dinghies became popular and provided excellent training in the basic skills. Club member Mattias Helstern went on to become European champion in this class in 1998. In the 1990s the 8-foot Optimist emerged as the single-handed boat for young people. For their size they are simple and perform exceptionally well in all weathers, with crews kitted out in waterproofs and wetsuits. Kinsale Yacht Club has also been prominent in providing access to sailing for physically challenged people. Club member John Twomey has represented Ireland at international level, sailing in a number of Paralympics.

Facilities ashore kept pace with development afloat. Initially, the sailing club had the use of a room at Dennis Quay where the signal flags, cannon and powder cartridges were stored and results were processed. Socially, members gathered after racing in the hostelries close to the pier where extensive post mortems were conducted. With the growing popularity of the sport, in the 1950s a clubhouse was built at Scilly which included meeting rooms, bar, stores and changing facilities. As access to the water was limited with little space for tenders and, more importantly, no shore-based storage facilities for dinghies, the location was considered unsuitable. An old Georgian house at Lower Fisher (O'Connell) Street with a fine open area stretching to the Pier road became available and was purchased. The building has been adapted and an old apple orchard cleared to provide a dinghy park with access to the Pier slipway. A major development in terms of facilities was the construction of the marina in 1978 which was significant not just for the club but for the town itself. Located in the most sheltered part of the harbour, its concentration of modern yachts identifies Kinsale as a major marine recreation centre, perhaps indicating what the immediate future holds for the harbour.

Kinsale Yacht Club has become a noted sailing centre particularly recognised for its ability to organise and cater for some of the most prestigious sailing events at a national and European level. Club member Alan Crosbie's expertise as an 'Officer of the Day' is recognised internationally. In terms of the numbers of boats, intricate logistics and the planning and conduct of racing, the Irish National Optimist Championships in 2006 under the direction of Eamonn Judge was a superb event. It drew over 220 boats to the harbour which included competitors from the UK and the US. In 2012 the club hosted the Edinburgh Cup for Dragons bringing over sixty boats to Kinsale in a superbly organised event.

The competitive racing element currently tends to dominate club activity on the water. Sailing for itself and the pure challenge of harnessing the wind and working the tide are now undertaken only as part of racing and rarely for the pleasure of simply 'going for a sail'. A great exponent of exploring the intrinsic challenge of sailing was Kinsale man Justin Coleman who, in his 12-foot *Wanda* built by himself, achieved some extraordinary feats in the 1950s. Over a four-day period, he sailed his little boat single-handed from Kinsale to Schull, scrambling ashore in remote coves at night for rest. Cruising is also a significant pursuit for some club members who seek out and have become familiar with some of the most beautiful sailing areas in Europe and further.

Another aspect of recreational sailing has been the development of ancillary services ashore, offering potential for employment. In 1962 Fred Good established one of the first sailing schools and yacht charter businesses in the country. Initially, he operated from a caravan on the Pier with a training fleet that consisted of Albacores, a National 18 and, for bigger boat experience, the Colleen class *Pinkeen*. The charter fleet was made up of Folkboats, comfortable small cruisers, brought in from East Germany and Sweden. Ahead of his time, Fred developed a boat chandlery and engine retail outlet at the Long Quay. Later, he with others put a boatyard and building facility in place at Kilmacsimon Quay. The yard was taken over by the Kingston family who later developed additional services and storage space for large craft at Middle Cove in the harbour. More recently, Gearoid Fitzgerald started a boatbuilding business at the Farm Lane and turns out fine vessels in fibreglass for fishermen and the leisure industry. Some of the world's finest sailing vessels are designed in Kinsale by renowned yacht designers and a successful sailmaking facility is available, together with top class service at Desmond Engineering and the maintenance of running and standing rigging.

In 1973 Kinsale Vocational School introduced sailing as a recreational activity for pupils at a time when the maritime environment was totally neglected in Irish education. The project, which was received enthusiastically by the pupils, stimulated a number of initiatives. Under a scheme for the introduction of pre-employment courses in 1977, Kinsale applied to the Department of Education and the County Cork VEC to run a Marine Skills course. While the focus was on providing practical training for marine-related careers in fishing, the merchant and naval services, there was a recreational and leisure element included. The course was first located on Lower O'Connell (Fisher) Street and in 1978 moved to the redundant boys' National School on St John's Hill. The full-time course was an exercise in curriculum development from which a number of interesting projects emerged.

From the boatbuilding and seamanship elements, the Department of Education agreed to sponsor a nationwide school's boatbuilding competition which was designed, planned and organised by the coordinator of the Kinsale course. The objective was for groups of five pupils, representing schools throughout the island of Ireland, to construct a boat as a woodwork project to the design of Jack Tyrrell. Prior to coming to Kinsale for assessment, the young people acquired and practised seamanship and handling skills (see plate 23) in the boats they had built. At Kinsale they were required to explain the method of construction and were individually interviewed ashore on safety, meteorology, rope work, etc. They were then assessed afloat on their ability to row, sail and on seamanship and handling skills. The aim was to promote an awareness of the maritime environment, develop seamanship skills and demonstrate the possibility of engaging with the sea. Apart from opening possible opportunities for careers, the objective was to develop an appreciation of the marine resource for use in a non-exploitative and sustainable way. The programme was designed to give access to boats and the sea, particularly to those who would not otherwise have had the opportunity. There was a strong emphasis on safety, seamanship and the importance of the marine environment. After two years the project was unexpectedly terminated in 1981. A possible reason was an emerging emphasis on recreation and adventure sports by the Department of Education, which was in line with Irish Sailing Association efforts to improve the standard of racing nationally. The high-performance competitive nature of this policy tended to limit appreciation of the maritime to the competitive and away from the wider objectives that were envisaged and pursued earlier at Kinsale.

Kinsale Outdoor Education Centre, which grew out of the original Marine Skills Course, continues to provide opportunities for recreational outdoor pursuits. The course itself is now taught at Kinsale Further Education College. The original objectives, which stressed training in vocational skills, evolved into FETAC-recognised modules that qualify students in a range of marine activities. It focuses strongly on an awareness of the marine environment, wind-powered energy and the importance of ecology and sustainability. In turn, this has led to the development of the Permaculture course which attracts students from all over the world to Kinsale. Many of those who complete the course get employment in various aspects of the marine industry, including adventure centres in Ireland and abroad as crew aboard ocean-going yachts.[15]

Fishing for sport and recreation has been pursued by Kinsale people from the middle of the nineteenth century. In 1907 it was reported that 'Kinsale once celebrated for its hookers ... has capital fishing grounds for the amateur'.[16] The formal founding of Kinsale Anglers Club took place at a public meeting held at the Courthouse on 31 May 1939.[17] The chairman's remarks at the initial meeting highlighted Kinsale as 'a fishing centre with its spacious harbour combined with estuary fishing available on the Bandon River and being entirely landlocked, offers shelter from all winds ... they had fishing second to none in Ireland'. With some prescience he went on to say that 'the newly formed Club would serve a very useful purpose in local efforts being made to develop the old and historic town as a tourist resort'. At the meeting it was decided to affiliate with the British Sea Anglers Society. Kinsale was included with 200 'fishing stations' in the Society's annual pocketbook which was circulated to thousands of anglers in the UK, and gave information on fishing available from the shore or afloat at Kinsale. It also provided data on tides, accommodation, availability of boats and the name of a local contact who would assist the visitor.[18]

The Kinsale Club drew up a fixture list for 1940 and circulated a programme. The busy season saw two or three competitions arranged each month from 1 May to 31 October at different grounds within the harbour. On a chart, marks were indicated where various species of fish could be caught. Bulman Sound produced whiting and pollack, which were also found at Bog Hole and Farmer Rock. Off the Crooked Ditch close to Eastern Point gurnet could be taken. The river under Ringrone Castle was known for bass. The rules stated that prizes were awarded on the basis of (a) the heaviest weight of fish of more than 9 inches in length and (b) the largest number of fish excluding mackerel. On occasions only 'edible' fish were permitted. This rule may have been included because of food scarcity during the war.

Fishing took place in rowing boats and salmon yawls hired for the day. Old fishing smacks, with small paraffin-smelling TVO engines fitted, made the odd foray outside the harbour. In the early days hand lines wound on timber frames were common but in time gave way to rods and sophisticated reels. Sustenance for the day consisted of sandwiches wrapped in paper and a bottle of stout or two. Then, after the day's fishing and weigh-in, the anglers and their friends adjourned to Murphy's Hotel on the Long Quay for a social evening. There they enjoyed the 'smoking concert', with each person present contributing their party piece, and continuing into the early hours.

The Kinsale anglers developed friendly relations with a Dublin club known by the chivalric-sounding title 'Knights of the Silver Hook'. For a number of years they came to Kinsale at the beginning of August and competed annually with the local anglers. The contact between the clubs inspired the idea of a nationwide Irish Federation of Sea Anglers which was established at Acton's Hotel in 1953.

At a later stage, in the 1960s, Kinsale emerged as the leading angling centre in Ireland, following the staging of the annual Kinsale

Sea Angling Festival, which emphasised deep-sea fishing. Thirty- and forty-foot boats took anglers to the Ling Rocks, the Old Head of Kinsale, east to Newfoundland Bay and the odd foray in the vicinity of the *Lusitania* wreck. Large skate, shark, ling, conger and other species were landed and weighed publicly on a platform at the Pier Head. Hundreds came to view the rather gruesome spectacle of these limp, dead creatures hanging from the weighing balance. With guts falling from the gaff-rent bellies, the fish, so magnificent in their natural environment, were presented for public gaze in a pathetic state. On occasions some exotic-looking fish were caught, which were examined and identified by the festival's resident marine biologist, Professor McMahon, who then proceeded to contribute some interesting observations.

Commercially, Kinsale had been in a state of economic depression for fifty years and the possibilities of developing the angling potential presented some hope. In the late 1950s Gary Culhane, who had spent time in Canada, established Kinsale Boats Ltd and facilities for anglers at the old Dockyard site, providing all the necessary equipment to engage in deep-sea fishing. Interestingly, it was the harbour and its qualities that first attracted Culhane, who was ably assisted by his sister Peggy Green. After years of stagnation, angling was the spark which ignited the tourist phenomenon and Kinsale once again created a unique niche for itself. The guarantee of a good haul attracted English, Dutch and German anglers in large numbers. New angling boats were built and experienced local men with seafaring backgrounds were employed as skippers (see plate 24). The growing number of visitors stimulated the growth of a range of services for tourists. The Rank Organisation built a hotel, now the Trident, in conjunction with the Angling Centre at the Dockyard site. Restaurants, bed and breakfast accommodation, general retail outlets and the full panoply of resources required to cater for many thousands of visitors each year were put in place. Festivals, based on themes relating to the harbour, were brilliantly marketed, with such logos as 'Catch me in Kinsale'. This started the process of making Kinsale one of Ireland's leading tourist centres which has been recognised nationally and acknowledged internationally by being awarded the initial European Prize for Tourism and the Environment in 1996.

Urban Council Development Plans since the 1970s have tended to focus on the promotion of tourism, with planning in relation to the harbour concentrating on what could be described as the development of a 'polite waterfront'. Commercial maritime activity and the fishing industry were perceived as secondary and on occasions even detrimental to the promotion of tourism. The Dockyard and associated warehousing has become a hotel. Open space adjacent to the Pier Head which would be useful for port-related activities has been converted to a roadway. An apartment complex now occupies the site which was once Robertson's fish yard and more recently the fish cannery. Much of the quayside and a number of slipways have been chained off to create a harbour promenade. The policy, if continued, runs the risk of removing the essential physical supports for the commercial development of marine-related industry. Tourism itself will suffer as the only experience presented to the visitor will be a banal, homogenised shadow of what was once a busy harbour town. Official policy in the period up to 2010 has run the risk of relegating port activity to little more than a reminder of what was once a vibrant seafaring community. Since then, recent improvements at the Pier Head, the Lobster Quay and the development of Adam's Quay would seem to indicate a change in official development planning. This augurs well for a regeneration of activity in the harbour, particularly in the area of fishing, which has seen a number of young fishermen invest in the purchase of larger craft.

Kinsale is unique among Irish towns. In cycles it has suffered the effects of economic depression and stagnation. Then, phoenix-like, it draws on a latent resilience, resurrecting itself and repeatedly emerging as a notable centre in Ireland. All of its significant prominence in history has been related to its connection with the sea. At a function in March 2013 to mark the handing over of Harbour Board control to Cork County Council, the essential significance of the sea to Kinsale was reiterated.[19] It is reasonable to conclude that, for future sustainable development, the potential that exists in Kinsale as a port and the qualities that nature has so generously bestowed will continue to provide the stimulus for innovative progress.

Glossary

Aback	Haul clew of sail to windward to assist in tacking.
Aft(er), Astern	Towards the stern or back of boat.
Aloft	Usually refers to positions above deck level.
Back sails	Trimming sails to catch wind on wrong side.
Back	Wind change in anticlockwise direction.
Ballast	Heavy material put aboard a vessel to give stability.
Barquentine	A vessel of three masts or more with square sails on foremast only.
Beacon furnace	Coal- or timber-fuelled light warning.
Beam	Maximum width of boat.
Bear away	Change direction away from the wind.
Berth	Accommodation aboard or to take vessel to allocated position.
Bend	Attach sail to yard or gaff.
Bilge	Underwater rounded section of hull.
Block	Pulley with one or more sheaves.
Boatswain (bo'sun)	Seaman responsible for vessel's sails, rigging and ropes.
Bounty	Share of benefits from maritime activity.
Bobstay	Stay at end of bowsprit to the cutwater on the stem.
Bowsprit	Spar that extends over the stem.
Box haul	Use of sails to assist in wearing around.
Breast hook	Knee to hold gunwales to stem of boat.
Breakwater	Artificial construction to provide protection from the sea.
Brig	Square-rigged two-masted vessel.
Bulkhead	Part of ship structure to increase rigidity and divide vessel.

243

Broach to	Tendency for vessel when off the wind to luff-up suddenly.
Call port	Ports at which orders for final destination were received.
Capstan	Used on ships for heaving on ropes and cables.
Cardinal marks	System of pillar buoys to show safest side to pass a danger.
Careen	Describes a vessel high and dry and leaning over on one side so that the bottom is exposed for repairs.
Carry away	Loss of masts, rigging or sails due to violent gust of wind.
Cat's paws	Outline of squall on water due to downward draught of wind.
Caulking	Process of serving oakum or rope into seams between planks.
Ceiling boards	Floor boards.
Chain plates	Iron plates on ship's side to which rigging is attached.
Characteristic	Distinguishing features or lights on navigational aids.
Chart	Information on waters and coastlines represented on paper.
Check	Ease a rope or sheet slowly.
Clearing line	Direction taken to avoid obstruction.
Clew	Lower or after corner of a sail.
Clinker	Overlapping timber planks in the construction of boats.
Complement	Number required to crew a ship.
Creaming	Making way quickly through the water.
Cringle	A rope loop worked into a sail.
Cutter	Single-masted vessel with main jib and staysail on bowsprit.
Deadeye	Wooden block through which shroud lanyards are rove.
Demurrage	Payment to owner when ship is delayed.
Drag	Anchor not holding on the bottom.
Drift	Distance made by floating object due to wind or tide.
East Indiamen	Ships of the East India Company.
Ebb	Tide receding or going out.
Fairway	Navigable part of channel.
Fathom	A measurement unit equal to six feet.
Feather oars	To turn blades horizontal when out of water.
Fetch	Sailing to windward, reaching objective in one tack.
Flood	An incoming or rising tide.
Foot, luff, leach	Sides of triangular sail.
Fore-and-aft rig	A vessel with all sails set in a fore-to-aft line with square sails on yards across the ship.
Forestay	Important support for mast at fore end of boat.
Futtock	Timber fitted to the frame of a ship.
Gaff	(i) spart at top of fore and aft sail to extend sail up or from mast; (ii) pole with iron hook used to get large fish aboard.
Garboard	Strake closest to keel.
Grappled	Use of grapple hook to draw objects closer.

Gunwales	Heavy timber around boat on top of upper strake.
Gybe	Change of direction so that stern passes through eye of wind.
Halyard	Rope used to hoist flags, sails and yards, etc.
Hands	Term used for crew – deckhands.
Harden to the wind	Sail closer to the wind.
Hard fast	Solidly aground.
Hawse pipe	Pipe through which cable from ship to anchor passes.
Head, tack, clew	Corners of triangular sail.
Hitch	Knot used in joining ropes and making fast to yards or posts.
Hove to	Arrangement of sails so that boat does not make way.
Hung on the ways	Slow to enter water when launched.
Hydrography	Gathering of information for use in charts.
Impressment	Recruitment of crewmen by force.
Knees	Grained timber pieces used to support thwarts, etc.
Ketch	Two-masted vessel with after mast stepped forward of rudder head.
Landfall	To see land after a long voyage.
Lanyard	Rope used to attach anything including shrouds to deadeyes.
Lateral	Buoys used to mark channel – red cone to port and green cone to starboard.
Leading lines	A heading or course identified by marks or transits ashore.
Lead line	Lead attached to line to take soundings.
Leathering	Attaching leather to oars to reduce wear.
Leeward	Anywhere downwind.
Littoral	Area close to the shoreline.
Lift	Wind direction change that assists sailing to windward.
Log	Record of a ship's voyage.
Lying off	Vessel anchored or stopped off a quay wall.
Mainsail	Largest sail in fore-and-aft rig.
Make way	Movement through water using sail, oars or power.
Manifest	Document containing details of cargo.
Mizzen	Small fore-and-aft sail set on mast in the after part of a boat.
Morse code	Signalling by means of light or sound to represent letters.
Nobby/Nickey	Inshore fishing vessels, traditionally used around Lancashire and the Isle of Man.
Pallace	Early form of fish-processing centre.
Painter	Rope at bow used to make boat fast.
Pitching	Bows of vessel plunging into troughs.
Pilot	Person taken on board to take vessels in or out of narrow entrances.
Planing	Moving through water with bows lifted clear.

Privateer	Privately financed ship used to attack enemy ships.
Port side	Left-hand side of vessel looking forward.
Reaching	Point of sailing with wind from abeam.
Rake	Slope of anything on a boat; rake of mast.
Rating	Classification of ships, 1 to 6, based on number of guns.
Ratline	Rope ladder attached to mast shrouds.
Race	Strong disturbed current, usually off headlands.
Range	Boat held in position within scope of her anchor cable.
Ride to anchor	Vessel held in position by anchor.
Rising	Timber battens on which tauts or thwarts are placed.
Rove	A halyard or rope passed through a sheave or block.
Rowing yawl	Term for working rowing boat.
Salvo	Firing of artillery as a salute.
Scandalise	To reduce sail quickly by adjusting height of gaff.
Scend	Surge created by a wave.
Schooner	Normally a two-masted vessel with mainmast taller than fore.
Scupper	Holes to allow water to flow overboard.
Sea kindly	Adequate boat for the local conditions.
Sextant	Instrument to measure angles at sea.
Set	Direction of the tidal current.
Sheer strake	Upper plank that gives longitudinal profile to boat.
Sheet	Rope used to trim sails.
Shoal	Shallow depth surrounded by deeper water.
Smack	Normally a small fishing vessel.
Sounding	Depth of water given in fathom, feet or metres.
Spill wind	Reduce the force of wind on sails by freeing sheets.
Spinnaker	Triangular sail hoisted when off the wind.
Spring tides	Highest and lowest tides that occur twice in lunar cycle.
Spritsail	Four-sided sail supported by sprit from tack to peak.
Squall	Sudden gust of wind.
Square rig	Square sails bent on to yards on one or more masts.
Starboard	Right-hand side of vessel looking forward.
Strake	The full length of plank from bow to stern.
Stroke	Oar astern which sets the rate followed by rowers.
Tabernacle	Three-sided fixture into which the foot of a mast is fitted.
Tack	(i) Hard Tack, or ship's biscuit; (ii) direction of sailing vessel in relation to which side the wind is blowing, i.e. port or starboard tack; (iii) to change direction of sailing, i.e. from port to starboard, or opposite; (iv) lower fore corner of any fore-and-aft sail.

Taut	A seat athwartship in a vessel. Also referred to as thwarts.
Thwarts	Seats athwartships in a vessel. Also referred to as tauts.
Tonnage	Ship measurement based more on cargo capacity than weight.
To weather	To sail a course to windward of a headland or a mark.
Transits	Markers ashore that identify direction lines.
Trim	How a boat floats and set of sails.
Up two blocks	Hoisted to full height when two blocks touch.
Victualling	Supply provisions to ships.
Veering	Clockwise change of wind direction.
Wake	The water immediately astern of a moving vessel.
Way on	(For a ship) to move through water.
Wear around	Change tack with stern to wind.
Weather	To pass around object on to which wind is blowing.
Well found	Vessel in good condition.
Weigh anchor	To lift anchor from the bottom.
Windward	In the direction from which the wind is blowing.
Yard	Spar across a mast to spread a sail.
Yaw	Due to sea, boat direction swinging from side to side.
Yawl	Two-masted vessel with after mast astern of rudder stock.

References

Chapter 1. On Entering Kinsale Harbour

1   Souhami, Diana, *Selkirk's Island*, Phoenix, London, 2001, p. 41.

2   O'Sullivan, F., *History of Kinsale,* Tower Books, Cork, 1976, p. 3; O'Rahilly, T.F., 'Dun Cearma', *Journal of the Cork Historical and Archaeological Society,* Vol. XLIV, Cork, 1939, pp. 16–20; Cremin, C., 'Some Prehistoric Remains near Kinsale' in the *Journal of the Cork Historical and Archaeological Society (JCHAS)* Vol. XXIX, Cork, 1923, pp. 73–74.

3   McSwiney, Fr P., 'Georgian Kinsale', *JCHAS* XLIV, Cork, 1939, p. 113.

4   O'Maidin, P. 'Today' in *Cork Examiner*, 1 November 1978; O'Sullivan, F., *op. cit.* 1976, p. 4; Bligh Talbot Crosbie, 'Antiquarian Remains, Part 1', *JCHAS* XVIII, (1912); Mulcahy, Michael, *A Short History of Kinsale*, Historical Guides, Cork, 1968.

5   Marsden, Philip, *The Levelling Sea*, Harper Collins, UK, 2011, p 87.

6   Taylor, Richard M., *The Lighthouses of Ireland,* The Collins Press, Cork, 2004, p. 16; de Courcy Ireland, John, *Ireland and the Irish in Maritime History,* Glendale, Dublin, 1986, p. 172.

7   Leather, John, *Gaff Rig,* Adlard Coles, London, 1970.

8   Kinsale Harbour Board, minutes of meeting for 2 January 1871.

9   Joyce, James, 'Cyclops' chapter, *Ulysses*, Penguin, 1960, p. 342; Jackson, J.W., *John Stanislaw's Joyce,* Fourth Estate, London, 1997.

10 Lewis, Samuel, *Topographical Dictionary of Ireland, II,* London, 1838, p. 232.

11 Caulfield, R. (ed.), 'Annals of Kinsale xliv, *The Council Book of the Corporation of Kinsale*, Surrey, 1879.

12 Murphy, Elaine, 'The Cromwellian Navy in Ireland, 1649–53' in *History Ireland*, July/August 2011, pp. 21–23; Mulcahy, M., *op. cit.*, 1968, p. 22.

13 Andrew, J.S., *Shapes of Ireland, Maps and their Makers, 1564–1839,* Geography Publications, Dublin, 1997.

14 Thuillier, John H., Private Papers.

15 Dinneen, P.S., *Foclóir Gaedhilge agus Béarla*, Dublin, 1979.

16 Many suggestions are put forward as to the origin of the name Bulman. The British Hydrographic Office indicated that it may be attributable to the name of a crewman aboard Captain MacKenzie's survey vessel in 1763. (Letter from Brian Thynne, National Maritime Museum, 29 December 2004.) This is incorrect as the name Bulman appears on charts from seventy years earlier.

17 Caulfield, R. (ed.), 'Annals of Kinsale, xliv', *The Council Book of the Corporation of Kinsale*, Surrey, 1879.

18 *Observations on Kinsale, 1758*, The Fercor Press, Cork, 1974.

19 Souhami, *op. cit.*, 2001, p. 41.

20 *Observations on Kinsale, 1758, op. cit.*, 1974.

21 Taylor, Richard M., *op. cit.*, 2004, p. 14.

22 *Kinsale Manorial Records, Vol. 5*, for 14 August 1695, Boole Library, University College Cork (UCC).

23 O'Connor, Anne, 'Cosimo de' Medici's Visit to Cork in 1669' in *JCHAS CXI*, 2006, p. 4.

24 Jim Lawton, Francie Dempsey and Jerome Lordan in conversation with the author.

25 Mitchell, F., and Ryan, M., *Reading the Irish Landscape*, Town House, Dublin, 1997, p. 65.

26 Kiely, Jerome, 'Cuirtapurteen' in *The Griffin Sings*, Chapman, Dublin, 1966, pp. 75–82.

27 O'Riordan, S.P., Hartnett, P.J., 'The Excavation of Ballycatten Fort', in *Proceedings of the Royal Irish Academy (PRIA)* 1943, pp. 1–43; 'The Excavation of the Large Earthen Ring Fort at Garrans, in *PRIA*.', 1942, pp. 77–150; Power, Denis, *et al.*, *Archaeology Inventory of Co. Cork, II*, OPW, Dublin, 1994, p. 78, Item 4329.

28 Stevans, Prof. G., Copenhagen University in Caulfield, R. (ed.), *op. cit.*, ii, 1879, p. 11; O'Brien, T.M., Letters to the Editor, in *The Irish Times*, 15 October 1945; Thuillier, John R., *History of Kinsale*, Kinsale, 2001, p. 3.

29 Lavery, B., *Ships*, National Maritime Museum, London, 2004, p. 42; de Courcy Ireland, John, *Ireland & the Irish in Maritime History*, Glendale, Dublin, 1986, pp. 57 &; Breen, C., & Forsythe, W., *Boats and Shipwrecks of Ireland*, Tempus, Gloucestershire, 2004, p. 71.

30 Vital, Laurent, 'Archduke Ferdinand's visit to Kinsale in Ireland'. An extract from *Le Premier Voyage de Charles-Quint en Espagne*, Translated by Dorothy Convery, celt.ucc.ie.

31 de Courcy Ireland, John, *Ireland and the Irish in Maritime History*, Glendale, Dublin, 1986, pp. 79, 81, 91.

32 Longfield, A.K., 'Appendix; Trade with Bristol, 1504–1505', in *Anglo-Irish Trade in the Sixteenth Century*, Routledge, London, 1929, p. 219.

33 Flavin S., Jones, E.J., *Bristol Trade with Ireland and the Continent, 1503–1601*, Bristol University, Rose Project, pp. 141, 153, 171, 173, 222, 676–77, 718.

34 Vital, *op. cit.*

35 Chambers, Anne, *Eleanor, Countess of Desmond*, Wolfhound Press, Dublin, 1986, p. 71.

36 Holohan, P., *JCHAS 109*, 2004, pp. 159–160.

37 O'Brien, A.F., 'Politics, Economy and Society' in O'Flanagan and Buttimer (eds.), *Cork: History & Society*, Dublin, 1993, pp. 94, 108, 133.

38 Caulfield, R. (ed.), *op. cit.*, xii, p. XII, 1 May 1395, Surrey, 1879.

39 Nicholls, K.W., 'The Development of Lordship in County Cork 1300–1600', p. 190, O'Flanagan & Buttimer, (eds.), *op. cit.*, 1993.

40 Ellis, Stephen G., *Tudor Ireland 1470–1603*, Longman, London, 1985, pp. 68–71.

41 O'Sullivan, F., 'Kinsale', in *JCHAS XI*, Cork, 1905, p. 1; Caulfield, R. (ed.), 'The Court Book', *op. cit.*, 1879.

42 Smith, C., *The Ancient and Present State of Cork City and County, Vol. I,* Reprint Cork, 1893 p. 205; McSwiney, Fr P., 'Eighteenth Century Kinsale', in *JCHAS XLIII*, Cork, 1938, p. 77, note 10.

43 O'Sullivan, F., *op. cit.*, Cork, 1976, P. 14.

44 Grand Jury presentment, October 1684.

45 T. Murphy, Lecture at Desmond Castle, September 2003.

Chapter 2. The Golden Age of Shipping

1 Mulcahy, M., (ed.), *Calendar of Kinsale Documents, A, Vol. 1,* 3 Oct 1692, pp. 90, 92; *Vol. 2,* Presentments 20 & 30, 1702; Presentment 20, 1703; *Vol. 2, 1707,* Presentment 9, 1707, Kinsale Regional Museum, Kinsale, 1988.

2 Kelleher, C., 'Connections and Conflict by Sea', Horning & Bannon (eds.), *Ireland and Britain in the Atlantic World,* Wordwell, Dublin, 2009, p. 57.

3 O'Sullivan, F., *The History of Kinsale,* Tower Books, Cork, 1976, p. 3; O'Sullivan, William, *Economic History of Cork City to 1800*, Cork University Press, 1937, p. 126; Evidence of trading uncovered during sewerage excavations in Kinsale, 2007 to 2010.

4 O'Flanagan, P., & Buttimer, C.G. (eds.), *Cork: History & Society,* Dublin, 1993, pp. 142, 351, 359 and 364, note 150; McCarthy Murrogh, M., 'English presence in Munster', *Natives & Newcomers,* Irish Academic Press, 1986, pp. 188–190.

5 Dorman, Rev. S.T., 'The Kinsale Knot of the Friendly Brothers of St Patrick', *JCHAS XX,* Cork, 1914, p. 178; Thuillier, John R., 'The Kinsale Knot of the Friendly Brothers of St Patrick', *Kinsale Record, Vol. 4*, Kinsale, 1992, p. 15.

6 Caulfield, R. (ed.), 'Annals of Kinsale', l, *The Council Book of the Corporation of Kinsale,* Surrey, 1879.

7 *Kinsale Manorial Records, Vol. III,* 1665–1675, Boole Library, UCC.

8 Smith, Charles 'Earl of Orrery's letters' in *The Ancient and Present State of the County and City of Cork, Vol. II*, p. 184; Caulfield, R. (ed.), *op. cit.*, li, 1879.

9 *Observations on Kinsale*, printed 1758, The Fercor Press, Cork, 1974, p. 10; 'Shipping News', *London Gazette*, No. 806.

10 Mulcahy, M., *A Short History of Kinsale, B,* Kinsale, 1968; Caulfield, R. (ed.), *op. cit.*, li to lviii, 1879; Bernard, T.C., 'Cork Settler Culture', O'Flanagan, P., & Buttimer, C.G. (eds.), *op. cit.*, 1993, p. 331; 'Shipping News', *London Gazette* Nos. 2679 and 2689.

11 *Kinsale Manorial Records, Vol. V and VI,* (1692 and following), Boole Library, UCC; Caulfield, R. (ed.), *op. cit.*, 1879; 'Shipping News', *London Gazette*, No. 3274.

12 'Shipping News', *London Gazette,* No. 4380.

13 Law, Ed. J., 'Vallancey's military surveys of 1776–1777 and 1796', *JCHAS* 116, Cork, 2011.

14 Rodger, N.A.M., *Safe Guard of the Sea,* (B), Harper Collins, London, 1997, p. 399; Lavery, Brian, *Ship,* National Maritime Museum, London, 2004, p. 147; Dickson, D., *op. cit.,* p. 417.

15 Rodger, N.A.M., *op. cit. (B),* 1997, pp. 359 & 407.

16 Souhami, Diana, *Selkirk's Island,* Phoenix, London, 2001, pp. 41–51.

17 Caulfield, R. (ed.), *op. cit.,* lvii, lxiv, 1879.

18 Souhami, Diana, *op. cit.,* p. 41.

19 Dickson, D., *op. cit.,* 2005, p. 418; Mulcahy, Michael (ed.), *op. cit. A,* Vol. I, p. 29, presentment 3 [October 1669], *Kinsale, 1988;* McSwiney, Fr. P., 'Georgian Kinsale', in *JCHAS* XLIV, A, Cork, 1939, pp. 108–111.

20 *Kinsale Manorial Records,* Vol. V, Boole Library, UCC.

21 Mulcahy, Michael, *op. cit. A,* Vol. 2, p. 17, Presentment 17, 1988; Caulfield, R. (ed.), *op. cit.,* lxvii, lxiv, 1879; Dickson, D., *op. cit.,* 2005, pp. 386–89.

22 Rogers Francis, *Three Sea Journals of Stuart Times,* Constable, London, 1937; McSwiney, Fr P., *op. cit. A,* 1939.

23 *Ibid.,* p. 113–114; Dickson David, *op. cit.,* 2005, p. 114.

24 Harbour Board receipts paid on 14 July 1879.

25 Klingelhofer, E., *Castles and Colonists,* Manchester University Press, 2010, p. 30; Kelleher, Connie, *op. cit.,* 2009, p. 59.

26 Orrery in correspondence with the Lord Deputy, seeking funds for the defence of the new harbour.

27 Southwell to the Lord Deputy, *Kinsale Manorial Records,* Vol. I, *1626–1661,* Boole Library, UCC, November 1637.

28 *Kinsale Manorial Records,* Vol. I, 14 June 1649, 26 June 1654, Boole Library, UCC; *The London Gazette,* March 1680, No. 1497; *New Oxford Dictionary of Biography,* p. 718.

29 *Kinsale Manorial Records, 1698–1764,* Vols. V & VI, Boole Library, UCC.

30 Caulfield, R. (ed.), *op. cit.,* lxiii, lxiv, 1879.

31 *Kinsale Manorial Records, 1698–1764,* Vols. V & VI, Boole Library, UCC.

32 Tomlin, Claire, *Samuel Pepys, The Unequalled Self,* Penguin, London, 2002, pp. 145, 441 (note 447); Caulfield, R. (ed.), *op. cit.,* lviii, 31 March 1688, 1879; Long, James & Long, Ben, *The Plot against Pepys,* Faber & Faber, London, 2007, pp. 123–125.

33 *Kinsale Manorial Records,* Vols. III, IV, V, Boole Library, UCC; Caulfield, R. (ed.), *op. cit.,* lx, 1879; Kings Weston Development Project, Correspondence, 2012.

34 Perdue, G., Bishop of Cork, Cloyne and Ross, fund-raising leaflet, 1969; Hornibrook, P., *Southwells Alms houses at Kinsale,* Unpublished Essay, 1971.

35 McSwiney, Fr. P., 'Eighteenth-Century Kinsale', in *JCHAS XLIII,* B, Cork, 1938, p. 86.

36 O'Connor, Anne, 'Cosimo de' Medici's Visit to Cork in 1669' in *JCHAS CXI,* Cork, 2006, pp. 1–6; McSwiney, Fr. P., *op. cit.* B, 1938, p. 80; McSwiney, Fr. P.,

op. cit. A, 1939, p. 106; McCarthy Morrogh, M., 'English Presence in Munster', in Brady, C., & Gillespie, R. (eds.) *Natives and Newcomers,* Irish Academic Press, Dublin, 1986, pp. 182–184; Crowley, John, et al, *Atlas of the Great Irish Famine, 1845–52,* Cork University Press, 2012, p. 359.

37 McSwiney, Fr. P., *op. cit.* A, 1939, p. 116.

38 Mulcahy, M., (ed.), *op. cit.* A, Vol. I, presentments 36 to 42, 30 September 1695, p. 107; presentments 17 to 24, 1 October 1694, p. 101; presentment 35, 4 October 1697 p. 118; Vol. II, presentment 30, 6 October 1712, p. 66, Kinsale, 1988.

39 *Ibid.,* presentment 26, 8 October 1666, p. 19; Caulfield, R. (ed.), lxxiii, *op. cit.,* 1879; Souhami, Diana, *Selkirk's Island,* Phoenix, London, 2002, p. 119.

40 Caulfield, R. (ed.), *op. cit.,* lxxv, 1879.

41 Dickson, David, *Old World Colony,* Cork University Press, 2005, p. 250.

42 Ní Chinnéide, Síle, 'A Frenchman's impressions of County Cork in 1790', *JCHAS Parts I and II,* Cork, 1973.

43 Walvin, James, *Black Ivory,* Harper Collins, London, 1992.

44 O'Callaghan Sean, *To Hell or Barbados,* Brandon, 2000, pp. 71, 72, 81, 114; Jolly, S., 'Remnants of an Indentured People', *The Irish Times,* and 'The Red Legs', *The Kinsale Record, Vol. 19,* pp. 51–53;

45 Caulfield, R. (ed.), 'The Court Book for 16 March 1679', *The Council Book of the Corporation of Kinsale,* Surrey, 1879.

46 TG4 Television, *The Celtic Connection,* transmitted 28 December 2009; Stuart, Andrea, 'Sugar in the Blood', *Granta 119,* May 2012.

47 Mulcahy, Michael, Letter 11 October 1998 to J.R. Thuillier; Quote from the *Shaftesbury Papers, Section IX, No. 14;* O'Callaghan, Sean, *op. cit.,* Brandon, 2000; Dickson, D. *op. cit.,* 2005, p. 49.

48 O'Flanagan, P., 'Villages and Towns in Co. Cork', O'Flanagan, P., & Buttimer C.G., *Cork: op. cit.,* 1993, p 398; Dickson, D. *op. cit.,* 2000, pp. 19, 113, 116; Caulfield, R. (ed.), *op. cit.,* xxxix, 1879.

49 Plumb, J.H., *England in the Eighteenth Century,* Penguin, 1962, pp. 179–185; Holohan Renagh, *The Irish Chateaux,* Lilliput, 1989; Wine Museum at Kinsale.

50 Caulfield, R. (ed.), *op. cit.,* liii, 1879; *Kinsale Manorial Records,* August 1675, *Vol. III, 1665–1675,*

51 Dickson, D., *op. cit.,* 2000, pp. 115; O'Sullivan, F., *op. cit.,* 1976, p. 130.

Chapter 3. Naval Presence – A Monitor of Rise and Fall

1 O'Sullivan, William, *An Economic History of Cork City from the Earliest Times to the Act of Union,* 1937.

2 Smith's drawing from Castlepark in 1750; Drawing of Dockyard by Vallancey, 1750.

3 Caulfield, R. (ed.), 'Annals of Kinsale', lvii, *The Council Book of the Corporation of Kinsale,* Surrey, 1879; McSwiney, Fr. P., 'Georgian Kinsale', *JCHAS XLIV,* A, Cork, 1939, p. 94.

4 McSwiney, Fr. P., 'Eighteenth-Century Kinsale', *JCHAS XLIII,* B, Cork, 1938, p. 76.

5 Williamson, J.A., *The English Channel,* Readers Union, Collins, London, 1961, p. 283.

6   Breen, C., Forsythe, W., *Boats & Shipwrecks of Ireland*, Tempus, 2004, pp. 118–119; de Courcy Ireland, John, *Ireland & the Irish in Maritime History*, Glendale, Dublin, 1986, p. 179.

7   McSwiney, Fr P., *op. cit. A*, 1939, pp. 96–98.

8   Caulfield, R. (ed.) *op. cit.*, lxiv, Surrey, 1879.

9   Rodger, N.A.M., *The Command of the Ocean*, Penguin, London, 2004, p. 159.

10 Caulfield, R. (ed.), *op. cit.*, liv, 1879.

11 Konstam, Angus, *Pirates, 1660–1730*, Osprey, UK, 1998, pp. 4, 5, 32.

12 Caulfield, R. (ed.), 'The Court Book of the town of Kinsale', *op. cit.*, 1879, p. 81; Coyle, Eugene, 'Irish Buccaneer', *History Ireland*, Vol. 7, No. 2; 'Privateers', *Irish Sword*, XV, p. 218.

13 Costello, Kevin, *The Court of Admiralty of Ireland 1575–1893*, Four Courts Press, Dublin, 2011, pp. 78, 81; Appleby, John C., & O'Dowd, Mary, 'Irish Admiralty: its organisation and development, 1570–1640', *Irish Historical Studies*, Vol. 24, Dublin, 1985, pp. 299–302.

14 Mulcahy, M., *A Short History of Kinsale*, Cork Historical Guides, Kinsale, 1968, p. 37.

15 O'Sullivan, F., *History of Kinsale*, Tower Books, Cork, 1976, p. 128.

16 Shipping News, *London Gazette*, No. 4751.

17 McSwiney, Fr P., *op. cit. A*, 1939, p. 115; Rodger, N.A.M., *op. cit.*, 2004, pp. 195–196.

18 'Antiquarian Remains in Kinsale District' in *JCHAS XVIII*, 1912, pp. 133–137.

19 Rodger, N.A.M., *The Safeguard of the Sea*, Harper Collins, London, 1997, p. 331.

20 Williams, J.A., *The English Channel*, Readers Union, Collins, London, 1961, pp. 209–308.

21 Fremont Barnes, G., *Nelson's Sailors*, Osprey, UK. 2005, pp. 9–12, 60.

22 Caulfield, R. (ed.), *op. cit.*, lxv, 1879.

23 Keohane, Anne, *School's Manuscript Collection*, 1938, Boole Library Archives, UCC.

24 Lewis, S., *Topographical Dictionary of Ireland, Vol. II*, London, 1839.

25 Dickson, D., *Old World Colony*, Cork University Press, 2005, p. 18.

26 Harrison, Richard S., *Merchants, Mystics and Philanthropists*, Cork Society of Friends, Cork, 2006, p. 182.

27 Rodger, N.A.M., *op. cit.*, A, 2004, p. 188; *Kinsale Manorial Records*, Vol. V, 26 September 1693, Boole Library, UCC.

28 Williams, J.A., *The English Channel*, Readers Union, Collins, London, 1961, pp. 282–283.

29 *Kinsale Manorial Records*, Vol. VI, 23 August 1698, Boole Library, UCC.

30 Vallancey, C., *Military Survey of Kinsale*, British Museum, 1778 – noted in McSwiney, Fr P., *op. cit. A*, 1939, p. 94.

31 McSwiney, Fr. P., *op. cit. B*, 1938, p. 76.

32 Black, Jeremy, 'Quiberon Bay', *BBC History Magazine*, November 2009; McSwiney, Fr. P., *op. cit. A*, 1939, p. 95.

33 Caulfield, R. (ed.), *op. cit.*, lxxxi, Surrey, 1879.

34 McSwiney, Fr. P., *op. cit.* B, 1938, p. 75; Law, Edward J., 'Vallancey's military surveys of 1776–1777 and 1796', *JCHAS 116*, Cork, 2011, p. 135; Vallancey, Charles, *Military Survey of Ireland, 1778*, British Museum, K.L.I. 13.2; de Courcy Ireland, John, *Ireland and the Irish in Maritime History*, Glendale, Dublin, 1982, Appendix 3, p. 365.

35 Lewis, S., *op. cit.*, 1839, p. 232.

36 Kennerley, Alston, 'A North West European Shipping Hub; Falmouth for Orders 1881–1935' in *International Journal of Maritime History*, Vol. XXII. No. 1, Hull, June 2010.

37 Petterson, Basil, *Turn of the Tide*, Irish Shipping Ltd, Dublin, 1962.

38 Kinsale Shipping Co., Crowley Papers, Cork Archives.

39 Anderson, R.M., *Sailing Ships of Ireland*, Morris & Co., Dublin, 1951, p. 90.

40 *Ibid.*, p. 280.

41 Thuillier, Joseph, Recollections, 1921.

42 Conversation with G. Gimblett, 20 June 1997.

43 Conversation with G. Gimblett, 24 September 1998.

44 Thuillier Joseph, (Jn.), *Warm Oceans Cold Seas*, Millington, Killiney, 1994; Stone, J., *Learning the Ropes: A Seaman's Apprenticeship*, Quack Books, York, 2000.

45 Conversation with: Jack O'Driscoll, Charlie Hurley, Denis O'Leary, Johnny Farren, John Alcock, Ted Coakley and Tim Sheehan.

46 *KPMG Consultant Report* on the state of regional ports and harbours in Ireland, 1998; Kiernan, Frank, *Marine Times*, September 2013.

Chapter 4. Fishing

1 De Courcy Ireland John, *Ireland and the Irish in Maritime History, (A)*, Glendale, Dublin, 1986, p. 83; *Irelands Sea Fisheries*, (B), Glendale, Dublin, 1981, p. 22; *Ireland's Maritime Heritage*, (C), An Post, Dublin, 1992, p. 28; Green, W.S., 'The Sea Fisheries of Ireland', *Agriculture and Industry in Ireland Report*, 1888, p. 370.

2 Longfield, A.K., *Anglo-Irish Trade in the Sixteenth Century*, Routledge, London, 1929, p. 51.

3 Caulfield, R. (ed.), 'Annals of Kinsale', xxxiii, *The Council Book of the Corporation of Kinsale*, Surrey, 1879; Went, A.E.J. 'Pilchards in the South of Ireland', *JCHAS* 51, 1946, p. 137.

4 Brabazon, Wallop, 'The Deep Sea & Coast Fisheries of Ireland', *Dublin University Magazine* Vol. XXXI, 1848, pp. 771–780.

5 Long, P., *Sea Heritage of Dingle*, Long, Dingle, p. 4.

6 Southwell, Robert, 'Facsimile of letter to Lord Deputy', de Courcy Ireland, John, *op. cit., (B)*,1981, p 34; Scott, R.J., *The Galway Hooker*, Ward River Press, Dublin, 1983; Townsend, Horatio, *Survey of the County of Cork, Vol. II*, Cork, 1815; Soé, G., 'The Dutch Herring-Boat of the Seventeenth Century' in *The Yachting Monthly, June 1909*, pp. 127–8.

7 Inspector's Report of the Commissioners of Fisheries, Ireland, House of Commons, *Report on Irish Fisheries*, 5 April 1836, p. 156.

8   Went, A.E.J., *op. cit.*, 1946, Cork, p. 137; Smith, Charles, *The Ancient and Present State of County and City of Cork,* 1750, pp. 310–311; O'Shea, John, *Seine Boats and Seine Fishing,* Allihies Folklore Group; Kittridge, Alan, *Cornwall's Maritime Heritage,* Twelve Heads Press, Cornwall, 1989, p. 16; *Kinsale Manorial Papers,* Vol. V, 'Walking in the Kinsale Area', 14 August 1695, Boole Library, UCC.

9   *Kinsale Manorial Records,* Vol. V, 14 August 1695.

10 De Courcy Ireland, John, *op. cit.,* A, 1986, p. 127.

11 De Courcy Ireland, John, *op. cit.,* C, 1992, p. 27.

12 Reynolds, Authur, 'Irish Fisheries', *Traditional Boats of Ireland,* The Collins Press, Cork, 2008, p. 18; 'Nairn Fisher Girls at the Cutting', *Dear Gremistra,* National Museum of Antiquities of Scotland, 1979; Conversations with Mona Thuillier and Gerald Gimblett.

13 Caulfield, R. (ed.), 'The Court Book of the Town of Kinsale', p. 5, *The Council Book of the Corporation of Kinsale,* Surrey, 1879.

14 Caulfield, R. (ed.), *op. cit.,* lxxxv, 28 May 1697, 1879; Mulcahy, Michael, *Calendar of Kinsale Documents,* Vol. 3, presentment 34, p. 99; Inspector's *Report on Irish Fisheries,* House of Commons, 5 April 1836, p. 156; *Parliamentary Gazetteer of Ireland for 1844–45,* Fullerton & Company, p. 568.

15 McSwiney, Fr. P., 'Eighteenth-Century Kinsale', *JCHAS* XLIII, 1938, p. 83; Caulfield, R. (ed.), *op. cit.,* lxiii, Surrey, 1879.

16 Smith, Charles, *Ancient and Present State of the County and City of Cork, Vol. I,* p. 212; O'Maidin, Padraig, 'Pocock's Tour of South and South West Ireland in 1758', *JCHAS LXIII,* Cork, 1958, p. 73.

17 Caulfield, R. (ed.), *op. cit.,* xxxviii, Surrey, 1879.

18 *Ibid.,* lxxii, lxxvi, lxxix, 1879.

19 *Ibid.,* lxxvii, 1879.

20 De Courcy Ireland, John *op. cit., (B),* 1981, p. 41; *Inspector's Report on Irish Fisheries,* House of Commons, 1843.

21 Symonds, Captain T.E., *Irish Quarterly Review,* Vol. 6, Royal Dublin Society, Dublin, March 1856, p. 191; *Cork Examiner,* 1 September 1868.

22 Rolleston, T.W. (ed.), 'Udalism and Feudalism', *Prose Writings of Thomas Davis,* Scott Library, London, 1889, p. 66.

23 *Inspector's Report on Irish Fisheries,* House of Commons, 1843.

24 *Irish Fisheries Commission Fourth Report* for 1822, (Appendix 14) shows that Kinsale had 7 decked vessels, 47 half decked, 53 open boats, 427 rowing boats crewed by a total of 2,822 men. Galway had 6,228 employed in fishing. By 1829, the Tenth Report of the Fisheries Office (Appendix 1) reported that Kinsale had 5 vessels which were decked, 160 half decked, 45 open sail and 625 row boats giving employment afloat for 4,612 men and boys as against 7,305 in Galway.

25 *Inspector's Report on Irish Fisheries,* Appendix IX, enumerated by coastguard officer Lieutenant Daish for House of Commons, 1836.

26 Note must be taken of the large number of deaths that occurred at Kinsale Workhouse during the Famine period. This loss was not of people from Kinsale but of victims from the much wider Poor Law area.

27 'Sea and Coast Fisheries', *Manx Sea Fishing 1840–1920,* National Heritage of the Isle of Man, 1992.

28 Worthington, Robert, 'Sea and Coast Fisheries', *Irish Quarterly Review*, Vol. 6, Royal Dublin Society, 1856/57, pp. 406–411.

29 'The Development of Irish Fisheries', *Irish Builder*, Vol. XVIII, No. 385, Dublin, 1876, p. 54; S. Fitzgerald, 'The Great Spring Mackerel Fishery', *Traditional Boats of Ireland*, The Collins Press, Cork, 2008, p. 27.

30 *Report of the Inspectors of Irish Fisheries, 1874*. House of Commons, p. 367.

31 Fitzgerald, S., *Mackerel and the Making of Baltimore*, Irish Academic Press, 1999, pp. 13–17; McCaughhan, M., 'Dandys, Luggers, Herring and Mackerel', *The Irish Sea*, Institute of Irish Studies, Belfast, 1989, p. 131.

32 In conversation with Frank Mills, maritime historian, Youghal.

33 McCaughan, Michael & Appleby, J.C., *The Irish Sea*, Belfast, 1989, p. 123.

34 National Heritage of the Isle of Man, 1840 to 1920, Peel; Correspondence with John Qualtrough, Port St Mary, Isle of Man, 7 November 1997; Fred Palmer, *Glimpses of Old Peel*, Amulree, 1993.

35 King, I.M., 'Going to Kinsale', in *Journal of the Isle of Man Family History Society*, Vol. 11, No. 1, Feb., 1989.

36 Caine, Hall, *The Manxman*, Isle of Man, 1894; O'Sullivan, F., *History of Kinsale*, Tower Books, Cork, 1976, p. 167.

37 Ó Síocháin, Conchúr, translated by R.P. Breatnach, *The Man from Cape Clear*, Mercier, Cork, 1975, p. 35.

38 Harbour Board minutes, 7 June 1774, 9 February 1880.

39 Robinson, Lennox, *Three Homes*, Joseph, London, 1938, p. 140.

40 Gibbings, R., *Sweet Cork of Thee*, Dent, London, 1951, p. 69; *Cork Examiner*, 15 March 1871.

41 Thuillier, Joseph, Recollections, 1921.

42 O'Sullivan, F., *State Aid for Fishermen – The Case for the Kinsale Fishermen*, Kinsale, 1911; Thuillier, Joseph, Recollections, 1921; Conversation with Mona Thuillier.

43 *Cork Examiner* for 12 May 1866 and 1 September 1868; O'Mahony, C., 'Fishing in nineteenth-century Kinsale', *JCHAS* 98, pp. 119, 121, 126.

44 Correspondence with the Heard Estate on the lease of the Dock Yard, March 1919.

45 Mitchell, Author, 'Thomas Johnson, 1872–1963, A Pioneer Labour Leader', in *Studies*, Vol. 58, No. 232, 1969; Robinson, L., *Three Homes*, Joseph, London, 1938, p. 137; de Courcy Ireland, John, *Ireland's Sea Fisheries*, B, Glendale, Dublin, 1981, p. 97.

46 Holohan, P., 'Kinsale Elections 1932', *JCHAS* 109, Cork, 2004, p. 167; Potter, M., 'The Rise & Fall of Local Democracy', *History Ireland*, Vol. 9, spring, 2011, p. 42.

47 Fitzgerald S., *Mackerel and the Making of Baltimore*, Irish Academic Press, Dublin, 1999, p. 51.

48 Harbour Board minutes, February and July 1879, December 1880, August 1881; Ordnance Survey, Plan of Kinsale waterfront, 1883, House of Commons, 6 July 1880.

49 Kinsale Harbour Board Minutes, December 1881; de Courcy Ireland, John, *op. cit.*, B, Dublin, 1981, pp. 66, 87.

50 Kinsale Harbour Board, Memorial to the Department of Agriculture and other Industries, 19 July 1900.

51 Report of the Inspectors of Irish Fisheries, 1880, p. 5; Green, W.S., Report on the Sea and Inland Fisheries of Ireland for 1900, appendices III and IV, pp. 24–25, Dept. of Agriculture and Technical Instruction.

52 Harbour Board minutes, 10 March 1896.

53 Fitzgerald, S., *op. cit.*, Dublin, 1999, pp. 13–14.

54 O'Sullivan, F., *op. cit.*, 1911, p. 29.

55 McKay, K.D., *A Vision of Greatness: The History of Milford*, Chevron, Milford, 1989, pp. 180–190.

56 Thuillier, Joseph, Recollections, 1921.

57 'The Development of Irish Fisheries', *Irish Builder, Vol. XVIII*, No. 385, Dublin, 1876, p. 54.

58 O'Flanagan P., 'Town and Village Life', O'Flanagan, P. & Buttimer, C.G., *Cork – History & Society*, Geography Publications, 1993, pp. 435–437.

59 O'Sullivan, F., *op. cit.*, 1911, p. 15–22.

60 Flynn, Majella M., 'The Geography of Marriage & Fertility in an Irish town: Kinsale 1901 and 1911', unpublished MA thesis, p. 7.

61 Conversation with G. Gimblett, 20 June 1997; *Cork Examiner*, 10 May 1927.

62 Nolan, Liam & Nolan, John E., *Secret Victory*, Mercier, Cork, 2009, p. 110.

63 Daly, Eugene, *Heir Island,* Heron's Way Press, Leap, County Cork, 2004; Levis, Cormac, *Towelsail Yawls*, Galley Head Press, Ardfield, 2002; Conversation with Danny Minihane, 1995.

64 *Cork Examiner,* 20 September 1958; McCarthy, C., *Archdeacon Tom Duggan*, Blackwater Press, Dublin, 1994, p. 183.

65 O'Grady, Desmond, *The Head Gear of the Tribe*, Peter Fallon (ed.), Gallery Books, 1979, p. 34.

66 Hurley, F., 'Kinsale Mercy Order Annals', *St Joseph's Convent of Mercy*, Kinsale, 1994, p. 49.

67 de Courcy Ireland, John, *op. cit.*, A, 1986, p. 352; *de Courcy Ireland, op. cit.,* B, 1981, pp. 122 & 170; de Courcy Ireland's correspondence with author 1978/1980.

68 Management Board Minutes, Technical School, 1903–1939.

69 Murphy Christina, 'Kinsale Pre-Employment Course', *The Irish Times,* 7 October 1977; Beausang, Sean, 'Their Classroom is a Shark Boat', *Cork Examiner*, 2 June 1979; Thuillier, J.R., 'Marine Skills Course', *Compass*, Vol. 2, No. 7, Irish Association for Curriculum Development, 1978; Thuillier, J.R., *County Cork VEC Reports*, 1976, 1977, 1978, 1979, 1981; Thuillier, J.R., 'The Marine Skills Pre-Employment Course'; McMahon, Leo, 'Marine Course', *Southern Star,* 22 August 1979.

Chapter 5. Threats and Harbour Defence

1 O'Rahilly, T.F., 'Dun Cearma', *JCHAS XLIV*, 1939, Cork, pp. 16–20.

2 Caulfield, R. (ed.), 'Annals of Kinsale', xii, *The Council Book of the Corporation of Kinsale*, Surrey, 1879.

3 Thuillier, J.H., Maps in *JCHAS XLIII,* Cork, 1938, pp. 80, 82; Mulcahy, Michael, (ed.), *Calendar of Kinsale Documents,* Vol. I, A, presentment 22, 6 October 1684, p. 83, Kinsale, 1988.

4 Mulcahy, Michael, (ed.), *op. cit. A,* presentment 43, 3 October 1692, Kinsale, 1988, p. 95; O'Neil, B. H. St. J. 'Fortifications of Kinsale Harbour', *JCHAS XLV,* Cork, 1940, p. 111.

5 Caulfield, R. (ed.), *op. cit.,* xvi, xxii, xxvi, Surrey, 1879.

6 Buffet, H.F., *Port Louis and its Citadel,* Musée de la Compagnie des Indes, Port Louis, 1992.

7 Graham Winston, *The Spanish Armadas,* Doubleday & Co., New York, 1972, pp. 258–267.

8 Silke, J.J., *Kinsale,* Four Courts Press, Dublin, 2000, pp. 74 & 87.

9 Map of Ireland, 1576, in the Museum of the Record Office, London.

10 Silke, J.J., *op. cit.,* 2000, pp. 123 & 127; *Pacata Hibernia,* 'Wars in Ireland', 1633, reprinted Dublin, 1810, pp. 374 & 383.

11 Morgan, Hiram, (ed.), *The Battle of Kinsale,* Wordwell, Wicklow, 2004; Thuillier, John R., *History of Kinsale,* Kinsale, 2001, p. 21–31.

12 Caulfield, R. (ed.), 'Appendix A, 28 May 1697', *op. cit.,* p. 305.

13 Caulfield, R. (ed.), 'Appendix E, Abstracts from the depositions of Cromwell's adherents in Kinsale 1654', *op. cit.,* Appendix E, Surrey, 1879, pp. 357 & 805.

14 'Antiquarian Remains in the Kinsale District', *JCHAS* XVIII, Cork, 1912, p. 82; O'Donnell, Mary, 'James Fort Excavation 1974–1998', *JCHAS* 107, Cork, 2002, pp. 1–70; Thuillier, John R., *op. cit.,* 2001, pp. 31–36; Caulfield, R. (ed.), *op. cit.,* lxiv, 1879.

15 O'Connor, Anne, 'Cosimo de' Medici's Visit to Cork in 1669', *JCHAS* CXI, Cork, 2006, p. 3.

16 O'Neil, B.H. St. J., *op. cit.,* 1940, p. 112.

17 O'Dowd, Mary, 'Gaelic Economy & Society', *Native and Newcomers,* Irish Academic Press, Dublin, 1986, pp. 124–128.

18 Power, Denis, *et al., Archaeological Inventory of County Cork,* Vol. 2, OPW, 1994, pp. 231, 223, 236; Fuller, J.F., *JCHAS* XIII, Cork, 1907, pp. 14–18; Healy, James N., *Castles of County Cork,* Mercier Press, Cork, 1988, pp. 256, 269, 282.

19 Samuel, Mark, 'A Tentative Chronology for Tower Houses in West Cork', *JCHAS* 103, Cork, 1998.

20 Keohane, Anne, 'Pupil of Ringrone National School', *Schools' Manuscript Collection, 1938,* Irish Folklore Commission, Dublin, 1938; Field Investigation, John R. Thuillier, 2003.

21 Canny, Nicholas, 'Early Modern Ireland, 1500–1700', *The Oxford History of Ireland,* R.F. Foster (ed.), Oxford University Press, Oxford, 1989, pp. 118–120.

22 Boyce, D. George, *Nationalism in Ireland,* Routledge, London, 1991, pp. 78–86.

23 O'Donoghue, Denis J., *History of Bandon,* Cork History Guides Commission, Cork, 1970, p. 21.

24 Depositions of the 1641 war held at Trinity College; Rodger, N.A.M., *The Safeguard of the Sea,* Harper Collins, London, 1997, p. 418; Bennett, George, *History of Bandon,* Henry & Coughlan, Cork, 1862.

25 Whetcombe, Tristram, 'Kinsale in 1641', *JCHAS* XIII, 1907, Cork; McCarthy, P., 'The River and its History', *The Ballinadee Way*, p. 45; Gillespie, R., 'Plantations in Early Modern Ireland', *History Ireland*, winter 1993, Dublin, p. 46.

26 *Ibid.*

27 Rodger, N.A.M., *op. cit.*, 1997, pp. 424–433; Kelsey, Sean, 'King of the Sea', *Journal of History Association*, Vol. 92, No. 308, p. 428; Murphy, Elaine, *The Cromwellian Army in Ireland, 1649–1653*, Routledge, London, 2012.

28 Bennett, George, *op. cit.*, 1862, p. 149.

29 de Courcy Ireland, John, *Ireland and the Irish in Maritime History*, Glendale, Dublin, 1986, *(A)*, 1986, p. 152.

30 Foster, R.F., *Modern Ireland 1600–1972*, Penguin, London, 1988, pp. 100–116.

31 Rodger, N.A.M., *The Command of the Ocean*, Penguin, London, 2004, p. 85.

32 Mordal, J., *Twenty-five Centuries of Sea Warfare*, Abbey, London, 1952, pp. 75–92.

33 Tomlin, Claire, *Samuel Pepys, The Unequalled Self*, Penguin, London, 2002, pp. 33, 106, 123.

34 Kelly, C., *The Grand Tour of Cork*, Cailleach Books, Beara, 2003, p. 21; Harrison, Richard S., *Merchants, Mystics and Philanthropists*, Cork Society of Friends, Cork, 2006.

35 Williamson, J.A., *The English Channel*, Readers Union Collins, London, 1961, pp. 248–263; Paintings and Objects in the Rijksmuseum, Amsterdam, Holland.

36 Caulfield, R. (ed.), *op. cit.*, liii, 1879; Kerrigan, Paul M., 'Charles Fort', *Irish Sword*, Vol. XIII, *Dublin, 1977–1979*, pp. 323–338; Dickson, David, *Old World Colony*, Cork University Press, Cork, 2005, p. 49.

37 Smith, Charles, *The Ancient and Present State of the County and City of Cork*, Vol. I, p. 213; Thuillier, J.R., *op. cit.*, Kinsale, 2001, pp. 40–43.

38 *Pacata Hibernia, Wars in Ireland*, 1633, reprinted Dublin, 1810, pp. 368–373; Thuillier, J.R., 'The Last Armada – Kinsale 1601', unpublished, 1999.

39 Kerrigan, Paul M., *op. cit.*, p. 330.

40 Mulcahy, M., *A Short History of Kinsale*, B, Historical Guides, Cork, 1968, pp. 27–30.

41 Caulfield, R. (ed.), *op. cit.*, lviii, 1879.

42 Dickson, David, *op. cit.*, 2005, pp. 55–59.

43 Mulcahy, M., *op. cit.* B, 1968, pp. 27–35.

44 Mulcahy, M. *op. cit.* A, *1988*, presentment 28, September 1695, p. 106.

45 'Antiquarian Remains in the Kinsale District', in *JCHAS* XVIII, Part II, 1912, p. 82; Caulfield, R. (ed.), *op. cit.*, lxiv, 28 May 1697, 1879.

46 Thuillier, J.R., *op. cit.*, Kinsale, 2001, p. 49.

47 Black, Jeremy, 'Quiberon Bay', *BBC History Magazine*, November 2009.

48 'Antiquarian Remains in the Kinsale District', *JCHAS* XVIII, 1912; Power, Denis, *et al.*, *op. cit.*, 1994, item 5878; Pochin Mould, D. *Discovering Cork*, Brandon, Kerry, 1991, p. 225.

49 Adams, T.A. 'Irish Naval Service', *The World Ship Society*, 1982, p. 15; Kennedy, Michael, *Guarding Neutral Ireland*, Four Courts Press, Dublin, 2008.

Chapter 6. Piracy, Smuggling and Wreck

1   O'Sullivan, William, *Economic History of Cork City to 1800*, Cork University Press, 1937, p. 102; de Courcy Ireland, John, *Ireland and the Irish in Maritime History*, A, Glendale, Dublin, 1986, pp. 141–144; de Courcy Ireland, John, 'An Outline History of Piracy', *Cultura Maritima*, Vol. 1, No. 1, Irish Branch, International Institute of Maritime Culture, Dublin, 1974, p. 19.

2   Fiant granted by Edward VI, October 1553.

3   Smith, Charles, *The Ancient and Present State of the County and City of Cork*, Vol. I, p. 188; Shipping News, *The London Gazette*, No. 1024.

4   Lavery, B., *Ships*, National Maritime Museum, London, 2004, p. 152; Konstam Angus, *Pirates 1660–1730*, Osprey, London, 1998, p. 57.

5   Breen, C., & Forsythe, W., *Boats & Shipwrecks of Ireland*, Tempus, UK, 2004, p. 77; Appleby, J.C., 'Merchants and Mariners, Pirates and Privateers', *The Irish Sea*, Institute of Irish Studies, Belfast 1989, pp. 47–58.

6   Childs, Wendy, 'Ireland's Trade with England in the Later Middle Ages', *Irish Economic and Social History, Vol. IX*, 1982, p. 12.

7   de Courcy Ireland, J., *op. cit.* A, 1986, p 82.

8   *Ibid.*, pp. 142–3.

9   *Ibid.*, p. 146; Ekin, Des, *The Stolen Village*, O'Brien Press, Dublin, 2008, pp. 98–122; Caulfield, R. (ed.), 'Annals of Kinsale', xxxiv, *The Council Book of the Corporation of Kinsale*, Surrey, 1879.

10 Costello, Kevin, *The Court of Admiralty of Ireland 1575–1893*, Four Courts Press, 2011, p. 261; Appleby, J.C., 'The Affairs of Pirates', *JCHAS* XCI, 1986. pp. 68–81; 'Irish Admiralty: its organisation and development, 1570–1640', *Irish Historical Studies*, Vol. XXIV, Dublin, 1985, pp. 322–325.

11 Appleby, J.C., 'Women & Piracy in Ireland', pp. 55, 61, 64 from MacCurtain, M. & O'Dowd, M. (eds.), *Woman in Early Modern Ireland*, Wolfhound Press, Dublin, 1991; Bowling, Tom, *Pirates and Privateers*, Pocket Essentials, Herts. 2008, pp. 119–138; 'Deadlier than the Male', *Kinsale Newsletter*, December 1984.

12 Winslow, Cal, *Albion's Fatal Tree, Crime and Society in Eighteenth-Century England*, Verso, Oxford, 1975, Dickson, David, *Old World Colony*, Cork University Press, 2005, pp. 135, 416; James, F.G., 'Irish Smuggling in the eighteenth century', *Irish Historical Studies*, Vol. XII, Dublin, 1961.

13 Keble Chatterton, E., *Kings, Cutters and Smugglers 1700–1855*, George Allen, London, 1912, chapter XIII.

14 Conversation with John H. Thuillier and Castlepark residents.

15 Ní Chinnéide, Sile, 'A Frenchman's Impressions of County Cork', *JCHAS* LXXVIII, Cork, 1973, p. 122.

16 McGough, E. 'Coast Watch', *Tracton Newsletter*, Vol. 26, No. 6, 2002; Cremin, C., 'Some Prehistoric Remains near Kinsale', *JCHAS* XXIX, Cork, 1924/5, p. 72.

17 Ó Síocháin, Conchúr, *The Man from Cape Clear*, translated from the Irish by Riobárd P. Breatnach, Mercier, Cork, 1975, pp. 41–59; Fitzgerald, S., *Mackerel & the Making of Baltimore*, Irish Academic Press, 1999, p. 47.

18 *The Dublin Evening Post*, 4 January 1735.

19 James, F.G., *op. cit.*, 1961, pp. 312, 314.

20 Dickson David, *Old World Colony,* Cork University Press, 2005, p. 416.

21 Cork County Council, *Report on Commoge Marsh Nature Reserve Project,* February 2005, p. 27.

22 McSwiney, Fr P., 'Eighteenth Century Kinsale', *JCHAS XLIII,* 1938, Appendix B. p. 92.

23 Caulfield, R. (ed.), *op. cit.,* lxxiii, 1879.

24 Kittridge, Alan, *Cornwall's Maritime Heritage,* Twelve Heads Press, 2003.

25 Bourke, Edward, J., *Shipwrecks of the Irish Coast, 1105–1993,* Bourke, Dublin, 1994, p. 118.

26 Thuillier, J.R., *History of Kinsale,* Kinsale, 2001, p. 75.

27 O'Donovan, Derry, *Ballinspitle and de Courcy Country,* Wordwell, Wicklow, 2003.

28 Luxton, Edward, 'Life at the Old Head of Kinsale, 1917–1922', Private Papers.

29 Smith, Charles, *op. cit., Vol. I,* (Cork), p. 210, note 10.

30 Conversation with Oliver Lynch, the last resident customs officer in Kinsale, 6 September 2010.

31 Bathurst, Bella, *The Wreckers,* Harper, 2006, pp. 10– 16.

32 Caulfield, R. (ed.), *op. cit.,* lvii for 9 March 1687, 1879.

33 O'Maidín, P., 'Loss of the *City of Chicago* off Kinsale, 1892', *Cork Examiner,* 3 September 1974.

34 O'Keeffe, Jim, 'Diving the *Falls of Garry', Coastline 90,* Kinsale Regional Museum, 1990, p. 39.

Chapter 7. Bandon River

1 Dickson, David, *Old World Colony,* Cork University Press, 2005, p. 420; O'Donoghue, D.J., *History of Bandon,* Historical Guides, Cork, 1970, pp. 9–17.

2 Lewis, Samuel, *Topographical Dictionary of Ireland, Vol. II,* London 1839, p. 232.

3 O'Donoghue, D.J., *op. cit.,* 1970, pp. 39, 51.

4 The date 30 October 1777 is given by Francis H. Tuckey in *The County and City of Cork Remembrancer,* 1837, which he describes as a 'waterquake' causing the tide at Kinsale to rise 'unusually high'. The variation in the dates is accounted for by the fact that a number of water disturbances occurred during these years, some of which are described in *The Kinsale Record, Vol. 20,* 'Great Lisbon Earthquake Tsunami at Kinsale', Graham Williams, 2012, p. 50.

5 Connolly, Sean, *The Bandon River from Source to the Sea,* Bandon, 1993.

6 O'Donoghue, D.J., *op. cit.,* 1970, p. 39.

7 Connolly, Paddy, 'A Canal through West Cork', *Bandon Historical Journal, No. 5,* 1989.

8 Bennett, G., *History of Bandon,* Cork, 1862, p. 315.

9 Brown, F. 'The Belgooly Mills and Distillery', *The Kinsale Record, Vol. 20,* 2012, p. 30; Collins, James F., 'Sources, Transport and Uses of Sea Sand', *Bandon Historical Journal, 1998/1999;* Caulfield, R. (ed.), 'Annals of Kinsale', xxxiv, and notes for 1666, 1669, 1671 in the 'The Court Book of the Town of Kinsale', *The Council Book of the Corporation of Kinsale,* Surrey, 1879.

10 Dickson, D., *op. cit.*, 2005, p. 237.

11 Donnelly, James S., *The Land and People of Nineteenth-Century Cork*, Routledge & Kegan Paul, London, 1975, p. 28.

12 Caulfield, R. (ed.), 'The Court Book', *The Council Book of the Corporation of Kinsale*, p. 112, Surrey, 1879.

13 Conversation with Christy Hurley, re loss of his uncle in 1948.

14 Levis, C., 'The Almost Forgotten Harbours', *Mizen Journal, No 4*, 1996; McCarthy, P., Quote from Rev. John Harding Cole, Church of Ireland curate in the 1860s, *The Ballinadee Way, p. 51*.

15 Thuillier, J.R., *History of Kinsale*, P. 68, Kinsale, 2001; Cork County Council, *Commoge Marsh Nature Reserve Project*, 2005, p.27.

16 O'Carroll, Michael, 'By the Banks of the Bandon', *Bandon Historical Journal, No. 1*, Bandon, 1984.

17 Bennett, G., *op. cit.*, 1862, p. 27; Pochin Mould, D.C., *Discovering Cork,* Brandon, Kerry, 1991, p. 168; Breen, C., & Forsythe, W., *Boats and Shipwrecks of Ireland*, Tempus, Gloucestershire, 2004, p. 111; O'Sullivan, P., 'English East India Co. at Dundaniel' in *Bandon Historical Journal, No. 4, 1988*, p. 9; McCracken, E., *Irish Woods since Tudor Times*, Newton & Abbot, 1971, p. 46; de Courcy Ireland, John, *Ireland and the Irish in Maritime History*, Glendale, Dublin, 1986, pp. 128–9.

18 Fremont–Barnes, Gregory, *Royal Navy, 1793–1815,* Osprey, London, 2007; O'Sullivan, P., *op. cit.*, 1988, p. 11; Pochin Mould, D.C., *op. cit.*, 1991, p. 169.

19 Connolly, Sean, *op. cit., 1993*, pp. 67–69; Thuillier, J.R., *op. cit.*, 2001, p. 68.

20 Connolly, Sean, *op. cit.*, 1993, pp. 62, 75.

21 Holohan, P., 'Kinsale Election 1832', *JCHAS 2004*, p. 167; 'Kinsale in the 1830s', *The Kinsale Record, Vol. 11*, p. 38; Ryan P., 'Heard's Bridge', *Kinsale Record, Vol. 5*, p. 31.

22 Kinsale Harbour Board correspondence with Board of Trade, White Hall, London, 26 August 1875.

23 *The Engineer*, 8 February 1878; Contract documents, 1878.

24 McCarthy, Dr. C., *Archdeacon Tom Duggan*, Blackwater Press, Dublin, 1994, pp. 175–192.

25 Longfield, A.K., *Anglo-Irish Trade in the Sixteenth Century*, Routledge, London, 1929.

26 Caulfield, R. (ed.), *op. cit.*, lxxv, Surrey, 1879.

27 Caulfield, R. (ed.), *op. cit.*, lxxiii, Surrey, 1879.

28 Went, A.E.J. 'History Notes on the Fisheries of the Bandon River', *JCHAS LXV*, 1960, p. 117.

29 Longfield, Robert, *Fishery Laws of Ireland*, Ponsonby, 1863, p. 57; McMahon, Bryan, *Irish Jurist*, Summer 1968, p. 21; Went, A.E.J., *op. cit.*, Cork, 1960, p. 119.

30 Lismore Papers (1), IV, 56, referred to in Went, A.E.J., *op. cit.*, 1960, p. 124.

Chapter 8. Tragedy at Sea

1 O'Mahony C. & Cadogan, T., 'Shipwrecks on the Co. Cork Coast', *Harbour Lights*, Cork, 1988, pp. 19–30; *Report to the Lords Justices of Ireland*, October

1693, Public Records Office; Bourke, Edward J., *Shipwrecks of the Irish Coast 1105–1993,* Bourke, Dublin, 1994; Letter from Ed Hoare to Sir R. Southwell, *Kinsale Manorial Records, Vol. V,* 11 December 1693.

2   Dinneen, P.S., *Foclóir Gaedhilge agus Béarla,* Dublin, 1927. From 'Muscan' in Irish – a place undermined by rats leaving a stench.

3   Various contributors, *JCHAS* 1, 1895, pp. 236–7; Vol. 7, 1901, pp. 43–46; Vol. 8, 1902, pp. 53–55; Vol. 9, 1903, pp. 131–132; White, Raymond, *Their Bones are Scattered,* Kinsale, 2003, pp. 108–115.

4   O'Maidin, Paidraig, 'To-Day Articles', *Cork Examiner,* 24 April 1985, 30 January 1969, 30 January 1975, 1 April 1975.

5   'Antiquarian Remains', *JCHAS* 18, part 2, 1912, p. 84.

6   O'Maidin, P. 'Loss of the *City of Chicago* off Kinsale in 1892', *Cork Examiner* 3 July 1974; Depositions taken by the Receiver of wrecks, at the Custom House, Kinsale, 23 June 1892.

7   Scott-Shawe, W.H. & Wykes, A., *Mariner's Tale,* Hamish Hamilton, 1959, p. 208; Depositions taken at the Customs Office, 22 April 1911; Barry, Jim, 'Diving the *Falls of Garry*', *Coastline 90,* Kinsale Regional Museum, 1990, p. 39; "Shipwreck near Harbour", *Freeman's Journal,* 24 April 1911.

8   *Cork Constitution,* 17 October 1898; *Cork Examiner,* 17 October 1898.

9   Depositions taken at the Custom House, Kinsale, 1 November 1892; Conversation with Gerald Gimblett, grandson of the skipper.

10 'Kinsale Funeral', *Isle of Man Family History Society Journal, Vol. II,* p.15, 1989; Preston, Diana, *Wilful Murder,* Corgi, 2003, p. 211.

11 Logbook of the submarine for 7 May 1915, p. VIII, presented by the German ambassador to Ireland at Kinsale Museum in 1996.

12 Saunders, Eric, & Marshall, Ken, *RMS Lusitania,* Waterfront publications, 1993; O'Sullivan, Paddy, *The Lusitania: Unravelling the Mysteries,* Sheridan House, 2000.

13 Preston, Diana, *op. cit.,* 2003, p. 306.

14 *National Geographic Magazine,* April 1994, p. 77.

15 F. Gregg Bemis in correspondence and conversation with the author.

16 Ó Síocháin, Conchúr, *The Man from Cape Clear,* translated by Riobárd P. Breatnach, Mercier, Cork, 1975, p. 122.

17 Connolly, T., 'The Boatmen of Kinsale', *The Kinsale Record, Vol. 3,* 1991; Forde, F., *The Long Watch,* New Island, Dublin, 2000, p. 51.

18 Harbour Board minutes, meeting held on 11 February 1946.

19 Roche, Richard, 'Irishman's Diary', *The Irish Times,* 19 January 2006; O'Callaghan, Patrick, The *Kinsale Record, Vol. 8,* 1998, p. 44.

20 Mortimer McCarthy, in fact, was presented with a harpoon gun from the *Terra Nova,* which may be seen in Kinsale Museum.

21 Smith, Michael, *An Unsung Hero,* The Collins Press, Cork, 2000; Various Contributors, *With Scott to the Pole,* Royal Geographical Society, Bloomsbury, London, 2004; Connolly, T., 'A Kinsale Hero of the Antarctic', *The Kinsale Record, Vol. IX,* 1999; Connolly, T., 'The McCarthy Brothers', *The Kinsale Record, Vol. X,* 2000; McCarthy, G., 'Mortimer McCarthy', *op. cit.,* 2000.

22 Ward, Nick, *Left for Dead, Tragic 1979 Fastnet Race*, A & C Black Publishers Ltd, London, 2007.

23 For comprehensive lists of ships lost check: O'Donovan, Derry, *Ballinspittle and de Courcy Country*, Wordwell, Wicklow, 2003; Bourke, E.J., *op. cit.*, 1994.

Chapter 9. Shipbuilding

1 McCaughan, Michael 'Irish Vernacular Boats', *Traditional Boats of Ireland*, The Collins Press, Cork, 2008, p. 6; *The Spray* was built by the Kinsale Thuillier boatbuilding firm.

2 Anderson, E.B., *Sailing Ships of Ireland*, Morris & Co., Dublin, 1951, p. 277.

3 Thuillier, John H., lecture notes on 'Shipbuilding in Kinsale', 25 March 1947.

4 Smith, Charles, *The Ancient and Present State of the County and City of Cork, Vol. I*, p. 210, Cork, 1893.

5 Plaque in St Multose Church, Kinsale; Caulfield, R. (ed.), 'Annals of Kinsale', xcv, *The Council Book of the Corporation of Kinsale*, Surrey, 1879; Darling, Rev. John L., *St Multose Church*, Kinsale, 1895, p. 34–36; O'Maidin, Padraig, 'Prefab Ships for Ross Castle Attack', *Cork Examiner*, 14 September 1971.

6 Caulfield, R. (ed.), *op. cit.*, xlix, 3 July 1667, 1879; Correspondence Fr. P. McSwiney and G.P.B. Naish, British National Maritime Museum, Greenwich, 1 December 1938.

7 Mulcahy, Michael (ed.), *Calendar of Kinsale Documents, Vol. 1*, presentment 26 October 1696, p. 111.

8 Rodger, N.A.M., *The Command of the Ocean*, Penguin, London, 2004, p. 607, Appendix II; Freemont-Barnes, G., *Royal Navy, 1793–1815*, Osprey, Oxford, 2007; McSwiney, Fr. P. 'Georgian Kinsale', [Notes of the model builder.], *JCHAS XLIV*, A, Cork, 1939, p. 98.

9 Eckersall, John, *The HMS Looe Story*, Looe Development Trust, 2008, pp. 6–10; Smith Charles, *op. cit.*, p. 213; & *Vol. II*, p. 222, Cork 1893.

10 Smith, Charles, *op. cit., Vol. I*, p. 210, Cork, 1893.

11 McSwiney, Fr. P. 'Eighteenth Century Kinsale', *JCHAS XLIII*, B, Cork, 1938, p. 85.

12 McSwiney, Fr. P. *op. cit.* A, Cork, 1939, p. 108.

13 Rodger, N.A.M., *op. cit.*, 2004, pp. 188–192.

14 McSwiney, Fr. P., *op. cit.* B, Cork, 1938, p. 75.

15 Thuillier, Joseph, Recollections, 1921.

16 De Courcy Ireland, J., *Ireland's Sea Fisheries*, Glendale, Dublin, 1981, pp. 74, 75, 81; *Cork Examiner* reports for 21 January 1882; 17 February 1885; 12 January and 8 March 1886;

17 O'Mahony, Colman, 'Fishing in nineteenth-century Kinsale', *JCHAS 98*, Cork, 1993, p. 124; *Cork Examiner*, 27 January 1887.

18 Robinson, Lennox, *Three Homes*, Michael Joseph, London, 1938, p. 108.

19 Southwell, R., 'Facsimile of Letter', de Courcy Ireland, John, *op. cit.*, 1981, p. 33.

20 McCaughan, Michael, 'Irish Vernacular Boats', *Traditional Boats of Ireland*, The Collins Press, 2008, p. 5.

21 Anderson, E.B., *op. cit.*, 1951, p. 277.

22 Copies of letters of Charles II and James II countersigned S. Pypes, *Yachting Monthly*, December 1906, pp. 148–150; Sisk, Hal, 'The Strange Origins of the Irish Hooker', *Traditional Boats of Ireland,* The Collins Press, 2008, p. 358; 'Dutch Influences on Irish Small Craft in the eighteenth century', *Cultura Maritima,* Institute of Maritime Culture, Autumn 1974.

Chapter 10. Regattas and Water Sports

1   Murphy, Maureen, *A Child of Two Continents,* RSP Design, London, 1995, p. 41.

2   Robinson, L., *Three Homes,* Michael Joseph Ltd, London, 1938, p. 125.

3   Harbour Board Minutes, June, July meetings, 1911.

4   Dickson, David, *Old World Colony,* Cork University Press, Cork, 2005, p. 423; Townsend, Rev. Horatio, *General and Statistical Survey of the County of Cork, Vol. II,* 1815, p. 22.

5   O'Sullivan, F., *History of Kinsale,* Tower Books, Cork, 1976, p. 158; Lewis, S., *Topographical Dictionary of Ireland,* Vol. II, London, 1837.

6   'Hunts Yachting Magazine, 1854', in Donegan, Harry, *South Coast Sailing,* Cork, 1912.

7   Kinsale Regatta programme, 1947.

8   Lewis, S., *op. cit.,* 1837, p. 232.

9   *Cork Examiner,* 29 August 1898.

10 *The Yachting and Boating Monthly, Vol. III,* No. 16, August 1907.

11 Kinsale Regatta Programmes for August 1886 and 1937.

12 Murphy, Maureen, *op. cit.,* 1995, p. 39; Kinsale Regatta Programme, 1947.

13 Virgil, *The Aeneid,* Book V, Translation, Penguin, 1985.

14 Sisk, Hal, 'The Strange Origin of the Irish Hooker', *Traditional Boats of Ireland,* The Collins Press, 2008, p. 359.

15 Thuillier, John R., *Marine Skills Course,* Unpublished M.Ed. Thesis, UCC, 1982; Conway I., 'Co Cork VEC Goes to Sea', *Cork Examiner,* 21 March 1976; Gubbins, M., 'Pupils on the Crest of a Wave', *Cork Evening Echo,* 5 September 1979; County Cork VEC, Annual Reports 1976 to 1981.

16 Bickerdyke, John, *Sea Fishing,* Longman, London, 1907, p 38.

17 Founding members were Tom White, Harry Acton, Dick Hegarty, Miss L. O'Connell, T.I. Alexander, H.P. Sweetman (Hon. Secretary) and John H. Thuillier, who was elected Chairman.

18 *Cork Examiner,* Report of the meeting, June 1939; *Pocket Book,* British Sea Anglers Society, 1940.

19 Murphy, Cllr K., former Vice Chairman of Kinsale Harbour Board, 7 March 2013. Speech at the County Hall.

Bibliography

Published Sources

Anderson, E.B., *Sailing Ships of Ireland,* Morris & Co., Dublin, 1951

Andrew, J.S., *Shapes of Ireland, Maps and their Makers, 1564–1839,* Geography Publication, Dublin, 1997

Balthurst, Bella, *The Wreckers,* Harper Collins, London, 2006

Barry, Jim, *Coastline 90,* Kinsale Museum, Cork, 1999

Bickerdyke, John, *Sea Fishing,* Longman, London, 1907

Bourke, Edward J., *Shipwrecks of the Irish Coast, 1105–1993,* Bourke, Dublin, 1994

Boyce, D., George, *Nationalism in Ireland,* Routledge, London, 1991

Brady, Ciaran, & Gillespie, Raymond, (eds.), *Natives and Newcomers,* Irish Academic Press, Dublin, 1986

Breen, C. & Forsythe, W., *Boats and Shipwrecks of Ireland,* Tempus, Gloucestershire, 2004

Buffet, H.F., *Port Louis and its Citadel,* Musée de la Compagnie des Indes, Port Louis, 1992

Caine, Hall, *The Manxman,* Heinemann, Isle of Man, 1894

Caulfield, R. (ed.), *The Council Book of the Corporation of Kinsale,* Surrey, 1879

Chambers, Anne, *Eleanor, Countess of Desmond,* Wolfhound Press, Dublin, 1986

Connolly, Sean, *The Bandon River from Source to the Sea,* Connolly, Bandon, 1993

Costello, Kevin, *The Courts of Admiralty of Ireland 1575–1893,* Four Courts Press, Dublin, 2011

Crowley, John, *et al.*, *Atlas of the Great Irish Famine 1845–52,* Cork University Press, 2012

Daly, Eugene, *Heir Island,* Heron's Way Press, Leap, County Cork, 2004

Bibliography

Darling, John, L., *St Multose Church,* Guy & Co., Cork, 1895

Davis, Thomas, *Prose Writings of Thomas Davis,* Scott Library, London, 1889

de Courcy Ireland, John, *Ireland and the Irish in Maritime History,* Glendale, Dublin, 1986

— *Ireland's Maritime Heritage,* An Post, Dublin, 1992

— *Ireland's Sea Fisheries – A History,* Glendale, Dublin, 1981

Dickson, David, *Old World Colony,* Cork University Press, Cork, 2005

Dinneen, P.S., *Foclóir Gaedhilge agus Bearla,* Irish Texts Society, Dublin, 1979

Donegan, H.P.F. ('Corinthian'), *History of Yachting in the South of Ireland 1720–1909,* Eagle, Cork, 1912

Donnelly, James S., *The Land and People of Nineteenth-Century Cork,* Routledge & Kegan Paul, London, 1975

Eckersall, John, *The HMS* Looe *Story,* Looe Development Trust, Cornwall, 2008

Ekin, Des, *The Stolen Village,* O'Brien Press, Dublin, 2008

Ellis, Stephen, G., *Tudor Ireland,* Longman, London, 1985

Fitzgerald, S., *Mackerel and the Making of Baltimore*, Irish Academic Press, Dublin, 1999

Flavin, S. & Jones, E.J., *Bristol Trade with Ireland and the Continent 1502–1601,* Bristol University, 2008

Foster, R.F., *Modern Ireland 1600–1972,* Penguin, London, 1988

— *The Oxford History of Ireland,* OUP, Oxford, 1989

Fremont-Barnes, G., *Nelson's Sailors,* Osprey, UK, 2005

— *Royal Navy, 1793–1815,* Osprey, London, 2007

Gibbings, R., *Sweet Cork of Thee,* Dent, London, 1951

Graham, Winston, *The Special Armadas,* Doubleday & Co., New York, 1972

Green, W.S., *The Sea Fisheries of Ireland: Agriculture and Industry in Ireland,* Department of Agriculture and Technical Instruction, Dublin, 1900

Harrison, Richard, S., *Merchants, Mystics and Philanthropists,* Cork Society of Friends, Cork, 2006

Healy, James N., *Castles of County Cork,* Mercier Press, Cork, 1988

Holohan, Renagh, *The Irish Chateaux,* Lilliput, Dublin, 1989

Horning & Banning (eds.), *Ireland and Britain in the Atlantic World,* Wordwell, Wicklow, 2009

Hurley, F., *St Joseph's Convent of Mercy,* Kinsale Newsletter, Kinsale, 1994

Jackson, J.W., *John Stanislaw's Joyce,* Fourth Estate, London, 1938

Joyce, James, *Ulysses,* Penguin, London, 1960

Kelly, C., *The Grand Tour of Cork,* Cailleach Books, Beara, 2003

Kennedy, Michael, *Guarding Neutral Ireland,* Four Courts Press, Dublin, 2008

Kiely, Jerome, *The Griffon Sings,* Chapman, Dublin, 1968

Kittridge, Alan, *Cornwall's Maritime Heritage,* Twelve Heads Press, Cornwall, 2003

Klingelhofer, E., *Castles and Colonists,* Manchester University Press, Manchester, 2010

Konstam, Angus, *Pirates, 1660–1730,* Osprey, UK, 1998

Lavery, B., *Ships,* National Maritime Museum, London, 2004

Leather, John, *Gaff Rig,* Adlard Coles, London, 1970

Levis, Cormac, *Towelsail Yawls,* GHO, Ardfield 2002

Lewis, Samuel, *Topographical Dictionary of Ireland, Vols. I and II,* London, 1838

Long, James, & Long, Ben, *The Plot against Pepys,* Faber and Faber, London, 2007

Long, P., *Sea History of Dingle*, Long, Dingle, 1980

Longfield, A.K., *Anglo-Irish Trade in the Sixteenth Century,* Routledge, London, 1929

Longfield, Robert, *Fishery Laws of Ireland*, Ponsonby, Dublin, 1863

Mac Cárthaigh, C. (ed.), *Traditional Boats of Ireland,* The Collins Press, Cork, 2008

McCarthy, Dr. C., *Archdeacon Tom Duggan,* Blackwater Press, Dublin, 1994

McCaughan, Michael & J.C. Appleby, (ed.), *The Irish Sea,* Institute of Irish Studies, Belfast, 1989

McCracken, E., *Irish Woods since Tudor Time,* David and Charles, Newton and Abbot, 1971

McKay, K.B., *A Victim of Greatness: The History of Milford,* Chevron, Milford, 1989

Marsden, Philip, *The Levelling Sea,* Harper Collins, London, 2011

Mitchell, F. & Ryan, M., *Reading the Irish Landscape,* Town House, Dublin, 1997

Mordal, J., *Twenty-five Centuries of Sea Warfare,* Abbey Library, London, 1952

Morgan, Hiram (ed.), *The Battle of Kinsale,* Wordwell, Wicklow, 2004

Mulcahy, Michael, *A Short History of Kinsale,* Historical Guides, Cork, 1968

Murphy, Elaine, *The Cromwellian Army in Ireland 1649–1653,* Routledge, 2012

Murphy, Maureen, *A Child of Two Continents*, RSP Design, London, 1995

National Heritage of the Isle of Man, *Manx Sea Fishing, 1840–1920,* National Heritage of the Isle of Man, Peel, 1992

Nolan, Liam, & Nolan, John, E., *Secret Victory,* Mercier Press, Cork, 2009

Observations on Kinsale, 1758, The Fercor Press, Cork, 1974

O'Callaghan, Sean, *To Hell or Barbados,* Brandon, Dingle, 2000

O'Donoghue, D.J., *History of Bandon,* Cork History Guides, 1970

O'Donovan, Derry, *Ballinspittle and de Courcy Country,* Wordwell, Wicklow, 2003

O'Flanagan, P. & Buttimer, C. G. (eds.), *Cork: History and Society,* Dublin, Geography Publications, 1973

O'Grady, Desmond & Fallon, Peter (ed.), *The Head Gear of the Tribe*, Gallery Books, Dublin, 1979

O'Mahony, C. & Cadogan, T., *Harbour Lights,* Great Island History Society, Cork, 1988

Ó Síocháin, Conchúr, Translator; Breatnach, R.P., *The Man from Cape Clear,* Mercier Press, Cork, 1972

O'Sullivan, F., *History of Kinsale,* Tower Books, Cork, 1976

— *State Aid for Fisheries, The Case for Kinsale Fishermen,* Acton Print, Kinsale, 1911

O'Sullivan, P., *The Lusitania: Unravelling the Mysteries,* The Collins Press, Cork, 2002

O'Sullivan, William, *The Economic History of Cork City,* Cork University Press, Cork, 1937

Palmer, Fred, *Glimpses of Old Peel,* Amulree, Peel, 1993

Parliamentary Gazetteer of Ireland, Fullerton & Co., Dublin, 1844–45

Patterson, Basil, *Turn of the Tide,* Irish Shipping Ltd, Dublin, 1962

Pacata Hibernia; A History of the Wars in Ireland, London, 1633; reprinted Dublin, 1810

Plumb, J.H., *England in the Eighteenth Century,* Penguin, Harmondsworth, 1962

Pochin-Mould, D., *Discovering Cork,* Brandon, Dingle, 1991

Power, Denis, *et al.*, *Archaeology Inventory of Cork, Vol. II*, OPW, Dublin, 1994

Preston, Diana, *Wilful Murder,* Corgi, London, 2003

Robinson, Lennox, *Three Homes,* Michael Joseph, London, 1938

Rodger, N.A.M., *Safe Guard of the Sea,* Harper Collins, London, 1997

— *The Command of the Ocean,* Penguin, London, 2004

Saunders, Eric & Marshall, Ken, *RMS* Lusitania, Waterfront Publications, Dorset, 1993

Scott, R.J., *The Galway Hooker,* Ward River Press, Dublin, 1983

Silke, J.J., *Kinsale,* Four Courts Press, Dublin, 2000

Smith, Charles, *The Ancient and Present State of County and City of Cork, Vols. I & II,* Guy & Co., Cork, 1893

Smith, Michael, *An Unsung Hero,* The Collins Press, Cork, 2000

Souhami, Diana, *Selkirk's Island*, Phoenix, London, 2001

Stone, T., *Learning the Ropes: A Seaman's Apprenticeship,* Quick Books, UK, 2000

Taylor, Richard M., *The Lighthouses of Ireland,* The Collins Press, Cork, 2004

Thuillier, John R., *History of Kinsale,* Thuillier, Kinsale, 2001

Thuillier, Joseph Jn., *Warm Oceans Cold Seas,* Millington, Dublin, 1994

Tomlin, Claire, *Samuel Pepys: The Unequalled Self,* Penguin, London, 2002

Townsend, Rev. Horatio, *General and Statistical Survey of County Cork,* Graisberry & Campbell, Dublin, 1810

Tuckey, Francis H., *The County and City of Cork Remembrancer*, Osbourn, Savage and Son, Cork, 1837

Virgil, *The Aeneid*, Translations, Penguin, London, 1985

Walvin, James, *Black Ivory,* Harper Collins, London, 1992

Ward, Nick, *Left for Dead,* A & C Black Publishers Ltd, London, 2007

Williamson, S.A., *The English Channel,* Readers Union, Collins, London, 1961

Newspapers, Periodicals

Annual Reports of the Inspectors of Irish Fisheries on the sea and inland fisheries of Ireland

Bandon Historical Journal, Bandon

BBC History Magazine, London

Dublin University Magazine, Dublin

Compass, Irish Association for Curriculum Development, Dublin

Cork Constitution

Cork Examiner

History Ireland, Dublin

International Journal of Maritime History, Hull

Irish Builder, Dublin

Irish Economic and Social History

Irish Historical Studies, Dublin

Irish Jurist, Dublin

Irish Quarterly Review, RDS., Dublin

Irish Sword, Dublin

Journal of the Cork Historical and Archaeological Society, Cork

Journal of History Association, London

Journal of the Isle of Man Family History Society, Peel

Kinsale Newsletter

London Gazette Shipping News

Marine Times

Mizen Journal

National Geographic

Proceedings of the Royal Irish Academy, Dublin

Southern Star, Skibbereen

Studies, Dublin

The Engineer, London

The Freeman's Journal, Dublin

The Kinsale Record

The Irish Times, Dublin

The Yachting Monthly, London

Tracton Newsletter, Tracton

Unpublished Sources

Correspondence: John de Courcy Ireland, Dublin; Eugene Dennis, Old Head of Kinsale, Gerald Gimblett, Kinsale & New York; Michael Mulcahy, Cork; Brendan O'Kelly, BIM., Dublin; Dept. of Education, Co. Cork VEC.; National Maritime Museum, Greenwich;

Cork County Council, Development Plans

Cork County Council, Report on Kinsale Marsh Nature Reserve, 2009

County Cork VEC., Annual Reports and Minutes of meetings

Depositions taken by Receiver of Wrecks, Custom House, Kinsale

Flynn, Majella, M., 'The Geography of Family and Fertility: Kinsale 1901 & 1911', M.A., UCC.

Hornibrook, P., 'Southwell's Alms Houses', Kinsale

Keohane, Anne, School's Heritage Survey, Irish Folklore Commission, Dublin, 1938

Kinsale Harbour Board Minutes, 1870–2012

Kinsale Manorial Records, Special Collection, UCC

Kinsale Shipping Co., Crowley Papers, Kinsale Museum

Kinsale Technical School Committee, Minutes 1899–1939

KPMG Report: The State of Ports and Harbours, Dublin, 1998

Purdue, Bishop G., Alms Houses Fund Raising Leaflet

Enquiry into loss of *St Albans,* Charles Fort, December 1693, PRO

Thuillier Bros. Boat Builders, Kinsale, Correspondence, diaries, account books, boat designs

Thuillier, John, H., Private correspondence, lecture notes, diaries

Thuillier, John, R., 'The Last Armada', Kinsale, 1999

— 'Marine Skills Pre-employment Course', M.Ed. Thesis, UCC, 1983

Thuillier, Joseph (Sr.), Recollections, 1921

Vital, Laurent, Translator D. Convery, Record of Archduke Ferdinand's visit to Kinsale, 1518, UCC

Oral Sources

John Alcock (Kinsale), Tony Bocking (Kinsale), Johnny Bowen (Castlepark), George Bushe (Crosshaven & Baltimore), Ted Coakley (Kinsale), Gary Culhane (Kinsale), John de Courcy Ireland (Dublin), Francie Dempsey (Old Head of Kinsale), George Farley (Kinsale), Johnny Farran (Kinsale), Freddie Fleming (World's End), Eugene Gillen (Kinsale), Gerald Gimblett (Kinsale & New York), Fred Good (Kinsale), Tony Hill (The Dock), Ned Hunt (Tisaxon), Charlie Hurley (Lower Cove), Christy Hurley (Scilly), Frank Kiernan (Kinsale), Jimmy Lawton (Duneen), Donie Lombard (Kinsale), Jerome Lordan (An Doras Breac), Billy Lynch (Scilly), Oliver Lynch (Kinsale), Barry Maloney (Kinsale), Frank Mills (Youghal), D. Minihane (Heir Island), Ger O'Donovan (Kinsale), Jack O'Driscoll (Summer Cove), Mick O'Driscoll (Kinsale), Don O'Herlihy (Summer Cove), Denis O'Leary (Kinsale), John O'Leary (Castlepark), Eamonn O'Neill (Kinsale), Timmy Sheehan (Kinsale), Jimmy Stapleton (World's End), Joseph A. Thuillier (Kinsale), John H. Thuillier (Kinsale), Mona Thuillier (Kinsale), Jack Tyrrell (Arklow), Johnny Walsh (Kinsale), Neddie Ward (World's End), Stanley Woods (Scilly).

Index

Brown, George 210–11
Buckley, Donie 197
Bulman Rock 11, 12, 13–14, 224
buoys 13, 15, 103, 175, 209
Burke, Edmund 141
Burrows, Thomas 120
Bushe, George 205
Butler family 45
Butler, James (12th Earl of Ormond) 86, 138
Butler, Thomas (10th Earl of Ormond) 28
Button, Sir Thomas 77, 147

Caine, Hall 93–4
Calnan, Tom and Timothy 196
cannery 115, 242
Carew, George 138
Caribbean 40, 51–4, 55, 122, 125, 134, 141, 149
Carmelite Friary 172
cartels (fish buyers) 99–100
Carthy, Jack 187
Casey's sail loft 71
Catholics/Catholicism 19, 20–1, 30, 32, 49, 54, 81, 87, 100, 121–2, 130, 131, 132, 134, 139, 140–1
Caulfield, Richard 22
Ceres 49–50
Charles Fort 15, 20, 23, 43, 47, 62, 137–9, 140, 141, 142, 143, 185
Charles I 77, 130, 131, 132, 133, 134, 135
Charles II 7, 44, 133, 134, 135, 137, 151, 167, 216
charter 26–8, 35, 119, 125, 156
charter business, yacht 237
charts 11–14, 77, 136, 183, 206
The Christofur of Kinsale 25
Chudleigh family 207–8
Chudleigh, Thomas 30, 207
Church of the Holy Trinity (Fort Hill) 20, 47, 138
Churchill, John (Duke of Marlborough) 140
Churchill, Winston 195
Cinque Ports 38–9, 40
Cistercians 23–4

City of Chicago 154–5, 160, 187–8
Civil War 141–2, 175
Clemen, Commander Martin 198–9
Club at Assembly Rooms 34–5
coastguard 154–6, 188, 190, 229, 232
Cogan, Richard 181
Cogan, Robert 77
Coleman, Justin 237
Colle, Richard 146
Colleen 71
Collins, Eugene 104
Collins, Greenville 12, 13, 14, 136, 206
Collins, Jack 197–8
collision at sea 191–2
Colman, Captain P. 72
colonisation 51, 57, 63, 121, 122, 125–6, 136, 162
Colthurst, Col. 104
Congested Districts Board 106, 212–13
Connolly, William 196
Connor, Bryant 53
Connor, Jack 152
conservation, fish 87
convoying systems 56, 58–60, 63, 210
coopers 40–1, 82, 88, 92, 210
Cork County Council 242
Cork Harbour 49, 65–6, 69, 76, 210, 224
Cormac, Anne 149–50
Cornish fishermen 89, 98, 103, 104, 107, 193
Corporation 26–8, 33, 34, 42–3, 42–4, 46, 50–1, 63, 64, 67, 69, 84, 85, 87, 102, 119–20, 125, 139, 141, 153, 156, 163, 172, 176
Corrin, Robert 92
Corry, James 100
Cotter, Michael 191
Coveney, Jerh 211
Cramer, David 191
crayfish 113
Crean brothers 190
Crean, Tom 199–200
Crofts, Sir James 120
Cromwell, Oliver 42, 46, 52, 126–7, 131, 132, 133, 134, 135, 207
Crosbie, Alan 237
Crowley family 70, 170

Germany 70, 72–3, 193–5, 196–7
'Gift' houses 48
Gillam, Captain 185
Gimblett, Denis 72–3, 192
Gimblett, Gerald 74, 180, 201
Glaramara 154
Glasgow 104
Good, Fred 237
grants (fishing) 88, 105, 109
Grattan's Parliament (1783–1800) 88
Green, Peggy 241
Guernsey 151

hake 77–8, 79–80
Hales, Tom 113
Halpin, George 8
Hammett, William 30
Hanyagh, Thomas 146
Harbour Act 1947 29
Harbour Board 10, 11, 14, 16, 29, 43,
    44, 69, 98, 101, 103–7, 110–11,
    112–13, 114–15, 164–5, 174, 175,
    178, 181, 196–7, 198, 211, 212,
    221, 222, 242
Hayles, Captain 185
Hazlitt, Rev. W. 63
Heard family 211–12
Heard, John 40
Hegarty, Dick 234
Helstern, Mattias 236
Henry Good Ltd 75
Henry II 23
Henry III 171
Henry VIII 32, 56, 164
Herrick family 131
herring 77, 80, 87, 88, 93, 110, 112,
    115, 214
Hill, Tony 176
HMS *Kinsale* 150, 170, 205, 206, 207–9
HMS *Looe* 209
HMS *Swallow* 184
Hoare, Alderman Edward 37, 41, 48, 66,
    67, 210
Holburne, Francis 67
holy well 20–1, 138
Honey Dew II 201
Hopkins, Gerald Manley 2
Howe, John 63

ice 90–1, 97
immigration 157
imports 24–5, 28, 30, 35, 54, 55, 65, 69,
    70, 72, 75–6, 81, 150, 165, 211
impressment 64–5
indentured servant 52–4, 141
informers 152
Invermore 71
Irish Pine 196–7
Irish speaking areas 18–20, 130
ironworks 169–70
Isle of Man 89, 109, 151, 205, 212, 214,
    217
    Manx fishermen *see separate entry*
Italy 24, 55
Ivye, Paul 11, 126

Jacob, Rob 231
Jagla, Tomas 201
James Fort (previously Castlepark Fort)
    77, 98, 125, 126–7, 129, 135,
    136–7, 139, 140, 141, 222
James I 35, 77, 130, 135, 147
James II 16, 36, 57, 127, 136, 139–40,
    141
James O'Neill 70
Jerome, Jerome K. 180
Johnson, Doctor 232
Johnson, Thomas 101–2
The John of Kinsale 25
joulters 84–5, 176
Joyce, James 10
Judge, Eamonn 237

Keating, Sean 21
Kelleher, Tom 142
Kelly, Pat 164
Keohane family 174
Keohane, Patrick 199–200
Kiely, Dan 164
Kiely, Jerome 21
The Kilfauns 192
Kilgobban Castle 128, 129, 131, 164
Kingston family 218, 237–8
Kinsale Development Association 112
Kinsale Fishermen's Benefit Society
    109–10
Kinsale Fishery Company 212